Winterthur Portfolio 4

Winterthur Portfolio 4

Edited by Richard K. Doud

Published for

The Henry Francis du Pont Winterthur Museum

by the University Press of Virginia

Charlottesville

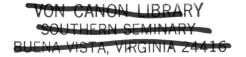

Statement of Editorial Policy

The objective of The Henry Francis du Pont
Winterthur Museum in publishing *Winterthur
Portfolio* is to make available to the serious student an
authoritative reference for the investigation and
documentation of early American culture.

The publication will present articles about many
aspects of American life. Included will be studies that
will extend current information about objects used
in America in the seventeenth, eighteenth, and
nineteenth centuries; or about the makers, the
manufacture, the distribution, the use, and the settings
of such objects. Scholarly articles contributing to
the knowledge of America's social, cultural, political,
military, and religious heritage, as well as those
offering new approaches or interpretations concerning
research and conservation of art objects, are
welcome.

Richard K. Doud, *Editor*
Carole J. Bower, *Editorial Assistant*

Editorial Committee
John A. H. Sweeney, *Chairman*
Charles F. Hummel
Dorothy W. Greer

Contents

Furniture of the Lower Connecticut River Valley

Nancy E. Richards

A Meeting of the Society of Cabinet-Makers, in Hartford and its vicinity, will be held at the house of Mr. AARON COLTON, in this City, on Monday next, at 3 o'clock P.M. A general and punctual attendance is requested.

THE appearance of this notice in the *Connecticut Courant* on August 27, 1792, implies the presence of an active and well-organized community of cabinetmakers in Hartford similar to that found in the major urban centers of Boston-Salem, New York, or Philadelphia. With the ever-growing interest in American furniture, it is strange that so little attention has been paid to the work of these craftsmen. Studies by Luke Vincent Lockwood, Irving W. Lyon, William S. Walcott, Jr., and Penrose R. Hoopes, written in the early years of this century, helped to stimulate an interest in Connecticut furniture; [1] but until the 1935 Wadsworth Atheneum exhibition, "Three Centuries of Connecticut Furniture," few writers considered this furniture sufficiently important to mention it more than casually. So little was known about the area's cabinetmakers that, until recently, every important piece of late eighteenth-century furniture was attributed to Aaron Roberts, Aaron or Eliphalet Chapin, or Samuel Kneeland and Lemuel Adams. [2]

Even today the serious investigation of Connecticut furniture is complicated by the fact that, unlike his fellow artisans, the cabinetmaker rarely signed or labeled his work, and few bills are available to help identify the furniture that survives. Account books, daybooks, or waste books for Hartford's cabinetmakers are nonexistent. Even the authors of those invaluable local histories written in the late nineteenth and early twentieth century seem to have conspired to maintain the mystery; when they mention the furniture crafts at all, their only reference is to the fact that the town had a cabinetmaker.

At a time when roads were poor and shipment overland was both difficult and expensive, water provided the quickest and most economical means of transportation. Located on the west bank of the Connecticut River just below the head of navigation, Hartford was ideally situated as a center for the dissemination of goods from Europe, the West Indies, and intercoastal ports to towns in Hartford County and to areas farther up the river. Above

[1] Among the writings on Connecticut furniture published prior to the Wadsworth Atheneum exhibition in 1935 are Luke Vincent Lockwood, *Colonial Furniture in America* (New York: Charles Scribner's Sons, 1913) ; Irving W. Lyon, *The Colonial Furniture of New England* (2d ed.; Boston: Houghton Mifflin Co., 1924) ; William S. Walcott, Jr., "A Kneeland and Adams Mirror," *Antiques,* XIII (Jan., 1928) , 30–32, and "Ten Important American Sideboards," *Antiques,* XIV (Dec., 1928) , 516–22; and Penrose R. Hoopes, "Aaron Chapin, Hartford Cabinetmaker," *Antiques,* XXIV (Sept., 1933) , 97–98.

[2] Since the publication of the Wadsworth Atheneum

catalogue, scholars and collectors have gathered much new material and information. More recent monographs on Hartford County craftsmen include Charles S. Bissell, *Antique Furniture in Suffield, Connecticut, 1670–1838* (Hartford: The Connecticut Historical Society and The Suffield Historical Society, 1956) ; *Frederick K. and Margaret R. Barbour's Furniture Collection* (Hartford: The Connecticut Historical Society, 1956) ; Penrose R. Hoopes, *Shop Records of Daniel Burnap, Clockmaker* (Hartford: The Connecticut Historical Society, 1958) ; and Frederick K. Barbour, *The Stature of Fine Connecticut Furniture* (Hartford: Privately printed, 1959) . A series of articles by Houghton Bulkeley which appeared in *The Connecticut Historical Society Bulletin* (hereafter *CHSB*) between 1957 and 1966 contributed much important primary information concerning local cabinetmakers. A checklist of Connecticut cabinetmakers up to 1820 appeared in *CHSB,* XXXII (Oct., 1967) , 97–144, and XXXIII (Jan., 1968) , 1–40.

Middletown, the Connecticut River was too shallow for the larger ocean-going vessels, and although some Hartford merchants traded directly with the West Indies, most goods—hardware, dry goods, wines and spirits, tea and spices, salt, textiles, glassware, and ceramics—were transshipped on coasters from Boston and New York.

Hartford has never ranked as a major city. When the Marquis de Chastellux passed through in 1780 on his way from Newport to West Point, he remarked critically: "The town of Hartford does not merit any attention either travelling through, or in speaking of it. It consists of a very long street, parallel with the river; it is regular, that is, the houses are not too distant from each other." [3] Even at the time of the first census in 1790, Hartford's 4,090 residents occupied an area of less than one square mile. In fact, the population of the entire county (including the towns of Berlin, Bristol, East Hartford, East Windsor, Enfield, Farmington, Glastonbury, Granby, Hartford, Simsbury, Southington, Suffield, Wethersfield, and Windsor) was 38,129 persons—only about five thousand more than that of New York City in the same year. [4] Nevertheless, during the early years of the Republic, Hartford provided the necessary economic and cultural climate to sustain some of Connecticut's most important cabinet- and chairmakers.

As Chastellux observed, the city was laid out in a modified grid pattern with the major business and residential streets parallel to the river and the access streets to the merchants' wharves at right angles to the river (Fig. 1). The most important commercial area was Main Street. The presence of hardware, dry goods, tailor, shoe, jewelry, blacksmith, book, and cabinet shops dotting the entire length of the street, both north and south of the "stone bridge," gave evidence that Hartford was primarily a city of shopkeepers and traders.

Because Hartford was the commercial center for the area, local merchants maintained close economic relations with the major northern seaports. Some of the city's more important merchants maintained factors in New York. Since these economic ties provided the *raison d'être* for periodic trips to that city, prominent Connecticut citizens became accustomed to the cultural activities available there. The appearance of a theater, museums, and panoramas in Hartford and the establishment of schools offering instruction in painting, dancing, French, and other genteel accomplishments contributed to the growing cosmopolitan air of the city.

Through their contacts in New York, Connecticut merchants were aware of the type of furniture being produced in the fashionable cabinet shops of Thomas Burling, Elbert Anderson, and George Shipley. It is not surprising that Oliver Phelps, a wealthy merchant and land speculator, partially furnished his newly remodeled house in Suffield, Connecticut, with New York furniture. Accounts with his New York factors show that over a period of several years Phelps purchased furniture from Burling, William Wilmerding, and James Ronalds (identified in Phelps's correspondence as J. Renolds). One particularly interesting bill, dated December 20, 1788, records these purchases:

to Cust p^d Thomas Burling for 1 Bureau		£ 6.0.0
" do p^d ditto for 8 Sattin hair bottom^d Chairs @ 45/		£18.0.0
" do p^d ditto for 1 Folding Table		£ 3.0.0
" do p^d J. Renolds for 1 Mahogany Bedstead & apparatus		£ 6.0.0 [5]

Even while some of Connecticut's most prominent citizens were purchasing furniture in New York, Hartford cabinetmakers were manufacturing pieces that compared favorably with those available in New York. The monopoly on Hartford's furniture production enjoyed by Robert Currier and Timothy Phelps, Jr., during the mid-1770's ceased with the dissolution of Currier's shop shortly after the end of the war and the untimely death of Phelps in 1784. Hartford was left without a major cabinetmaker—a vacuum that was to attract a number of trained craftsmen to the city.

One of the best known, Aaron Chapin, was already in residence in 1783. He had served as an apprentice and a journeyman in the East Windsor

[3] Marquis de Chastellux, *Travels in North-America in the Years 1780, 1781, and 1782* (London: C. G. J. and J. Robbinson, 1788), I, 36–37.

[4] U.S. Bureau of the Census, *Heads of Families at the First Census of the United States Taken in the Year 1790: Connecticut* (Washington: Government Printing Office, 1908), pp. 32–56.

[5] Phelps-Gorham Papers (New York State Library, Albany). The author wishes to thank Mr. Arthur Leibundguth, of the Antiquarian and Landmark Society of Connecticut, and Dr. Frank H. Sommer III, of the Winterthur Museum, for making available their notes and photostats of these papers.

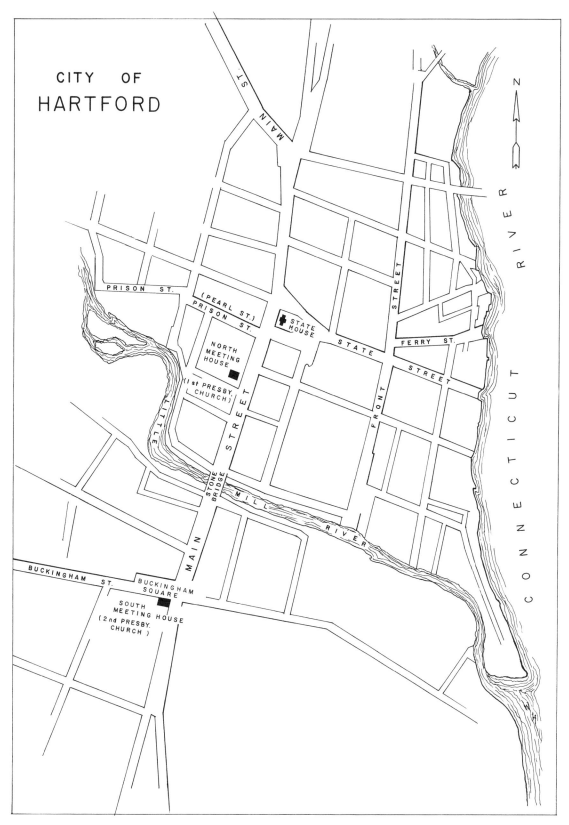

Fig. 1. Map of Hartford, Connecticut, 1790–1800. Drawn by Winifred W. Heath, 1967. (Winterthur.)

shop of his cousin Eliphalet. As the largest shop in that town (possibly the largest in the state), it afforded young Chapin the opportunity to work with the only Hartford County cabinetmaker who had trained in Philadelphia. Vigorous local competition and the hope of obtaining new commissions in an expanding commercial center may have prompted his move to Hartford. On December 3, 1783, he advertised in the *Connecticut Courant:*

Cabinet Furniture!
Aaron Chapin

Begs leave to acquaint the public, as well as his former customers, that he has lately removed from East-Windsor to Hartford, and now improves the shop opposite Mr. Samuel Burr's, Merchant; where he now carries on the Cabinet and Chair making business, in as great variety perhaps as is done in any one Shop in the State, in both Mahogany and Cherry Tree, of which he has now a good stock. . . . He has now on hand a few good Tea and Kitchen Tables, [and] a variety of Tea and Wine Servers to dispose of on reasonable terms for good pay in hand.

Chapin employed one or two workmen in his small shop on Main Street. Periodic references in the newspapers suggest that at least part of his time was devoted to the cleaning and repairing of watches. However, in the *Connecticut Courant* of July 19, 1788, he reassured his customers that "he still carries on the Cabinet and Chair making business, in its great variety of articles—among which are Sofa's Swel'd or pla[i]n, easy Chairs—Clock Cases, Gun Stocks, weavers Shuttles, Pitch Pipes, Flutes, Fifes, &c." Unfortunately, no labeled or otherwise documented piece from this period survives. The absence of labeled pieces suggests either that Chapin's work was so well known and easily identifiable as to make labeling unnecessary, or that he did not wish to go to the added expense of having the labels printed.

Chapin's position as the only cabinetmaker in Hartford soon was challenged by Samuel Kneeland. In contrast to Chapin's modest notice, Kneeland's initial advertisement in the *American Mercury*, August 14, 1786, contained an impressive list of items. Although his shop was not large (probably about the same size as Chapin's, with one or two workmen), he was prepared to sell:

SWELL'D front, and plain Desks, with or without Book-cases, Swell'd and plain Bureaus, Clock-Cases, Cases of Drawers, Merchant's writing Desks, Dineing Tables, Tea, Card, Pembroke and Tray ditto, Tea and Dineing Trays, Ladies wash Stands, Fire Screens, Parlour Chairs, Chamber ditto, Sofas, Easy Chairs, Elbow ditto, and Chairs of various other kinds; High post, Camp and Common Bedsteads, Light Stands, Back-Gammon Boxes, Ches and Cribbage Boards, Looking Glass Frames, plain or gilt; Also Furniture of various other kinds, made of Cherry or Mehogany.

Kneeland's origins are obscure. There is no record of where he learned his craft, but the presence of such established cabinetmakers as Timothy Phelps, Jr., in Hartford, Thomas Bulkley (Buckley) in Farmington, and Eliphalet Chapin in East Windsor supports the contention that he probably was trained locally. In any event, Kneeland was already a well-trained craftsman when the notice appeared.

No record exists of the day-to-day work of his shop; but, in addition to the manufacture of household furniture, a considerable portion of his time was devoted to the routine repair of old furniture, the recaning of chairs, and the making of coffins. Persistent notices, in both Hartford newspapers, advertising the repair and resilvering of looking glasses suggest that this work accounted for a sizable part of his income. Advertisements offering "Old Looking Glasses repaired, fram'd and gilt in the neatest manner, so as to look equal to new ones," [6] and "those who have old Glasses that is defac'd in the silvering, may, (if the plate is whole) have an entire new Looking-Glass, at a small expense," [7] appeared with regularity. A lack of active local competition afforded Kneeland a limited monopoly in this field. [8]

Another lucrative side of Kneeland's business was supplying finished cases for local clockmakers. Although no labeled examples are known, Daniel Burnap's shop records indicate that between April, 1788, and March, 1792, Kneeland provided that East Windsor clockmaker with seven cherry clockcases ranging in price from £4.6.0 to £5.0.0 each, or a total of £32.6.0. During the same period, Kneeland purchased three additional clock movements ranging in price from £10.0.0 to

[6] *American Mercury*, Nov. 12, 1789.
[7] *American Mercury*, July 25, 1789.
[8] Although several Hartford merchants imported looking glasses from New York, Nathan Ruggles did not establish his looking-glass manufactory, the first firm devoted solely to this purpose, until 1803, several years after Kneeland left Hartford.

£11.10.0 each, or a total of £32.6.0.[9] Presumably he sold these in cases made in his shop.

The increasing prosperity of his business is demonstrated by the fact that between 1786 and 1791 Kneeland moved his shop three times, to successively larger quarters.[10] In view of this, it is strange that so few documented examples of this period survive. One particularly important piece is a small cherry chest (Fig. 2) made to house an

FIG. 2. Samuel Kneeland, Chest. Hartford, Conn., *ca.* 1786. Cherry; H. 9″, W. 19″, D. 18½″. (Connecticut Historical Society.)

oriental export porcelain punch bowl belonging to Jeremiah Wadsworth of Hartford.[11] Ogee bracket feet, geometric string inlay on the front, and an inlaid patera on the lid add distinction to its simple dovetail construction. Pasted on the inside of the lid is a printed label (Fig. 3) dated August 14, 1786. Identical, except for its size and spelling, to Kneeland's first advertisement in the *American Mercury,* this label identifies the earliest known piece of Kneeland furniture.

Competition also came from Aaron Colton, a Massachusetts-born craftsman who had settled in Hartford and opened a small shop prior to 1787. Although his shop was active, his first recorded public announcement did not appear until 1792, suggesting that his products were so well known as to need no advertising.

The opening of a fourth cabinet shop in 1789

[9] Hoopes, *Daniel Burnap,* pp. 45–56.

[10] In June, 1787, Kneeland moved to a shop on Wells Street just a few yards west of the "stone bridge" on Main Street. Two years later he informed his customers that he had "removed to his house near Mr. Blis' tan works." In 1791 he moved again, this time to a house west of Mr. Jonathan Butler's tan works.

[11] "The Wadsworth Punch Bowl, c. 1780," *CHSB,* XX (April, 1955), 33–41.

brought to an end the dominance exercised by Chapin, Colton, and Kneeland. On August 17 of that year, John Wells advertised in the *American Mercury:* "CABINET WORK, of all kinds . . . he is now carrying on the Business of Cabinet, Chair, and Bedstead making, in their various branches; at the shop lately belonging to and occupied by Mr. Samuel Kneeland, a few rods west of the great bridge." Just twenty years old, Wells had recently completed his apprenticeship. With whom he trained is not known, but either Kneeland or Aaron Chapin in Hartford or Eliphalet Chapin in East Windsor could have taught the East Hartford youth.

During this early period, competition within the furniture trades was not sufficiently brisk to cause any cabinetmaker to resort to prolonged periods of newspaper advertising. In fact, during the entire year of 1790 no Hartford cabinetmaker advertised in the local papers. The appearance of George Shipley's notice in the *American Mercury* on December 20, 1790, must have had an instant impact on the cabinetmaking community.

CABINET MAKERS

WANTED several good workmen in the Cabinet making business—such will meet with constant employment and good wages by applying to

George Shipley,

No. 161 Water-Street, Between Beekman and Burlin[g] Slip, New York.

Imagine the appeal that the possibility of working

FIG. 3. Kneeland, Label on Chest in Figure 2. Paper; H. 3″, W. 3½″. (Connecticut Historical Society.)

in the shop of this London-trained cabinetmaker would have for a young craftsman. It may have been just this advertisement that encouraged Wells to undertake this additional training in New York. Certainly, there would have been a place for a young journeyman in Shipley's newly opened shop.

After spending nearly a year in New York, Wells announced the reopening of his shop in December, 1791, and advised his customers that "he has lately returned from one of the most noted Cabinet Shops in New-York, furnished with a variety of the most modern patter[n]s." [12] Armed with his advanced technical training and a knowledge of the competitive business techniques of New York cabinetmakers, he launched a campaign in the local newspapers that impelled the other craftsmen to advertise more actively.

Increased activity within the local community, given added impetus by an awareness of problems shared by cabinetmakers in other urban centers, led the Hartford craftsmen to unionize. In 1792 they formed an association, known as the Hartford Society of Cabinet Makers, which attempted to standardize prices and improve conditions in the trade. Patterning themselves on the precedent set forth in the 1788 edition of *The Cabinet-Makers' London Book of Prices,* they resolved to "form . . . into a Society for the purpose of regulating the prices of our work; on the principal of dealing in CASH, and of establishing a uniformity in our trade for the general interest of ourselves and customers." [13]

Within a month after its inception, Aaron Colton called a meeting of the members of the society. Of whom was this society composed? Had its price book survived *in toto,* this and other relevant questions would have been answered. Unfortunately, only a fragment of the original manuscript remains; several pages of itemized prices and the all-important final page with the list of the subscribers are missing. Probably every qualified cabinetmaker and chairmaker in the county joined. Included would have been: Lemuel Adams, Aaron Chapin, Aaron Colton, Samuel Kneeland, Daniel Phelps, 2d, Stacey Stackhouse, John Wadsworth,

and John Wells in Hartford; Eliphalet Chapin, Simeon Loomis, and Bethuel Phelps in East Windsor; Thomas Bulkley and Eli Wood in Farmington; Silas Easton in East Hartford; and Whitehead Howd and Nathaniel Jones in Southington.

Cohesion of purpose within the cabinetmaking community stimulated activity, which was reflected in advertisements in the *Connecticut Courant.* Daniel Phelps, 2d, a hitherto unknown craftsman, advertised for a journeyman and an apprentice on February 20, 1792. On December 3 of the same year, Aaron Colton advertised: "WANTED IMMEDIATELY. A JOURNEYMAN that is a good workman at the Slegh making or Cabinet business—Also a likely BOY, about 15 years of Age, as an Apprentice to the CABINET business." And on September 10, 1792, Samuel Kneeland, a respected and well-established cabinetmaker, formed a partnership with Lemuel Adams, an unknown artisan. The *Courant* reported:

SAMUEL KNEELAND & LEMUEL ADAMS

RESPECTFULLY inform the public, that they carry on the Cabinet and Chair-making business, in its various branches, under the firm of *Kneeland & Adams* —They have on hand a compleat assortment of well season'd Stuff, and make all kinds of Cabinet Work, of Mahogany, and Cherry tree, in the newest fashion.

Also, Quicksilver, Frame, and Gilt *LOOKING GLASSES* of every kind—all to as great perfection as in America.

N. B. A good workman at Common Chairs, may have constant employ, and ready pay, by applying to said Company.

Above this notice is the same cut of a serpentine-front chest of drawers, a pembroke table, and a ladder-back side chair that Kneeland had used in his 1787 advertisements, suggesting that furniture in the Chippendale style continued to be fashionable in Hartford even as new styles were introduced.

Evidently the firm prospered, for on November 12, 1792, Kneeland and Adams advertised for two or three journeymen and two "likely active lads" as apprentices, thus making their shop one of the largest in Hartford. Certainly, it was a well-established and confident firm that could offer "Mahogany Furniture of every kind equal to any made in

---

[12] *American Mercury,* Dec. 5, 1791.

[13] This document has been published in its entirety by Lyon, *Colonial Furniture,* pp. 267–70. The original manuscript is now in the Watkinson Library, Trinity College, Hartford.

Fig. 4. Samuel Kneeland and Lemuel Adams, Chest of Drawers. Hartford, Conn., 1793. Cherry; H. 35½″, W. 46½″, D. 20¾″. (Winterthur 51.66.1.)

New York or Boston."[14] Judging by the documented furniture that survives, this was no idle boast.

A handsome, serpentine-front chest of drawers (Fig. 4), constructed of cherry rather than the more fashionable mahogany, bears a startling resemblance to the piece shown in the firm's first advertisement. Distinguished by canted front corners, fluted quarter columns, and a combination

[14] *American Mercury*, Nov. 12, 1792.

of bracket and claw-and-ball feet, the well-proportioned chest retains its original brass column stops, escutcheons, and drawer pulls. Inside the top drawer is an engraved Kneeland and Adams label (Fig. 5) with a pencil inscription across the top, "bought Dec 23ᵈ 1793," which seems to date the piece rather accurately.

A receipt accompanying a set of six cherry side chairs also bears the date December 23, 1793 (Fig. 6). Written on the back of an advertising handbill, the receipt records Mrs. Dickerson's purchase

FIG. 5. Kneeland and Adams, Label on Chest in Figure 4. Paper; H. 8″, W. 6½″. (Winterthur.)

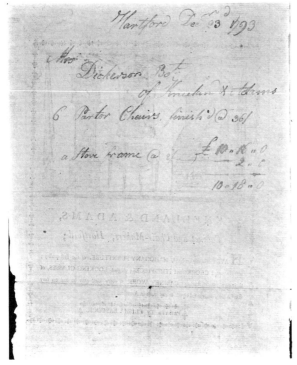

FIG. 6. Bill for the Kneeland and Adams Side Chairs. Paper; H. 8⅞″, W. 7″. (Winterthur.)

of "6 Parlor Chairs, finish'd @36/ £10.16.0." These chairs (Fig. 7), made in the newest fashion, have survived in remarkably good condition; five of the set retain their original black-painted canvas upholstery. According to family tradition, the chairs were bought at the time of Mrs. Dickerson's marriage. A penciled notation on the front of the advertisement, "1793 / When grandmother was married," appears to be in the same hand as the writing on the label on the chest of drawers previously shown, suggesting that both pieces were once owned by the same family.

Although the prototype for these chairs can be found in Hepplewhite's *The Cabinet-maker and Upholsterer's Guide,* the immediate inspiration was the work of New York's fashionable cabinetmakers. Men like George Shipley, whose connection with the Hartford cabinetmaking trades has already been mentioned, produced chairs adapted from designs in Hepplewhite's *Guide.* One example is the set of eight mahogany side chairs made for the Lawrence family of Flushing, New York (Fig. 8). Still upholstered in the original horsehair, one of the chairs has Shipley's label glued to the underside of the webbing (Fig. 9). The visual parallels between the Kneeland and Adams chairs (Fig. 7) and these chairs by Shipley are obvious. Certainly, as two of Hartford's most prominent cabinetmakers, Kneeland and Adams were aware of these new designs and were familiar with the work of Shipley's shop.

Between 1792 and 1795, Kneeland and Adams operated a lucrative, if highly competitive, business. John Wells's advertising campaign in the local newspapers had challenged their position as the city's leading firm. To indicate the capabilities of their shop, they offered the following inducement to their customers:

They can supply them with every kind of Cabinet work, on very short notice, as they have in constant employ the best workmen, from New-York and Boston. —They have now on hand, and ready for sale, an elegant assortment of Cabinet furniture, consisting of Parlour, Chamber and Hall Chairs, Mahogany, with swelled and Concave seats, neatly covered with Satten-Hair Seating—Mahogany and Cherrytree Desks and Book-Cases—ditto Commode and plain Beauroes—Mahogany Secretarys and Sideboards—Dining, tea, and Breakfast Tables—Mahogany Card and Pembrook Tables, square, round and oval, inlaid and plain—Pier, Writing, and Kitchen Tables—Highpost, Field, Cross and Cord Bedsteads—Clocks and Time-Pieces—Clock Cases, of various prices—Candle-Stands, Tea-

FIG. 7. Kneeland and Adams, Side Chair (one of a set of six). Hartford, Conn., 1793. Cherry; H. 38¾", W. 21½", D. 20". (Winterthur 67.151.)

FIG. 8. George Shipley, Side Chair (one of a set of eight). New York City, 1791–1795. Mahogany; H. 38½", W. 21", D. 17½". (Martha Lawrence Read; photo, Art Institute of Chicago.)

Trays and Sarvers—Kitchen Chairs—Elegant Looking-Glasses, from one to thirty Dollars each and a good assortment of China faced Clo[a]k Pins.[15]

Their success is a subject of speculation.

Of the few documented pieces known, two scrolled looking glasses support Kneeland and Adams' claim that they could supply "elegant looking glasses of their own manufacture."[16] The first, a modest piece, consists of a simple, molded frame embellished by scrolled fretwork with outflaring ears at both top and bottom (Fig. 10). In contrast, the second looking glass has more exuberant fretwork and the addition of a gilt phoenix incorporated in the cresting (Fig. 11). Both are fashioned of mahogany veneer on pine, are identified by a Kneeland and Adams label (similar to the type illustrated in Fig. 5) pasted on the backboard, and have a history of ownership in Spring-

[15] *American Mercury*, Oct. 14, 1793.
[16] *American Mercury*, July 22, 1793.

field, Massachusetts. The more elaborate example bears the added ink inscription: "from Thomas Bagg / family West Springfield / Mass."

Only one other labeled example of the firm's work is known. Fashioned in cherry, this straight-front chest of drawers (Fig. 12) is in marked contrast to the contoured façade of the other Kneeland and Adams chest (Fig. 4). Attention to decorative details—banding on the edge of the top, cock beading edging the drawers, and shaped bracket feet—adds interest to the "plain style" piece.

In common with most Hartford firms, the greatest part of Kneeland and Adams' business came from small individual commissions—a table or two, a single case piece, or even a set of chairs. Imagine, then, the effect on the whole cabinetmaking community of the plans to furnish the new State House. Competition for the available jobs must have been vigorous, with every firm anxious to secure a part of this sizable commission.

As might be expected, the major share of the cabinet work was awarded to Samuel Kneeland and Lemuel Adams. According to the artisans' bills, now in the archives of the Connecticut State Library at Hartford, Adams supplied most of the seating for the Senate Chamber (twenty armchairs for the senators, armchairs for the governor and the speaker, and ten window stools), while Kneeland furnished the tables.[17] John Wadsworth, a Windsor chairmaker in Hartford, made twenty-five Windsor settees and twelve Windsor chamber chairs, which were painted green. Jonathan Bright, an East Windsor-trained cabinetmaker turned upholsterer, is credited with upholstering the chairs and window stools. The size of the commission (£105.6.0 to Lemuel Adams, £52.10.0 to Samuel Kneeland, £70.13.0 to John Wadsworth, and £60.4.6 to Jonathan Bright), a total approaching £300, may have been a contributing factor to the sudden influx of cabinetmakers from other areas.

Adams' invoice is less explicit than one would wish. Because of the large number of surviving examples, however, the State House chairs are tra-

ditionally described as having a shield-shaped back with an urn-shaped splat (Fig. 13). The chairs are adapted from Plate V of Hepplewhite's *Guide* of 1788 and enlivened by an inlaid segmented icicle, stringing, and a banded cuff. This same decoration appears on the legs of the window stools. Over the period of a century and a half, the tables have vanished, but a number of the chairs, re-covered in red morocco to simulate the original upholstery, have been installed in their original setting.

With the awarding of these commissions, the partnership altered noticeably; the State House work must have occupied most of the partners' time. In any event, the firm ran no new advertisements in 1794, and on March 9 of the following year, the *American Mercury* carried the following notice: "THE CO-PARTNERSHIP of Kneeland & Adams, is this day by mutual consent dissolved. SAMUEL KNEELAND. LEMUEL ADAMS. Hartford, March 5, 1795."

Thus ended one of the city's most successful partnerships. Each opened his own shop—Kneeland at his old location on Main Street north of the bridge and Adams at a new shop on Ferry Street.

FIG. 9. Shipley, Label on Side Chair in Figure 8. Paper; H. 5", W. 3½". (Martha Lawrence Read; photo, Art Institute of Chicago.)

---

[17] Bills to the state dated in Jan., 1796 (Archives, Connecticut State Library, Hartford). Adams asked payment for:

To 20 Mahogany Armed Chairs inlaid and carved exclusive of Upholstery Work @ 72 /	£ 72– 0– 0
To 2 d° for the Gover[n] & Speaker @ 87 /	£ 8–14– 0
To 10 Windsor Stools Mahogany inlaid exclusive of Upholstery Work @ 27 /	£ 13–10– 0
To a Writing Desk for the Secretary's room with 4 falls—pigeon Nests in each—with Drawers & a Sliding table—Brass-Nails—springs + trimmings—including every thing but the f[inishings]	£ 10–10– 0
To 2 Mahogany Vote Boxes	. –12– .
	£105– 6– 0

Kneeland asked payment for:

To a large Circular Mahogany Table 29 feet in length 18 Draws leggs inlaid & strung Exclusive of Trimmings	£ 30– 0– 0
To 1 Large Oval Ditto 12 feet long 2 Draws Mahogany leggs inlaid &c.	£ 9– 0– 0
To 1 Cherry Ditto 10 feet long 2 Draws & Streechers leggs Inlaid &c.	£ 7–10– 0
To 9 Clerks Tables with Draws & Strechers leggs inlaid & Strung @ 60 /	£ 6– 0– 0
	£ 52–10– 0

FIG. 10. Kneeland and Adams, Looking Glass. Hartford, Conn., 1792–1795. Mahogany veneer on pine; H. 31″, W. 18″. (Connecticut Historical Society.)

In the years that followed, Kneeland was a restless businessman. In December, 1796, he announced his intention to leave Hartford and offered for sale his dwelling house, outhouses, and other buildings, which he described as

pleasantly situated, about five minutes walk from the bridge, with an excellent garden containing 30 or more young fruit-trees of the best kind . . . 1 rood of land [and] the house 2 stories high, 28 by 38 feet on the ground, exclusive of a Lintoo, 38 feet long and 8 feet wide. . . . Said house is handsomely finished, painted and papered on the lower floor, which contains five rooms.[18]

[18] *American Mercury,* Dec. 19, 1796.

FIG. 11. Kneeland and Adams, Looking Glass. Hartford, Conn., 1792–1795. Mahogany veneer on pine; H. 37″, W. 18½″. (Winterthur 59.794.)

In March, 1797, he moved to a vacant shop on Main Street, which was formerly used by William Dexter as a comb factory. That same month his house with property was sold at public auction, and in April, John Thomas of Hartford purchased from him an additional plot of land (10 rods deep by 4 rods wide) for the sum of $1,000.[19]

[19] Register of Deeds, 1795–1801, XXI, 609 (Connecticut State Library). Kneeland had already sold Thomas a quarter-acre plot in 1792 for £40.

FIG. 12. Kneeland and Adams, Chest of Drawers. Hartford, Conn., 1792–1795. Cherry; H. 35", W. 43", D. 19". (Maxwell Brainard.)

With the capital from these sales, he moved to Farmington, where, in a notice dated January 20, 1798, he advised his customers that "he has lately removed from Hartford to the noted stand lately occupied by Mr. Thomas Bulkley, cabinet-maker, deceased; where he intends to carry on the above business in all its various branches, in the most modern fashions, of cherry or mahogany." [20] Advertisements for workmen, which appeared later that year, are the last record of his work in Connecticut. Presumably, Kneeland moved to New York State in the early years of the nineteenth century, for he died in Geneseo, New York, in 1828.

[20] *Connecticut Courant,* Feb. 5, 1798.

Of the furniture made by Kneeland, only a square, tilt-top table with serpentine outline and rounded corners can be assigned to the postpartnership period (Fig. 14). Handsomely proportioned, the mahogany table with its simple, turned pedestal and snake feet is branded "S. KNEELAND" in a serrated rectangle (Fig. 15) on the top of the pedestal. This unusual brand, which resembles a metalsmith's mark, also appears seven times on the base of the pedestal.

Adams, apparently wishing to capitalize on his recent prominence, opened his new shop on Ferry Street in January, 1796. He undertook to expand his business by advising his customers that he "has constantly on hand a general assortment of Mahogany furniture, made in the neatest and most approved fashions, which he offers for sale at the New-York prices . . . all kinds of Cabinet Work, Chairs, Soffa's &c. on the shortest notice as he employs the best workmen from New-York and Boston." [21] Late that same year, he entered into a limited association with Erastus Dewey, a Windsor chairmaker, who provided him with chairs. During the last years of the decade, business continued to expand; and, to compensate for this growth, Adams constantly sought workmen. Just why he decided to close his shop is not known, but in May of 1800 he advertised both in the Hartford newspapers and in such distant journals as the *Hampshire Gazette* in Northampton: "To be leased . . . the best CABINET SHOP in Connecticut; a good

[21] *Conn. Courant,* Jan. 18, 1796.

Fig. 14. Kneeland, Table. Hartford or Farmington, Conn., 1796–1810. Cherry; H. 27¼", top (square) 31½". (Old Sturbridge Village Photo.)

Fig. 13. Lemuel Adams, Armchair. Hartford, Conn., 1794–1796. Mahogany; H. 40½", W. 22½", D. 18½". (Connecticut Historical Society.)

Fig. 15. Brand on Table in Figure 14. H. ¼", W. 1⅜". (Old Sturbridge Village Photo.)

workman that will come well recommended, may have the privilege of buying on credit, all the Stock, Tools, &c, that may be wanted to carry on said business." [22] Late in 1800, Adams disappeared from the scene; no record of him after this year is known.

The types of furniture he produced are unknown, since no labeled examples endure. However, a number of chairs related to those made for the State House can be attributed to Adams' shop on the basis of stylistic similarities.

With both Kneeland and Adams working on the furnishings for the State House, John Wells sought a larger share of the individual commis-

[22] *Conn. Courant,* March 31, 1800.

sions. His frequent advertisements for workmen attest to his continued activity, and, by his own admission, he had at his shop "many articles of mahogany and cherry tree furniture already made, and free for inspection." [23] One measure of his financial success was that he was able to invest in property. In March, 1794, he purchased a small plot of land (about one-eighth acre) on the west side of Main Street, north of the bridge, from Daniel Hinsdale for £126. On this site he built his new shop. The following year he added, on the

south, a strip ten feet wide; and in 1796 he bought another ten-foot strip. The next year Wells purchased a house with about a quarter acre of land on the east side of Main Street near the South Meeting House. [24]

Certainly one of the outstanding entrepreneurs in Hartford, Wells demonstrated his ability as a craftsman by the skillful handling of the complex façade of a reverse serpentine-front chest of drawers (Fig. 16). Although it is contemporary with a serpentine-front chest by Kneeland and Adams

[23] *Conn. Courant,* May 27, 1793.

[24] Register of Deeds, 1795–1801 (Connecticut State Library), XIX, 199; XX, 464.

FIG. 16. John I. Wells, Chest of Drawers. Hartford, Conn., 1791–1810. Birch; H. 33¼", W. 39", D. 20". (Connecticut Historical Society.)

(Fig. 4), this piece is more modest in its over-all design and execution. Content solely to experiment with the shape of the façade, Wells framed the chest with a simple, straight top and claw-and-ball feet. Made of birch, the chest was "refinished" sometime during the last century and stained to simulate mahogany; the brass pulls and escutcheons are old but not original. The chest is branded "J. WELLS" on the inside backboard (Fig. 17).

Advertisements during the 1790's suggest that Wells was competent at making a wide variety of items—case pieces, beds, chairs, and tables. His notice in the *American Mercury* on January 25, 1796, set the tone for the work of his shop:

JOHN I. WELLS, has constantly on hand, some Mahogany, and most kinds of Cherry-Tree FURNITURE: —Those who favour him with their custom, may depend on his exertions to please them:—He would engage to furnish them with any kinds of Furniture that can be expected from a Cabinet-Maker's shop, as cheap as at any shop in this City; and from his making it with his own hands, is enabled to warrant it as durable, as what New-York affords.

A persistent characteristic of Wells's furniture is its durability. An over-all substantial feeling is evident in a small, oval, mahogany-veneered table (Fig. 18), despite attempts to lighten the design with stringing and bold panels of light woods inlaid on the legs. The table is branded on the underside of the frame (Fig. 19). Comparison with the brand on the chest of drawers shows that the same branding tool was used.

The affluence, both real and apparent, of Hartford's leading cabinetmakers attracted other craftsmen to the area in the mid-1790's. Two New York furniture makers moved north to take advantage of the city's expanding market. William Flagg (formerly of 19 Cliff Street, New York City) opened a shop on Main Street, north of Elisha Babcock's printing office, where he was prepared to sell "all kinds of Mahogany or Cherry Furniture, such as Sideboards, [bolection] or straight Fronts, Sofas, easy Chairs, Secretaries, Bureaus, oval Breakfast Tables, circular Card Tables, Chairs of different patterns, all made in the neatest New-York fashions." [25] And at his shop on Front Street, north of Ferry Street, Sylvester Tylee (formerly of 456 Pearl Street in New York City) informed the public "that he has commenced the

Cabinet and Chair business, in all its various branches; and has on hand a handsome assortment of Mahogany and Cherry Furniture, of the first quality, and at as cheap as can be bought in this City, or New-York." [26] Apparently, neither man was successful, since no record of them exists after 1797, and there are no known examples of their work.

In contrast, some Windsor chairmakers found sufficient work. Stacey Stackhouse, a New York-trained chairmaker, opened a shop in Hartford in the mid-1780's and remained in business there until 1795, when he moved to Claverack, New York, after selling his shop to John Wadsworth. Locally trained, Wadsworth may have served as an apprentice in the Stackhouse shop. Other Windsor chairmakers were less fortunate: Jacob Norton's small shop closed in 1789, and Erastus Dewey, who supplied Lemuel Adams with Windsor chairs, disappeared from the Hartford scene in 1797.

Certainly, Hartford was the center of cabinetmaking activity for the county, but the difficulty of transporting heavy furniture across the Connecticut hills encouraged the establishment of independent cabinet shops in the interior. Skilled and semiskilled artisans supplied most of the furniture for local use. Most towns could boast of a local craftsman, although many are known only through literary references since no documented furniture exists. Thomas Bulkley and Eli Wood both operated small cabinet shops in Farmington where they made and repaired furniture. Silas Easton advertised the sale of Windsor chairs at his

FIG. 17. Brand on Chest in Figure 16. (Connecticut Historical Society.)

shop a little south of the paper mill in East Hartford. In Southington, Nathaniel Jones offered any article of furniture from cradle to coffin, vying with Whitehead Howd for local commissions.

East Windsor, the county's second largest cabinetmaking center, boasted several craftsmen. Eliphalet Chapin's large shop has been mentioned already. Simeon Loomis and Jonathan Bright (for-

[25] *Conn. Courant*, July 4, 1796.

[26] *American Mercury*, Oct. 3, 1796.

Fɪɢ. 18. Wells, Table. Hartford, Conn., 1791–1800. Mahogany; H. 28¾″, W. 24″, D. 15″. (Connecticut Historical Society.)

mer Chapin apprentices) made and sold furniture in that city and supplied Daniel Burnap with clock cases, as did Joseph Bartlet and James Flint.[27] One of the most interesting of these local artisans is George Belden, a Hartford-trained cabinetmaker, who opened a shop in East Windsor in 1793. Belden's work has been identified only recently.[28] Of particular interest is a reverse serpentine, fall-front secretary and bookcase with a flat top and ogee bracket feet now owned by Philip H. Hammerslough. Inscribed in pencil, "George Belden / Hartford / May 6, 1791," the secretary was made just before Belden finished his apprenticeship in that city.

In Hartford, a new generation of cabinetmakers was beginning to make its mark. John Porter, 2d, after completing his apprenticeship in Aaron Chapin's shop in 1800, opened a shop about thirty rods east of the State House on State Street. Employing a technique used successfully by Kneeland and by Wells, Porter enlivened his advertisements by including illustrations of the type of furniture he could supply. One advertisement, used repeatedly in 1801 and 1802, shows a large serpentine-front sideboard flanked by a shield-back side chair and a semicircular side table. Another notice has a pair of serpentine-front, slant-top knife boxes on a sideboard and a pair of card tables. Below these cuts he ran the following statement:

JOHN PORTER

Manufactures all kinds of Cabinet work in the best manner, the latest and most approved patterns, and at the shortest notice. An assortment of the most fashionable and common articles constantly on sale at his cabinet shop.[29]

Porter's untimely death on October 25, 1802, at the age of 29, brought to an end the career of one of the city's most promising young cabinetmakers. No documented examples of his work have been found, but the list of items offered for sale by the administrators of his estate is a good summary of the kinds of things he made.

1 Elegant Mahogany Sideboard—1 ditto Secretary— 1 ditto Washstand—1 ditto Candlestand—2 pair ditto

Card Tables—1 Cherrytree Bureau—4 ditto Portable Desks—3 ditto Dining Tables—1 ditto Washstand— 1 Pine Toilet Table—A number of Traveling Trunks —1 low post Bedstead—1 sett unfinished Bedposts— 1 Crown Tester—A few Looking Glass Frames—two or three Maple Planks, and some refuse Boards—A quantity of Broken Stuff, some of it valuable—3 Work Benches, and sundry Tools and Utensils—Long Hair for Stuffing—Skins for covering Trunks.[30]

The inventory of his estate, taken July 18, 1803, provides an excellent index of the prices of furniture made by Hartford cabinetmakers. In the absence of account books or daybooks for these cabinetmakers, it is the only known index of fair market values; therefore, it seems pertinent to quote from it at length.

1 Mahogany Sash-Cornered SideBoard	$55.00
2 Ditto Swealed Front Beaurows	
$27.50	55.00
2 Ditto Dᵒ Dᵒ 24	48.00
1 Sash Cornerᵈ Side Board	55.00

Fig. 19. Brand on Table in Figure 18. (Connecticut Historical Society.)

1 Serpentine Ditto		45.00
1 Slash Band Secretary		38.00
1 Cockᵈ-Beeᵈ Ditto		25.00
1 Mahogany Dining Table & Ends		37.00
2 pr Card Table with Ditto & Sash Cornerd		62.00
1 pr. Ditto $25 & 1 pr Cimma		50.00
1 pr. Dᵒ Pembroke $19 & 1 pr Oval Pembroke $21		40.00
1 pr Mahogany Round Candle Stands		7.00
1 pr. Ditto $25 & 1 pr Cimma		50.00
1 Sweald Front Wash Hand Stand		10.00
4 Large Looking Glass Frames		8.00
9 Smaller " " "	1.75	15.75
2 Cockᵈ Beaded Cherry Bureau	11—	22.00
3 Dining Tables at $6—1 Breakfast Table	4.25	22.25

[27] Hoopes, *Daniel Burnap*, pp. 53–55.
[28] See Houghton Bulkeley, "George Belden and Erastus Grant, Cabinetmakers," *CHSB*, XXVII (July, 1962), 65–73. Bulkeley points out the similarities in construction of this secretary to one inscribed "E. Grant / Westfield," owned by L. Marsden Hubbard, and to a chest of drawers, inscribed "Erastus Grant," owned by Paul Godard.
[29] *Conn. Courant*, Aug. 17, 1801.
[30] *American Mercury*, June 16, 1803.

2	Round Candle Stands & 1 Square Dº	1.50	4.50
1	Wash hand Stand		2.00
2	Large Portable Writing Desks	4.50	9.00
3	Smaller Ditto "	3.50	10.50
2	Cross Bedsteds with Sackings	5—	10.00
1	Bedsted with Cannapa Testers		5.50
1	Ditto Field Dº & Tester		5.50
1	High Post & Tester		5.50
1	Common Post & Corded		2.50 [31]

The tools, materials, and finished furniture in his shop were valued at $1,119.73 by the administrators of his estate. With the addition of his personal belongings and other household items, the total value of his estate was listed at $1,347.58—an impressive amount for a young cabinetmaker.

Porter's contribution may never be understood fully. Certainly, he was a more than competent craftsman. Possibly several pieces formerly attributed to Aaron Chapin (or at least to Chapin's school) properly belong to Porter.

Young Laertes Chapin, another of Aaron's apprentices, probably joined his father's firm about 1800, for it is about this time that Aaron began to devote more time to the business of furniture making.[32] Possibly the competition from Porter and Wells encouraged him to advertise. After a few tentative notices listing cabinet furniture, "well made and fashionable," and picture frames, plain or gilt, Aaron Chapin resorted to the type of advertising popularized by Wells.

AARON CHAPIN . . . Has on hand elegant Sideboards, made in the newest fashion, and of the best mahogany, sashcornered and circular Card Tables, oval Tea Tables, square dining and breakfast Tables, Secretary's and Book cases, Bureaus, and all other kinds of furniture of mahogany and cherry tree. He flatters himself that by having the best of timber, and workmen, he shall be able to furnish setts of furniture on short notice, that shall be both handsome and good.[33]

The number of pieces attributed to Aaron Chapin is vast. Of these, only a handsome, eight-leg sideboard can be assigned to his firm. Made in 1804 for Frederic Robbins, the sideboard (Fig. 20) accompanied by its original bill of sale was presented to the Wadsworth Atheneum by a direct descendant of Robbins. The bill is particularly interesting. Dated November 22, 1804, it records "Mr. Frederic Robbins / Bout of Aaron Chapin / 1 Mahogany sashcornered 8 leg sideboard $68.00 / 1 Candle stand $1.67 / $69.67." Receipted at the bottom "Recᵈ Pay in full for Aaron Chapin / Laertes Chapin," it predates the Chapins' official partnership by three years. This particularly handsome piece is fashioned of matched panels of mahogany veneer. It is decorated with string inlay in geometric patterns on the doors, drawer fronts, and legs; large oval inlays of light wood above the legs; and pendants of string-inlay ovals on the legs. A well-constructed and complex form, this sideboard compares favorably with those available in New York.[34]

Two plain-style bookcases (Figs. 21 and 22) are often assigned to Chapin's shop. The evidence for the attribution of these pieces is based on entries in the diary of the Rev. Thomas Robbins and is, at best, tenuous. Admittedly, Robbins' diary does contain several references to Chapin's firm:

Sept. 1, 1806: Talk of getting some cabinet work of Mr. Chapin. He has some very good.

. . . . .

March 2, 1807: Got a very fine cherry book-case at Hartford which Mr. Chapin had made for me. Paid for it forty-four dollars.

March 3, 1807: Rode home with the lower part of my book-case safely.

. . . . .

July 4, 1807: Received the remainder of my book-case from Hartford. It is an exceedingly good one.

. . . . .

June 23, 1813: Paid Mr. Chapin, my cabinetmaker $20.

. . . . .

Feb. 24, 1814: Paid Chapin cabinetmaker $20. I closed their accounts.[35]

[31] Probate Records for Hartford District (Connecticut State Library).

[32] A sideboard made by B. Colton for Aaron Chapin & Son, dated Sept., 1801, now owned by The Connecticut Historical Society, confirms that father and son worked together for several years before their partnership was announced officially. See "Connecticut Cabinetmakers," *CHSB*, XXXII (Oct., 1967), 112 and 117.

[33] *Conn. Courant*, July 13, 1803.

[34] Compare this example with the elaborately inlaid mahogany sideboard made about 1795 by Mills and Deming of New York for Lt. Gov. Oliver Wolcott of Connecticut and illustrated on the cover of the Dec., 1928, issue of *Antiques*. This sideboard is veneered in carefully matched mahogany panels with large oval satinwood insets. It is further enriched with swags, garlands, urns, and shells inlaid in a variety of colored woods. Brought to Hartford in 1796, the year Wolcott became governor, it was certainly the most elaborate sideboard in the state at the time.

[35] The author is indebted to Mr. Thompson R. Harlow, director of The Connecticut Historical Society, for making available his notes on the furniture owned by the Rev. Mr. Robbins, first librarian of the society.

There is, however, no way to determine whether these entries refer to either of the bookcases assigned to Chapin.

The announcement of the formation of the partnership of Aaron Chapin & Son appeared in the Hartford newspapers on January 1, 1807.

AARON CHAPIN and LAERTES CHAPIN, having formed a connection in business, under the firm of AARON CHAPIN & SON, offer for sale, CABINET FURNITURE, such as Sideboards; Secretarys and book Cases; Bureaus; Card and Pembroke Tables; dining and breakfast Tables; bason Stands, candle Stands; Sofas and easy Chairs; Bedsteads; swing Cradles, &c. made in the best manner and on liberal terms.[36]

In the years that followed, they continued to make a wide variety of household furniture. The firm remained in business after Aaron's death in December, 1838, finally ceasing its operations when Laertes moved to East Hartford in 1845.

Aaron Colton, another of the city's leading craftsmen, vied with the Chapins for cabinetmaking commissions. In the years following the establishment of the society, his shop expanded to include a journeyman and two apprentices. In addition to furniture, he could supply window frames and sashes. In 1796 he moved from his original stand on Prison Street to a more advantageous location on Main Street east of the theater, where he offered for sale:

An assortment of Cabinet Furniture, such as Side Boards and Bureaus, of various kinds and prices, Secretarys, Desks and Book Cases, Dining and Circular end Tables, breakfast, kitchen and toilet Tables, &c. &c. Bedsteds of all kinds, Candle Stands and Swing Cradles, Boston Stands, portable Desks, easy Chairs and Sofas, Bed Chairs and night Stools. Likewise the newest and best kind of washing Machine, and many other articles made in the newest and best manner.[37]

The inclusion of a washing machine in his list of available items is an unusual departure from prec-

---

[36] *Conn. Courant,* Jan. 14, 1807.

[37] *Conn. Courant,* Feb. 26, 1806.

FIG. 20. Aaron Chapin, Sideboard. Hartford, Conn., 1804. Mahogany; H. 41¼″, W. 78½″, D. 26¼″. (Courtesy Wadsworth Atheneum, Hartford.)

FIG. 21. Secretary-Bookcase. Probably Hartford, Conn., 1800–1820. Cherry; H. 96¾″, W. 52⅛″, D. 20″. (Connecticut Historical Society.)

FIG. 22. Bookcase. Probably Hartford, Conn., 1800–1820. Cherry; H. 93¼″, W. 52½″, D. 19″. (Connecticut Historical Society.)

edent. Unfortunately, no model of this ingenious machine has survived.

Documented examples of his work seem to have vanished; the only exception is an interesting chest of drawers (Fig. 23). Made of cherry, the shaped bracket feet, the simple cock beading framing the drawers, and the concave molded top add interest to this straight-front chest. A penciled inscription on the bottom of the case identifies the maker: "A Colton / July 1801." Colton continued to advertise until about 1815, when he is believed to have retired from business.

Encouraged by the increased competition around him in the early nineteenth century, John Wells expanded his business. Besides employing men to make the usual cabinet furniture, he advertised for journeymen experienced at flag or rush seating and Windsor chairmaking and for a dexterous young man to make gun stocks. Recurrent pleas for "*long* Horse and Cattle HAIR" [38] for stuffing suggest that Wells sold many upholstered chairs. One such is the Martha Washington armchair, or "Lolling" chair, branded "J WELLS" in several places on the frame (Fig. 24).

[38] *Conn. Courant,* July 13, 1801.

The serpentine crest, the concave arm supports, and the prominent outline of bellflowers and string inlay on the arm supports and front legs recall similar pieces of Massachusetts origin. Traditionally, this chair has been assigned the date of 1789–1791; however, it is more reasonable to assume that it was made between 1800 and 1810, when this type of chair was most popular in Massachusetts.

Wells did not devote all his energies to cabinetmaking. He speculated in land in upper New York State on a limited scale, at a time when huge tracts were being purchased by Connecticut businessmen. Some of this property was held for investment; part was rented out for farming. Wells also farmed a section of his Hartford land. Newspaper advertisements show that during the 1790's he raised fruit trees for sale.

In 1804, Wells apparently contemplated leaving Hartford, for in the *Connecticut Courant* of August 22, he offered

For sale his dwelling house, with other buildings, &c connected with it. Also the Shops which he occupies, with the pleasant lot on which they stand; with possession next June.

His reasons for remaining in Hartford are not known, but subsequent advertisements indicate that he continued his trade. On March 7, 1807, he announced the formation of a partnership with Erastus Flint. Nothing is known about Flint until he opened a small shop on Main Street in June, 1806, offering for sale, "CABINET FURNITURE in all its variety, made in the newest and most approved fashion. Also Sofa's, Chairs, Bedsteads, &c. made to order, with neatness and dispatch." [39]

Under the partnership, new items were introduced and business flourished. For example, Wells and Flint offered sofas "made upon a new, cheap and improved plan . . . [and] an elegant assortment of gilt fancy Chairs of the newest patterns." [40] This is the earliest Connecticut advertisement for the sale of gilt furniture other than looking glasses. During the next few years the firm carried a variety of gilt, fancy, bamboo, and fan-back chairs. Anticipating an increase in business, the firm moved to larger quarters in July, 1808, where "a new and elegant furniture warehouse" was opened. Perhaps the partners overestimated

FIG. 23. Aaron Colton, Chest of Drawers. Hartford, Conn., 1801. Cherry; H. 37½″, W. 45″, D. 20½″. (Richard Mills.)

the size of their market; in any event, they terminated the partnership on March 28, 1809, although both men continued working for several years.

Indicative of Flint's new business venture is his notice for workmen stipulating that "none need apply unless well acquainted with making sideboards." [41] Meanwhile, Wells reopened a shop at his home near the South Meeting House. Not to be outdone by Flint, he confidently advertised that he could furnish an entire house on short notice; but about the same time he began to curtail his cabinetmaking activities and for the second time offered for sale his dwelling, shop, tools, and furniture. Although he continued to make sofas and easy chairs, much of his time was devoted to experiments with the grinding of paints and the making of ink. A partnership formed in 1810 with Samuel Beckwith, Jr., a cabinetmaker, in which Beckwith managed the cabinetshop, allowed Wells ample time for his other projects.

Although it is not labeled, one other piece, which has descended in his family, can be attributed to Wells. It is a simple, cherry secretary that is assigned to him by family tradition. Illustrated

[39] *Conn. Courant,* June 25, 1806.
[40] *Conn. Courant,* July 1, 1807.

[41] *Conn. Courant,* March 28, 1810.

FIG. 24. Wells, Upholstered Easy Chair. Hartford, Conn., 1795–1810. Cherry; H. 43″, W. 24″, D. 20½″. (Herbert T. Darlington.)

in *The Connecticut Historical Society Bulletin* (July, 1961), the secretary is rectangular in shape with a heavy, molded cornice and a slant-top desk. Unornamented except for narrow beading edging the drawers, the piece has bracket feet which are similar in profile to those on the Kneeland and Adams chest of drawers (Fig. 12).

Eli Wood, a Farmington cabinetmaker, moved to Hartford in 1800. There he established his business in the shop on Ferry Street formerly occupied by Lemuel Adams, where he employed one apprentice and two journeymen. The following year he formed a partnership with Nathaniel Watson, another cabinetmaker from Farmington.

Nathaniel Watson, Eli Wood & Co. Have commenced partnership to the Cabinet and Chair making business under the firm of WATSON, WOOD, & Co. In the shop lately occupied by Eli Wood, where they have constantly on hand a general assortment of Mahogany and Cherry-tree Furniture and Chairs, of all kinds made in the newest and most approved fashions.[42]

The success of the firm was such that the partners advertised for two or three journeymen cabinetmakers. Although they undoubtedly produced many items, no documented pieces have survived.

Most of the Hartford cabinetmaking firms were successful; however, a firm operated by Joel and Charles Huntington was less fortunate. The announcement of its establishment appeared in the *American Mercury* on July 30, 1801:

Joel & Charles Huntington, (CABINET-MAKERS), Respectfully inform the public that they have taken a shop in Prison-street opposite the Bank, where they intend to carry on their business in its several branches.

The firm disappeared from the local records the next year, and there is no indication of the type of goods produced.

Outside the city limits, a variety of less well-known craftsmen plied their trade. Nathaniel Jones continued his business in a small shop in Southington. About 1805, Hempstead and Graves opened a shop which furnished goods for the residents of Hebron. That same year, Luther Jones set up a shop in West Simsbury and Edward Shepard opened one in Wethersfield. Whitehead Howd of Southington moved to New Hartford in 1807. Two years later, Orrin Winchell advertised the opening of his shop in Wallingford. The work of

these men is known only through literary sources. It is clear from their advertisements, however, that they carried a full line of cabinet furniture, in both mahogany and cherry, as well as a handsome assortment of chairs.

The variety of items advertised by these cabinetmakers indicates that they were well informed about the type of work available in Hartford and that they were equipped to furnish similar pieces in their own communities. Support for this statement can be found in the account books of John Fitch Parsons, a Suffield cabinetmaker. These books, now in the Kent Memorial Library in Suffield, provide an accurate record of the work done in his shop between September, 1804, and December, 1825.[43] Included are a wide variety of tables, candlestands, sideboards, clock pieces, bureaus, secretaries, bedsteads, and bookcases. Where Parsons received his training is not recorded, but his confidence in undertaking a variety of complex forms suggests that he had worked in the shop of a master craftsman in Hartford or East Windsor. His account book also contains a wide range of less expensive items: coffins, a clotheshorse, carriage seats, cupboards, fireboards, pitch pipes, frames for portraits, rockers for chairs, boot trees, rolling pins, and an occasional tavern sign. As the major cabinetmaker in Suffield, Parsons repaired and altered furniture as well as supplying new pieces.

Even though he was some distance from Hartford, Parsons' prices for finished furniture were comparable to those of the city cabinetmakers and were probably based on the price list agreed on by the Society of Cabinetmakers. Most sideboards cost $50.00. Bureaus varied in price from $17.50 to $25.00, depending on style and ornament. The price of tables varied according to size: candlestands were $1.50 to $2.00 each, kitchen tables were $3.50 each, pembroke tables were $5.50 to $6.00 each, and dining tables were $7.00 to $10.00 each. The price of a secretary averaged between $25.00 and $30.00. Depending on the material used, clock cases cost from $7.00 to $20.00.

Considering the myriad entries, quantities of documented Parsons furniture should have survived; but Parsons apparently neither labeled nor signed his work, for no known piece can be authenticated. Because of their direct descent in the

---

[42] *Conn. Courant,* Aug. 17, 1801.

[43] These account books were published in part in Bissell's *Antique Furniture.*

Fɪɢ. 25. John Fitch Parsons (attributed), Sideboard. Suffield, Conn., 1807. Mahogany; H. 40½″, W. 72½″, D. 27″. (The Suffield Historical Society, Gift of Mr. and Mrs. Samuel Reid Spencer: photo, Lomis Studio.)

Fɪɢ. 26. Shipley, Sideboard. New York City, 1791–1795. Mahogany; H. 40⅜″, W. 74⅞″, D. 33¾″. (Mrs. James Hale Steinman: photo, Winterthur.)

family of the original owner, four pieces—a pair of semicircular side tables, a rectangular candle-stand, and a sideboard—are generally attributed to Parsons.[44] Of particular interest is the serpentine-front sideboard with its complex pattern of concave and convex planes decorated with geometric patterns of string inlay (Fig. 25). Highly sophisticated in its arrangement of parts, this piece relates to the Chapin sideboard (Fig. 20) and to the type of New York sideboards available in Connecticut, as shown in the example by George Shipley (Fig. 26).

Connecticut's furniture craftsmen, both in Hartford and in some of the larger towns, were more sophisticated than most writers have been willing to admit. With the help of one or two journeymen and a few apprentices, they made the

[44] *Ibid.*, p. 32.

same wide range of items that was available in any major city. Admittedly, these craftsmen were not innovators; their inspiration came from English furniture designs as translated by New York cabinetmakers. With the close economic ties between Hartford and New York, it is only natural that the cabinetmakers in Hartford looked to the work of their counterparts in the country's fastest-growing city. Yet the style that evolved was their own. Working primarily in cherry, with some important pieces in the more fashionable mahogany, they skillfully manipulated their materials, allowing inlaid and carved decoration to enhance rather than detract from the form. Their preference for certain ornament owes more to the easy transfer of ideas from shop to shop within a closely knit community than to any organized "school."

Detail of Figure 4, page 32.

Wallpaper from the Shop of William Poyntell

Horace L. Hotchkiss, Jr.

WITH its dignified, five-bay façade of beaded wood siding, extensive interior carving and paneling, and floor plan of a central hall with four corner rooms, the Imlay house in Allentown, New Jersey, is a typical, although rather late, example of the small-town Georgian "mansion."[1] The builder of the house, John Imlay (1754–1813), had antecedents in Allentown; but when he started construction, presumably in the early 1790's, he was continuing his career as a Philadelphia shipping merchant in the West Indies trade.[2] The wallpaper and borders that adorned one of the front bedrooms on the second floor of the house are now at The Henry Francis du Pont Winterthur Museum in a parlor known as the Imlay Room (Fig. 1).

The paper, with its accompanying borders, is an important artifact because it came from the walls of an old house still standing in a village near Trenton and Bordentown, New Jersey. Its historical interest is reinforced by the original bill of sale now owned by The Metropolitan Museum of Art in New York.

Mr Imlay	Phil^a April 18, 1794 Bo^t of Wm Poyntell		
8 Pieces Paper Hanging	@ 3/9	£	1..10..0
8 Yards narrow black border	1/		0.. 8..0
8 Yards festoon d°	1/		0.. 8..0
10 Pieces Elegant Paper	11/3		5..12..6

24 Yards Elegant broad fruit border	1/10½	2.. 5..0
120 Yards d° narrow rose border	@ 6	3.. 0..0
	£ 13 3 6	

Rec^d payment
  for Wm Poyntell
  R^t Caldcleugh

Having only 10 pieces of the Elegant Paper, I have pack'd it all up, but at Mr Imlays option whether he chuses to keep or return what is left on putting it up, supposing that it might be agreeable to him to have some to spare in case of accident, as the same pattern cannot be replaced in case a small portion should be wanted at a future time.

W. P.

American wallpaper bills of this period are rare. Poyntell's bill refers not only to the Winterthur-Imlay paper but to an "Elegant Paper" of classical medallions (Fig. 2) that also hung in the Imlay house and was later removed to the American Wing of The Metropolitan Museum. From the bill we learn that John Imlay purchased his wallpapers and borders from the Philadelphia firm of William Poyntell (1756–1811), stationer and jeweler.

In 1924 when Nancy McClelland wrote *Historic Wall-Papers,* she, knowing the importance and rarity of eighteenth-century wallpapers found in place in American houses, included in her book photographs of the two papers then still hanging in the Imlay house. A transcription of the bill, at that time the property of the owner of the mansion, Mrs. Mary Emma Gordon, was also given in Miss McClelland's book.[3]

[1] Now Farmer's (private) Hospital. A description of the house, some of its history, and illustrations are found in John Taylor Boyd, Jr., "The House of John Imlay, Esq., an Eighteenth Century Dwelling, Allentown, New Jersey," *Monograph Series,* XV, No. 3 (1931), 59–60, Plates XXXII–XLV. The Winterthur-Imlay wallpaper is shown in part in Plate XLIV.

[2] *Ibid.,* p. 59.

[3] Nancy McClelland, *Historic Wall-Papers: From Their Inception to the Introduction of Machinery* (Philadelphia: J. B. Lippincott Co., 1924), pp. 256–59.

Fig. 1. Imlay Room, Winterthur, showing wallpaper from the John Imlay house, *ca.* 1790, Allentown, N.J. (Winterthur 3S–4 [see also Figures 5–7].)

The word "pieces" in the bill refers to a roll of wallpaper, the roll being of a length that cannot be readily determined. From the size of the original Imlay house rooms, however, it may be deduced that the "pieces" referred to here might have measured between twenty-four and thirty feet. In accord with the practice of the time, these rolls were made up of smaller segments or squares pasted together. On old wallpapers before about 1830 (when rolls of "endless paper" began to come into use), the horizontal seams occur at intervals of approximately fifteen to thirty inches.[4] Because of the soft, fine quality of the rag paper, they are not distracting.

The "Elegant Paper," mentioned in the bill, is now owned by The Metropolitan Museum and was installed for several years in the Haverhill

Room in the American Wing (Fig. 3).[5] It is in the "Pompeiian" style (Fig. 4) with medallions and arabesques such as those favored by Jean-Baptiste Reveillon (1725–1811), who made ordinary, non-flocked wallpaper fashionable in the Paris of the 1770's. Arabesque designs of this sort were often associated in the public mind with Raphael's Loggia for Pope Leo X. In the year Imlay purchased his "Elegant Paper" from Poyntell, the Englishman Henry Wansey, on a visit to Philadelphia, noted in his journal: "I dined this day with Mr. Bingham. . . . I found a magnificent house and gardens in the best English style. . . . The room was papered in the French taste, after the style of the Vatican in Rome."[6] The Metropolitan-Imlay

[4] The Winterthur-Imlay segments are 20½ by 18 inches.

[5] The wallpaper was removed from exhibition in 1947.

[6] Henry Wansey, *An Excursion to the United States of North America in the Summer of 1794* (2nd ed. rev.; Salisbury, [Eng.]: J. Easton, 1798), p. 123.

FIG. 2. Wallpaper, French, *ca.* 1790, from the Imlay house. (The Metropolitan Museum of Art, Sage Fund, 1924 [see also Figures 3 and 4].)

paper must have resembled Mr. Bingham's, and, since it was the most expensive of the lot, was probably imported from France. In the illustration of the Haverhill Room, the "Elegant broad fruit border" can clearly be seen at frieze height.

The Winterthur-Imlay paper (undoubtedly the one listed first in the bill) is of a different type —a design of flowering branches that owes little to classical precedent (Fig. 5). Flowered papers were known in England and France late in the seventeenth century and were generally related to textile designs. The flowers of the mid-eighteenth century were often large in scale and—like several papers installed in the Jeremiah Lee Mansion, Marblehead, Massachusetts, in the 1760's—of a relaxed, open design unlike the succeeding, more mechanical compositions seen in the *Directoire*. The Winterthur-Imlay paper, flowing and asymmetrical in its design, goes back to this earlier style. Its leaves and flowers also convey another impression, a definite feeling of *chinoiserie* in the manner of Jean Pillement (1728–1808), French tapestry designer and court painter. Pillement was well known for his graceful arabesques incorporating Chinese animal and architectural motifs as well as fantastic flowers and seed pods.

Old, unused lengths of wallpaper that have been shielded from the light reveal the startling eighteenth-century tolerance for bright color. Some of the color of the Winterthur-Imlay sidewall paper has been lost, and one must bear this in mind when looking at its mellowed tints. The remaining colors are principally browns and grays on an off-white background. Although generally printed from wood blocks, papers of this sort were often also partially stenciled and "penciled" (hand-painted). That an eighteenth-century customer could have a greater color choice in wallpaper than we have today is shown by the statement in Poyntell's advertisement in *Dunlap's American Daily Advertiser*, March 21, 1791: "Paper made to any particular desire of Ground and Colours, at 3 days notice."

It is interesting that a set of borders designed in the crisp manner of the 1790's was used with this wallpaper of a somewhat earlier style (Figs. 6 and 7). Throughout the eighteenth century, borders were used along cornices and chair rails and to outline windows, doorways, and chimney pieces. As in the Winterthur Imlay Room, it was common practice to hang "busy" borders in juxta-

position with strongly patterned, unrelated wallpapers. The borders in this room have retained most of their original color and employ relatively large areas of black for contrast.

It is surprising to find in the Poyntell bill that only eight yards each of these two borders are called for; this would seem more appropriate for a closet six feet square than for a room. In this period, however, three or four widths of border were often printed longitudinally on an ordinary roll of wallpaper stock, to be later cut and separated. Such was probably the case here.

It is possible that the relatively inexpensive Winterthur-Imlay paper was not imported, but made by Poyntell. If so, it is doubtless a copy of a French or English design, since American manufacturers copied European wallpapers as a matter of course. It is unlikely that the economy could have supported many commercial designers as we know them. Although Poyntell advertised in the *Pennsylvania Packet,* December 4, 1797, "Print Cutters wanted. Neat workmen at drafting and cutting," these men would probably not have created original designs, but would have transferred already existing patterns to wood blocks and stencils for the process of wallpaper printing.

In choosing his wallpapers, John Imlay may have looked over a sample book, for on October 9, 1792, Poyntell had advertised in the *Federal Gazette* that "A Pattern Book is now ready for inspection: amongst them are, a great variety of Fashionable and Handsome Borders." This statement is of special interest in the history of American wallpaper, as the writer knows of only one existing American wallpaper sample book that may date from the eighteenth century.[7]

When he started to make wallpaper, Poyntell said: "That he [Poyntell] may stand responsible

---

[7] A wallpaper sample book covered with an Irish newspaper, *D. E. Post,* showing dates of 1795, is in The Joseph Downs Manuscript and Microfilm Collection (66X141), Division of Libraries, Winterthur Museum. A handwritten inscription on the inside of the front cover reads, in part, "This Book of Patterns / belonged to Archibald Hamilton Rowan Esqʳ / he had it in America." The book, whose cover reads, "Book of Wallpapers of the 18th Century lent by Lt Colonel Elliot," contains 142 samples of decorated papers. The wallpaper designs are very small in scale, and some undoubtedly were meant to be used as end papers for books and linings for trunks and boxes. Despite the eighteenth-century cover, the papers appear to be of the 1800–1830 period. Sample no. 44 in the book, a tiny geometric design resembling widely spaced berries, has the watermark "BRANDYWI[NE]."

for the quality of his manufactures, each piece will in future be stamped with his name."[8] A recent investigation of several widths of the Winterthur-Imlay paper did not reveal the stamp, and the protective cloth backing applied several years ago makes impractical a thorough search. In a letter to the writer, Abbott Lowell Cummings mentioned Zachariah Mills of Hartford, Connecticut, who (at a slightly later date) also marked his wallpapers.[9] Cummings continued:

Two or three papers have been found which bear the Mills mark and it is of interest to note that the mark occurs very infrequently. As a matter of fact, Mills says that he only stamps each roll and that would mean a very infrequent interval indeed, once the paper was applied to the walls. In one case, a room in Connecticut,

[8] *Federal Gazette* (Philadelphia) , March 23, 1790.
[9] Letter dated Jan. 6, 1967, to the writer, from Abbott Lowell Cummings, assistant director of The Society for the Preservation of New England Antiquities.

I believe, the mark was found only once or twice in the entire room.

William Poyntell, born in Oxfordshire, England, was by 1781, at the age of twenty-five, selling wallpapers at his stationery store at "Second Street, three Doors below Market Street."[10] Poyntell also sold a great many other things. An advertisement in the *Pennsylvania Packet* of December 9, 1783, lists among his merchandise, "a variety of jewellery ware, best violin strings, harpsichord wires, guitar strings, parchment, money scales and weights." Later he supplied workmen to hang wallpapers, and by 1790 he started making wallpapers rather than merely importing them.[11] Plunkett Fleeson, an upholsterer prominent in Philadelphia town affairs, is credited with being the first American to manufacture wallpaper, having

[10] *Freeman's Journal* (Philadelphia) , June 6, 1781.
[11] *Federal Gazette*, March 23, 1790.

FIG. 3. Wallpaper Panels, French, *ca.* 1790, from the Imlay house. (The Metropolitan Museum of Art, Sage Fund, 1924.)

FIG. 4. Wallpaper, French, *ca.* 1790, from the Imlay house. (The Metropolitan Museum of Art, Sage Fund, 1924.)

FIG. 5. Detail of Wallpaper, *ca.* 1790, from the Imlay house. (Winterthur 3S–5.)

announced this venture in 1739.[12] Throughout the early eighteenth century, wallpaper manufacturing, selling, and hanging were usually in the province of the upholsterer, like Fleeson, or the stationer, like Poyntell.

In 1795, a year after he had sold wallpapers to Imlay, Poyntell moved his shop to 70 Chestnut Street.[13] It is indicative of Poyntell's prominence that President Washington, during his residence in Philadelphia, purchased wallpaper from him.[14] Poyntell, established in the heart of the business area, had a considerable investment in wallpaper. In the *Philadelphia Gazette* of April 4, 1796, he advertised, "In addition to the extensive stock of his own manufacture he has for sale twelve thousand pieces of French papers, together with Borders, Landscapes and Chinese Pieces for ornamenting Breast Work and Chimney Boards."

Poyntell is not listed in the tax records for Chestnut Ward after 1798. In his will, made shortly before he died in 1811,[15] he referred to himself as "Gentleman," and considering his English upbringing this might indicate an earlier decision to disassociate himself from "trade." In any event, at his demise he was a wealthy landowner who made generous provision for his widow and five children, left cash bequests to relatives in England, and provided an annuity of twenty-five pounds for his brother residing there.[16]

Although astute and canny in business matters, Poyntell had the delightfully diffuse interests of an eighteenth-century man of means. In 1805, he was one of the founding directors of the Pennsylvania Academy of the Fine Arts.[17] He left to his younger son, William, then a minor, his share in the Library Company of Philadelphia "Together

[12] McClelland, *Historic Wall-Papers*, p. 241.

[13] *Philadelphia Gazette,* Nov. 3, 1795.

[14] "Washington's Household Account Book, 1793–1797." *Pennsylvania Magazine of History and Biography,* XXXI, No. 3 (1907), 322, 340, 343.

[15] A short obituary in *Relf's Philadelphia Gazette and Daily Advertiser,* Sept. 12, 1811, confirms indirectly the birth year and death date (1756–1811) given in Rev. William White Bronson, A.M., *The Inscriptions in St. Peter's Church Yard, Philadelphia,* ed. Charles R. Hildeburn (Camden, N.J., 1879), p. 45. In 1966, the birth and death dates on Poyntell's gravestone were worn away and unreadable.

[16] Estate of William Poyntell, Philadelphia County Will Books, 1811, Will Book 3, p. 519 (City Hall, Philadelphia).

[17] Charles Coleman Sellers, "Rembrandt Peale, 'Instigator,'" *Pennsylvania Magazine of History and Biography,* LXXIX (July, 1955), 339.

with all my maps Prints in sheets Surveyors Compass and chain Camera obscura antient coins." To his son-in-law and former business associate, Robert Caldcleugh, he left "my stained glass which I brought from Europe." [18]

Poyntell declared in the *Pennsylvania Packet,* December 9, 1783, when he was only importing wallpapers, that his low prices would make papering as cheap as whitewash. It is true that the wall of the time (unless a paneled fireplace wall) was ordinarily whitewashed plaster; but wallpaper had probably come into moderate use by the 1740's and was doubtless fairly common at the time John Imlay purchased the paper now at Winterthur. Considering this, one sees too few eighteenth-century American rooms with original wallpapers. The Imlay Room helps to give a picture of a certain scale and subject matter in eighteenth-century wallpaper design and illustrates a reliance on borders that greatly transcends our own. Only on the subject of color does the room fail to instruct completely.

[18] Estate of William Poyntell, Philadelphia County Will Books, 1811, Will Book 3, p. 519 (City Hall, Philadelphia).

FIG. 6. Detail of Cornice Border, *ca.* 1790, from the Imlay house. (Winterthur 3S–6.)

FIG. 7. Detail of Chair-Rail Border, *ca.* 1790, from the Imlay house. (Winterthur 3S–7.)

Detail of Figure 1, page 37.

Henry Dawkins and the Quaker Comet

Wilford P. Cole

If the comparison be admissible, he appeared rather like a comet, which threatens, in its irregular course, the destruction of the worlds near which it passes, than as one of those tranquil orbs which hold their accustomed place, and dispense their light, in the harmonious order of heaven.[1]

WITH these words, Benjamin Lay was presented to early nineteenth-century readers by his biographer, Roberts Vaux. Lay was an English Quaker with a penchant for controversy, who came to the American colonies about 1731 and launched a singular antislavery crusade in the Philadelphia region. Several depictions (all prints) of this eccentric reformer exist. They show a short, cruelly deformed old man with a white beard, dressed in knee breeches, frock coat, and hat. His extended right hand rests on a walking stick and holds an open book. His left hand is raised slightly above waist level in an ambiguous gesture.

These portraits are based on a rare, etched and engraved print, signed "W Williams Pinx'" and "HD.Fecit." (Fig. 1). The engraver's signature is that of Henry Dawkins, and the painter's name probably refers to William Williams, a leading painter in Philadelphia in the mid-eighteenth century. Williams' painting is now lost.[2] Two copies of the Dawkins print are in the Quaker Collection of the Haverford College Library, Haverford,

Pennsylvania. One (hereafter, "the first Haverford copy"), formerly in the collection of Caroline Allison, is a heavy but clear impression on laid paper, frayed at the bottom right corner, stained by water along the bottom and by a spot of glue on the left margin, and glued to a sheet of modern paper. The other (hereafter, "the second Haverford copy") is a lighter impression of the same state on wove paper, which has turned slightly gray-brown. The copy in The Henry Francis du Pont Winterthur Museum, of unknown provenance, appears to be of the same impression as the second Haverford copy and on the same paper (Fig. 2). It has now been cleaned and the paper de-acidified.

Benjamin Lay was born in humble circumstances in Colchester, Essex, on November 26, 1681/82.[3] In 1702/03, after a brief apprenticeship to a glover and a short period working on a brother's farm, he went to sea. During his voyages to the Near East, seamen's tales exposed him to the terrors of slavery among the Moslems.[4] In 1710, he returned to Colchester and married Sarah (last

---

[1] Roberts Vaux, *Memoirs of the Lives of Benjamin Lay and Ralph Sandiford; Two of the Earliest Public Advocates for the Emancipation of Enslaved Africans* (Philadelphia: Solomon W. Conrad, W. Brown, Printer, 1815), p. 16.

[2] William Sawitzky, "William Williams, First Instructor of Benjamin West," *Antiques*, XXXI (May, 1937), 240–42; and Wilford P. Cole, "Henry Dawkins, Engraver" (unpublished Master's thesis, University of Delaware, 1966), pp. 58–60.

[3] Biographical details about Lay are scattered, often conflicting, and frequently legendary. Lay's own book (see Note 4) gives only the barest documentation of his experiences, but mentions the Near Eastern voyage and his spiritual unrest in Barbados. Vaux's biography pieces together fragments from Lay's book with traditional material and apologetics and has become the immediate source for most biographical notes. The first solid additions to Lay's story, since Vaux, were contributed by C. Brightwen Rowntree, "Benjamin Lay," *Journal of the Friends' Historical Society* (London), XXXIII (1936), 3–19. Rowntree discovered documents regarding Lay's relations with Quakers in England and clarified certain chronological questions. Unless otherwise noted, biographical details in this article are from Vaux and confirmed, or at least repeated, by later writers.

[4] Benjamin Lay, *ALL SLAVE KEEPERS that keep the Innocent in Bondage, APOSTATES Pretending to Lay*

name unknown), who was also a hunchback and of a stature similar to his own.

Over the next ten years, he involved himself in political and religious controversy in London to the dismay of fellow members of the Devonshire House Monthly Meeting. It is not clear which issues so aroused Lay and aggravated the Friends. According to one legend, he was granted an audience with George I (and another with George II), to whom he presented a copy of Milton's tract, *Considerations Touching the Likeliest Means to Remove Hirelings Out of the Church.* In 1720, after many warnings, his contentiousness finally moved the Meeting to disown him. The action failed to effect the desired change in him, however, and the Colchester Two Weeks Meeting, in whose jurisdiction he was living in 1723, officially repudiated him and his practices. This prompted considerable correspondence between Lay, Devonshire House Monthly Meeting, and the Colchester Two Weeks and Monthly Meetings concerning his attempt to be reinstated. Finally, in 1729, the Colchester Monthly Meeting accepted Benjamin and his wife, who had not been disowned.[5] This brought the Meeting under censure from the Quarterly Meeting for the County of Essex, but Lay was retained.

About 1731, Lay and his wife moved to Barbados, where he engaged in some form of merchant trade.[6] Details of his life there are sparse, but it appears that the excesses of slavery practiced by the English settlers caused him great mental and moral anguish and provided a focus for his reformer's zeal. The Lays' consciences were so burdened that they moved to Philadelphia in 1732.

Claim to the Pure & Holy Christian Religion; of what Congregation so ever; but especially in their Ministers, by whose example the filthy Leprosy and Apostacy is spread far and near; it is a notorious Sin, which many of the true Friends of Christ, and his pure Truth, Called Quakers, has been for many Years and still are concern'd to write and bear Testimony against; as a Practice so gross and hurtful to Religion, and destructive to Government, beyond what Words can set forth, or can be declared of by Men or Angels, and yet lived in by Ministers and Magistrates in AMERICA. THE LEADERS OF THE PEOPLE CAUSE THEM TO ERR. Written for a General Service, by him that truly and sincerely desires the present and eternal Welfare and Happiness of all Mankind, all the World over, of all Colours, and Nations, as his own Soul; BENJAMIN LAY (Philadelphia: Printed for the author [by Benjamin Franklin], 1737), p. 16. The publication and date of this book are discussed in Note 11.

[5] Rowntree, *Journal*, XXXIII (1936), 10.

[6] *Ibid.*, pp. 11 ff., establishes this date, rather than 1718, the generally accepted date.

The acrimony of his controversies followed them there in a letter, dated June 27, 1732, from the Colchester Two Weeks Meeting, warning that he was a troublesome Friend and that he had not given satisfaction for grievances against him in England.[7] Although Sarah was eventually accepted in Philadelphia, Lay never gained membership in Meetings in America. This did not prevent him from attending Meetings throughout the Philadelphia area, nor did it cause him to forsake his exaggerated brand of Quaker piety. He wore plain clothing made of tow and linen of his own weaving, refused to ride a horse or coach, and eschewed the use of any meat or other product of animal suffering. He was an ardent student of the Bible and religious literature, and was reputed to have collected an unusually large library. He objected to capital punishment, arguing that wantonness and idleness were sinful and might be reformed in prison, but that no repentance was possible from the grave.[8] To these ideals few Friends could object in principle, but his fulminations against slavery kept him continually at odds with the Quaker community.

Lay's objection to slavery was on moral and humanitarian grounds, and his campaigns were carried on with great fervor. He lost no opportunity to prick the consciences of Quaker slaveowners and rub them with the salt of his own anguish. He harangued Meetings with annoying length and frequency, and more than once was forbidden entry to Meetings or bodily removed for harassing brethren and ministers who were testifying. If Whittier's story is true, he may have staged America's first sit-in, or "sit-out," as it were. Offering no resistance to his removal from one Meeting, he was unceremoniously deposited in a street gutter by a burly attendant. According to the story, he lay there until the Meeting closed, refusing to participate in the violent act that had put him there by picking himself out.[9] At times, however, his adherence to peaceable Quaker principles was more questionable. When a neighbor refused to free a slave girl, Lay kidnaped the neighbor's son to demonstrate the agonies the girl's family must have felt when she was taken from them.[10]

Unlike Ralph Sandiford, Anthony Benezet,

[7] *Ibid.*, p. 12.

[8] Vaux, *Memoirs*, pp. 39–40.

[9] John Greenleaf Whittier's introduction to *The Journal of John Woolman* (Boston: James R. Osgood and Co., 1871), pp. 13–14.

[10] Vaux, *Memoirs*, p. 28.

FIG. 1. Henry Dawkins, *Benjamin Lay*. Philadelphia, probably about 1760. Etching and engraving after lost painting by William Williams; plate, H. 9¹⁵⁄₁₆″, W. 7⁷⁄₁₆″. (Quaker Collection of the Haverford College Library.)

Fɪɢ. 2. Dawkins, *Benjamin Lay* (later impression). Philadelphia, probably after 1810. Etching and engraving; plate, H. 9¹⁵⁄₁₆″, W. 7⁷⁄₁₆″. (Winterthur 66.110.)

John Woolman, and other early abolitionist Quakers, Lay was not moved to wage a pamphlet war. One of his most curious performances, however, was his book, *All Slave Keepers That Keep the Innocent in Bondage . . .* , dated 1737.[11] This mélange of letters, quotations, meditations, and diatribes was, as Vaux remarked, "so intemperate as to confirm the usage, rather than to reform it." [12]

Benjamin and Sarah Lay lived in a cottage, "resembling, in its construction, a cave," located about six miles north of Philadelphia between Germantown and the Old York Road, near Mileston (e) .[13] How they supported themselves is not clear. Vaux and others have suggested that Lay may have continued his old trade as a glover, or possibly as a draper, as might be inferred from the uncharacteristically fine textiles listed in his estate inventory.[14] He may have carried on the same merchant trade he maintained in Barbados, the nature of which is not revealed in known documents. The Lays remained in the cottage until ill health forced them to move. They settled on the farm of John Phipps, near the Abington Meeting

House, where Sarah died late in 1735.[15] Benjamin died on February 3, 1759, at the home of Joshua Morris, and was buried in the Friends' burial ground at Abington.[16]

The Dawkins print shows Lay standing in front of the opening to a cave. This probably does not represent his home, but, rather, the secluded spot to which he retired to read and meditate:

[Lay] selected an interesting spot, on the farm of the person with whom he resided, and improved a natural excavation in the earth, near a fine spring of water, so as to afford himself a commodious apartment. The interior part of the room of his cave was neatly ornamented with festoons of evergreen, and in other respects, the room was conveniently fitted for his purpose. Here was kept his library of books, which amounted to nearly two hundred volumes, comprising some of the works of the best authors in theology, biography, poetry, and history. In that seclusion he reflected, read, and wrote.[17]

The spring of water is shown in the lower right corner of the print, and by it a bowl, knife, and basket of fruit or turnips, alluding to his vegetarian habits. An open book (no title shown) and two turnips appear in the left foreground.

In his right hand, Lay holds an open book inscribed "TRION on Happiness." This probably represents a treatise entitled *The Way to Health, Long Life and Happiness . . .* , written by Thomas Tryon, an English Quaker, under the pseudonym "Philotheos Physiologus." [18] The message of the book was that peaceful, healthful, and

---

[11] For full title and imprint see Note 4, taken from the copy in the Rare Book Division of the Library of Congress (hereafter LCRB) . Some inaccuracies appear in citations given in Charles Evans, *American Bibliography* (Chicago: Privately printed, 1904), II, Entry No. 4149, and in Joseph Sabin, *A Dictionary of Books Relating to America from Its Discovery to the Present Time* (New York: J. Sabin & Sons, 1878) , X, Entry No. 39465. Benjamin Franklin printed the book, although his name does not appear on the title page. There is some question about the imprint date. Although Franklin thought he remembered printing it in 1736, and the title page reads 1737, several passages are dated as late as "3rd month, 1737/8" (e.g., p. 147). In a letter dated November 4, 1789, Franklin remarked to John Wright:

"And about the year 1736, I printed another book on the same subject for Benjamin Lay, who also professed being one of your Friends, and he distributed the books chiefly among them. By these instances it appears, that the seed was indeed sown in the good ground of your profession, though much earlier than you mention, and its springing up to effect at last, though so late, is some confirmation of Lord Bacon's observation, that *a good motion never dies;* and it may encourage us in making such, though hopeless of their taking immediate effect."

This letter is in Albert Henry Smyth (ed.), *The Writings of Benjamin Franklin* (New York: Macmillan Co., 1907) , X, 61–62.

[12] Vaux, *Memoirs*, p. 31.

[13] *Ibid.*, p. 23.

[14] Amelia Mott Gummere, *The Quaker, A Study in Costume* (Philadelphia: Ferris & Leach, 1901) , pp. 44–46, enumerates selected items from the inventory, but does not reveal where it is located. Rowntree (*Journal*, XXXIII [1936], 18 and 19) mentions that it is fifteen pages long but also neglects to give its location.

[15] "Early Anti-Slavery Advocates," *The Friend, A Religious and Literary Journal*, XXIX (1856) , 196.

[16] Vaux, *Memoirs*, pp. 52–53.

[17] *Ibid.*, pp. 43–44.

[18] [Thomas Tryon], *The Way to Health, Long LIFE and HAPPINESS, or, A Discourse of Temperance AND The particular NATURE OF ALL THINGS requisit for the Life of Man, as ALL sorts of MEATS, DRINKS, AIR, EXERCISE, &c. with special Directions how to use each of them to the best Advantage of the BODY AND MIND. Shewing from the true ground of Nature whence most Diseases proceed, and how to prevent them. To which is added, A Treatise of most sorts of English Herbs, With several other remarkable and most useful Observations, very necessary for all Families. The Whole Treatise displaying the most hidden secrets of PHILOSOPHY, and made easie and familiar to the meanest Capacities, by various Examples and Demonstrances, The like never before Published. COMMUNICATED TO THE WORLD FOR A GENERAL GOOD, By Philotheos Physiologus* (London: Printed and sold by Andrew Sowle, 1683) . This book (a copy of which is in LCRB) was an amplification of a 1682 pamphlet under Tryon's own signature, *A TREATISE of CLEANNESS in Meats and Drinks, OF THE PREPARATION of FOOD,*

moral living could be achieved through observance and practice of the fundamental harmonies of the Four Qualities, the Four Complexions, the Seven Perfect Colors, and the Seven Tones. Much more than a philosophical treatise, it offered a rationale and practical suggestions for the choice and preparation of foods, hygienic management of the household, and happy marital relations. Probably more important to the vegetarian Lay was the fourteenth chapter, "Of Flesh, and its operation on the Body and Mind: That the common eating thereof does awaken the wrathful Nature of Mankind, &c."

The inscription beneath the picture reads:

W William Pinx!/HD.Fecit.

BENJAMIN LAY. / LIVED to the Age of 80, in the Latter Part of Which, He Observ'd extreem Temperance, in his Eating, and Drinking. / his Fondness, for a Particularity, in Dress and Customs, at times Subjected him, to the Redicule of the Ignorant, but his Friends, / who, were Intimate with Him, thought Him, an Honest Religious man.

Henry Dawkins, engraver of the portrait, was also a colorful character, if much less endowed with high purpose. Like Lay, he appears infrequently and dimly through the veil of history; but the few episodes known seem, in their preposterous situations and sudden reverses, rather like snippets from an eighteenth-century farce.[19]

Dawkins is first recorded in New York as the engraver of John Burnett's bookplate in 1754. The following year, he advertised that he had been working for Anthony Lamb, mathematical instrument maker (Fig. 3), but was then setting up in business for himself as an engraver of ornament on metal. By 1757, he was in Philadelphia, where he was married, worked for the engraver James Turner, and again established his own shop. He remained in Philadelphia for about fifteen years. During that time, he worked for some of the most prominent men and institutions in the colonies—Sir William Johnson, Francis Hopkinson (Fig. 4), the College of New Jersey at Prince-

FIG. 3. Dawkins, Trade Card of Anthony Lamb. New York, ca. 1754. Engraving; image, H. 11″, W. 7⁷⁄₁₆″. (Courtesy of the New-York Historical Society.)

ton, Pennsylvania Hospital, and the American Philosophical Society. His work ran the gamut from some of the most skillfully executed American prints, such as the Lamb trade card or the bookplates, to some of notably low quality, such as the relief-cut fable illustrations for Thomas Dilworth's *New Guide to the English Tongue* (Fig. 5).[20] He appeared later in New York, a drunkard on trial for counterfeiting during the Revolution, and, subsequent to imprisonment, petitioned the court for his own execution. After a mysterious disappearance, his fortunes suddenly rose when he ornamented Governor Trumbull's Thanksgiving Day Proclamation in 1777 and the first New York State coat of arms in 1778. Even more ironically, he was paid for helping engrave official Continental currency in 1780. Virtually nothing is known of him after

THE Excellency of Good Airs, AND THE BENEFITS OF Clean Sweet Beds. Also of the Generation of Bugs, AND THEIR CURE. To which is added A SHORT DISCOURSE OF THE PAIN in the TEETH, Shewing from what Cause it does chiefly proceed, and also how to prevent it (London: Printed for the author, and sold by L. Curtis near Fleet-Bridge, 1682). A copy of this pamphlet is in LCRB.

[19] Cole, "Henry Dawkins," pp. 9–26.

[20] 93rd ed.; Philadelphia: John Dunlap, 1772.

this mercurial chain of events until, in 1786, his plates were sold in Philadelphia.[21]

As a work of art, Dawkins' engraving of Lay is of indifferent quality. It is comparable to most of his work, being adequate for representation, but is neither imaginative nor subtle in execution. Dawkins' forte was ornamental *chinoiserie* and *rocaille*, generally applied to minor variations of two basic bookplate designs, trade cards, and certificates.[22] Pictorial work was outside his sphere of competence, but there are numerous examples of his attempts in this field, including, in 1764, *Pennsylvania Hospital, Nassau Hall,* and *The Paxton Expedition,* and, in 1772, the illustrations for Dilworth's *New Guide.*[23]

It is important to note that the Benjamin Lay

[21] He may, however, have passed his last years with his son John, a mariner. The 1790 census listed five free white males older than sixteen living in John's household on the south side of South Street, Southwark, Philadelphia. See U.S. Bureau of the Census, *Heads of Families at the First Census of the United States Taken in the Year 1790* (Washington: Government Printing Office, 1907), IX, 87. Those listed, however, could have been tenants and not family members.

[22] Cole, "Henry Dawkins," pp. 27–38.

[23] A number of these prints are extant. Copies of *Penn-*

Fig. 4. Dawkins, Bookplate of Francis Hopkinson. Philadelphia, 1757–1772. Engraving; plate, H. 3¾", W. 3". (University of Delaware Library, Brewer Bookplate Collection: photo, author.)

Fig. 5. Dawkins, *The Old Woman and Her Maids.* Philadelphia, 1772. Wood- or type-metal-cut, illustration from Thomas Dilworth's *New Guide to the English Tongue;* border, H. 2¹⁵⁄₁₆", W. 3". (Princeton University Library, Sinclair Hamilton Collection: photo, author.)

portrait is partly etched, partly engraved. About half the lines exhibit the blunt ends, erratic direction, or imprecise edges that characterize etching. Others have the precise profiles and finely tapered ends characteristic of engraving. For example, outlines of the major forms and surfaces of the ground and rocks are etched, while the surface of Lay's costume and the "Trion" book are engraved. Here and there engraved lines are superimposed over a field of etched lines to intensify shading, as on the ground between Lay's left foot and the fruit basket. Microscopic examination provides abundant evidence that most of Dawkins' intaglio prints contain at least some etched linework and that all his "engraved" pictures (but not the bookplates, certificates, or advertisements) contain a preponderance of etching. Most writers, when discussing "American copperplate engraving," imply that engraving was the only intaglio technique used in America until late in the eighteenth century. They tend to overlook the fact that etching was an established technique in Europe long before the eighteenth century, and that as

sylvania Hospital can be found in The Joseph Downs Manuscript and Microfilm Collection (hereafter DMMC), Division of Libraries, Winterthur Museum; The Historical Society of Pennsylvania (hereafter HSP); and the Library Company of Philadelphia (hereafter LCP). Prints of *Nassau Hall* are in the John Carter Brown Library; LCRB; the Lenox Collection, The New York Public Library; and Princeton University Library. Examples of *Paxton Expedition* are located at LCP and the Stokes Collection, The New York Public Library. A copy of Dilworth's *New Guide* is in the Sinclair Hamilton Collection, Princeton University Library.

early as 1645 a French book of instructions illustrated the tools and techniques necessary to make etchings closely imitate the line qualities of fine engraving.[24]

Among the questions raised by the print is that of the very reason for its existence. If it was indeed copied from a portrait by William Williams, under what circumstances was the original painted? Certainly Lay, in all his pious austerity, would not commission a portrait of himself by one of the leading artists of his time.[25] If his papers existed, they might provide a clue; but according to Vaux, they were destroyed during the Revolution.[26]

The painting may still exist, but its location is unknown to the author. It may have been what Benjamin Franklin, then in London, referred to when he wrote to Deborah Franklin, on July 10, 1758, "I wonder how you came by Ben. Lay's Picture." [27] This "Picture" was almost certainly not the Dawkins print, whose inscription implies that it was executed after Lay's death in 1759. No such painting was listed in Franklin's will, nor is the author aware of any mention of it by visitors to Franklin's home. It is apparently not among the possessions of Franklin's descendants.[28] On December 11, 1763, Franklin wrote Alexander Dick of Prestonfield, Edinburgh, "Be pleased to present my Respects to . . . Pythagorus who, from his Temperance I conclude is still living and well. I send him the Picture of a Brother Philosopher in this Country." [29] Leonard Labaree identified "Pythagorus" as John Williamson of Moffat. Much earlier, Franklin had called Lay "the Pythagorean-cynical-christian Philosopher." [30] The similarity of phrasing applied by Franklin to both Williamson and Lay (who was also known for his temperance) suggests that he could have been

sending a portrait of Lay—probably the Dawkins print, but possibly the Williams painting. If it seems peculiar to suggest that such a painting might have been shipped across the Atlantic, it is interesting to note that another painted portrait of Lay was intended for shipment from England to America a generation later. Thomas Pole of Bristol wrote to Roberts Vaux on November 8, 1817:

Lay lived before my remembrance or knowledge. . . . I have an oil painting of him which I have employed some of my leisure hours before breakfast to copy in order to present to thee, but the mornings have now become so dark, from the awakening of the days, that I have not been able to compleat it to send by a Vessel this Autumn, as the Baltic, in which this letter is to go, is the last expected to sail and she does not sail for Philad⦂ a Philadelph[i]a Vessel may be going in the Spring, when I hope to forward it immediately to your City, but I almost doubt its being worth thy acceptance from the hand of so imperfect an artist.[31]

Unfortunately, Pole failed to describe his portrait, name the artist, or give its provenance; nor did he mention whether there was any similarity between it and the frontispiece of Vaux's recently published biography of Lay (Fig. 6). In a second

[31] Letter from Thomas Pole, November 8, 1817, to Roberts Vaux (Roberts Vaux MSS, HSP).

Fig. 6. William Kneass, *Benjamin Lay*. Philadelphia, *ca.* 1815. Stipple engraving; image, H. 3″, W. 3″. (Library Company of Philadelphia: photo, Winterthur.)

[24] Abraham Bosse, *Traicté des manieres de graver en taille douce sur l'airin, par le moyen des eaux fortes, & des vernix durs & mols* (Paris, 1645).

[25] If the fine goods in his inventory were not trade goods, if they truly represented his personal possessions, then this "pious austerity" was only a public face and not his real inclination. For the present, since there is no evidence to the contrary, the author assumes Lay's sincerity.

[26] Vaux, *Memoirs*, p. 44.

[27] Leonard Labaree (ed.), *The Papers of Benjamin Franklin* (New Haven: Yale University Press, 1959–1966), VIII, 92.

[28] Author's conversation with Dr. Whitfield J. Bell, Jr., librarian, American Philosophical Society, Philadelphia, Pa.

[29] Labaree, *Papers of Franklin*, X, 386.

[30] *Pennsylvania Gazette* (Philadelphia), March 25, 1742, quoted by Labaree, *Papers of Franklin*, II, 357.

letter, dated January 19, 1819, he apologized for his delay in sending his copy of the portrait, but again failed to describe it.[32] None of these paintings have been located by the author.

If William Williams' painting is elusive, the history of the print is even more aggravating. The inscription implies that it was engraved after Lay's death in 1759, but how soon thereafter is not known. In his *Essays, Literary, Moral and Philosophical,* first published in 1798, Benjamin Rush wrote: "In the print of him [Lay], which is to be seen in many houses in Philadelphia, he is represented with 'Tryon on Happiness' in his hand, a book which he valued very much, and which he frequently carried with him in his excursions from home."[33] Since no other early print of Lay is known, this reference fixes a forty-year span during which the first print must have been cut. Dawkins' life cannot be documented past 1786, when his plates were sold in Philadelphia, so it is likely that the print was made before this date. Since Lay would best have been remembered and his portrait would have had the greatest topical interest within a few years of his death, the print probably goes back to the early 1760's.

Of the copies known to the author, the first Haverford copy, which is printed on laid paper, is the earliest. The Winterthur and second Haverford copies are printed on wove paper. Dard Hunter states that the earliest use of wove paper occurred in England in the 1750's, and that it was but infrequently used there even into the 1760's and 1770's. The earliest American book on wove paper was printed in 1795 by Isaiah Thomas of Worcester, Massachusetts, but this paper was not commonly used in America until the second decade of the nineteenth century.[34] Therefore, there is great likelihood that the first Haverford copy is an early impression, probably soon after 1759, and that the Winterthur and the second Haverford impressions date from a later period, probably after 1810.

Undoubtedly, other copies of the Dawkins print exist; references have been made to some whose present locations are not known. Henkels'

catalogue of Washington letters and relics, December 15 and 16, 1891, lists a copy: "476 Benj. Lay. Engraved by Henry Dawkins. Folio. Line. Full Margin The first copperplate portrait engraved in Philadelphia. Excessively rare." The purchaser was listed as "Judge," who bought the print for $15.00.[35] The author has been unable to trace "Judge," but Edwin Wolf, 2nd, librarian of The Library Company of Philadelphia, has suggested to the author that this may be a pseudonym for one of the better-known jurist-collectors of the period—perhaps Samuel Pennypacker or Hampton L. Carson. Indeed, at the 1908 sale of the Pennypacker Collection, Henkels sold a copy of the Dawkins print for $10.00 "Damaged on the right hand margin and mounted on white paper." [36] When acquired in 1966, the Winterthur copy had the Henkels catalogue entry pasted to it.

Stauffer listed Dawkins' print in his *American Engravers* in 1907, but failed to tell where the copy was located.[37] It may well have been in his own collection, since a tracing in ink was placed in his extra-illustrated copy of Scharf and Wescott's *History of Philadelphia, 1609–1884,* now in the Historical Society of Pennsylvania.[38] The original is not in his collection in the New York Public Library, however, and has not been successfully traced.

A copy was offered for sale in 1916 or 1917 by the Franklin Bookshop.[39] Another was once in the

---

[32] Letter from Thomas Pole, January 19, 1819, to Roberts Vaux (Roberts Vaux MSS, HSP).

[33] 2nd ed.; Philadelphia: Printed by Thomas and William Bradford, 1806, p. 299.

[34] Dard Hunter, *Papermaking; The History and Technique of an Ancient Craft* (New York: Alfred A. Knopf, 1943), pp. 94–95.

[35] *An Extraordinary Collection of Washington's Letters, Washington Relics, Revolutionary Documents and the Rarest Works on American History; Also Scarce American Portraits, Maps and Views; To Be Sold . . . December 15 and 16, 1891, . . . Catalogue Compiled and Sale Conducted by Stan. V. Henkels; Thos. Birch's Sons, Auctioneers, 1110 Chestnut St., Philadelphia, Cat. No. 677* (Philadelphia: Thos. Birch's Sons, 1891); *Stan. V. Henkels, Prices and Names of Purchasers, Sale of Washington Letters and Relics, December 15 & 16, 1891* (Philadelphia, 1891).

[36] *The Library of the Hon. Samuel W. Pennypacker, Former Governor of Pennsylvania . . . April 10th, 1908, . . . Catalogue No. 943, Part VI,* comp. Stan. V. Henkels (Philadelphia: [Stan. V. Henkels], 1908), p. 41, Lot No. 358.

[37] David McNeely Stauffer, *American Engravers upon Copper and Steel, Part II: Check-List of the Works of the Earlier Engravers* (New York: The Grolier Club, 1907), p. 78, No. 461.

[38] J. Thomas Scharf and Thompson Wescott, *History of Philadelphia, 1609–1884* (Philadelphia: L. H. Everts & Co., 1884).

[39] Franklin Bookshop (Philadelphia), *Americana curiosa et Quakeriana, A Remarkable Collection of Printed and Manuscript Archives Relating to the Colonization and Religious History of the United States;* Cat. 35 ([Philadelphia, 1916–1917]), Lot 190a. The Dawkins portrait, classed as an etching, was offered for sale at $45.00. It was described as "a

Fridenberg Gallery of New York. A photograph of the latter, deposited with the Wallace Photograph Collection in the Historical Society of Pennsylvania, was reproduced in William Murrell's *History of American Graphic Humor*, in 1933.[40] Shortly thereafter, the gallery went out of business, and its unsold prints were distributed among the New York Public Library, The Metropolitan Museum of Art, and possibly some private collectors whose names are not recorded.[41] The author has been unable to find this print in either institution and cannot trace it further.

In the early 1800's there was a revival of interest in Benjamin Lay. William Kneass[42] stipple-engraved a rather poor figure of Lay for the frontispiece of the Vaux biography (Fig. 6).[43] The image was obviously based on Dawkins' print, being identical in pose, costume, and proportion. Its modeling is cruder and less detailed, and the figure is shown without background or inscription; however, the image is substantially the same. Significantly, the title of the book in Lay's hand reads "African Emancipation," which represents a considerable change in emphasis from Dawkins' version. It is extremely curious that Dawkins' inscription and iconography avoided any reference to Lay's antislavery crusades, which were at least as noticeable as, and certainly more memorable than, his simple style of living and vegetarian diet. There is, of course, no problem in explaining the change in emphasis for the 1815 version, since the

good copy of the original print, the size of the engraved portion being 9-1/2 × 7-1/8 inches. Mounted on heavy cardboard and suitable for framing. With this is an example of Lay's autograph written on the fly-leaf of an old book, once belonging to him."

[40] New York: Whitney Museum of American Art, 1933, I, 20–21, Fig. 17.

[41] Author's conversation with Miss Elizabeth E. Roth, New York Public Library.

[42] Kneass (1780–1840) was a commercial engraver in Philadelphia from 1804 to 1824, when he was appointed engraver and diesinker at the United States Mint. See George C. Groce and David H. Wallace, *The New-York Historical Society's Dictionary of Artists in America, 1564–1860* (New Haven: Yale University Press, 1957), p. 373.

[43] Copies are located in HSP, LCP, QCHC, the Friends' Historical Library at Swarthmore College, Swarthmore, Pa. (hereafter FHL), LCRB, and others. All copies seen by the author have been trimmed in binding inside the plate mark. The dimensions of the image, exclusive of the inscription, are 3" high by 3" wide. Several reproductions of this print exist (PFL, FHL, QCHC [2 copies], HSP). They are virtually line-for-line copies but lack some of the lighter stip-

point of Vaux's biography was Lay's antislavery activities.[44] This was the earliest of a long series of pictures derived from the Dawkins print.

Another version of the image, whose origin the

pling and line ends of the original Kneass print. Each is printed on a folio sheet of what appears to the author to be mid- to late-nineteenth-century white paper, without plate mark. They may be early photographic reproductions. The FHL copy has written on the reverse "Presented by Charles Roberts," with the stamped marks "12/28, 1887" and "142 N. 16TH STREET, / PHILADELPHIA."

[44] The following year, Vaux received a letter from William Dillwyn of Higham Lodge, England, dated April 12:

"I am also gratified by thy Description of your occasional Retreat in a Neighborhood familiar to my Recollection in early life . . . where commenced my personal acquaintance with the principal Hero of thy well written Narrative, Benj Lay, who verbally related to me several of the anecdotes thou records, with some other descriptions of his eccentric Character. M Phillips is reprinting thy History

FIG. 7. John Palmer, *Benjamin Lay*. Place and date unknown. Etching (line and stipple); image, H. 3", W. 3". (Quaker Collection of the Haverford College Library.)

author has been unable to trace, is an etching signed "John Palmer sc" with the inscription: "Benjamin Lay. / one of the earliest Advocates of / Negro Emancipation. / 1718" (Fig. 7) .[45] Perhaps it was a frontispiece, since the right margin is torn, as if from a book. John Palmer may have been the "J. Palmer" noted by Groce and Wallace as the illustrator of a Bible published in New York in 1826, but he is otherwise unknown to the writer.[46] The print is a direct steal from Kneass's: superimposed Xerox copies of the two align almost perfectly. The date, 1718, probably refers to the date when Lay was assumed by Vaux and other early writers to have left England for Barbados.

In 1842, the American Anti-Slavery Society in New York published its *Memoir of Benjamin Lay*, based on Vaux's biography, bearing an unsigned image of Lay on its frontispiece (Fig. 8).[47] This etching is a considerably degraded version of the original image, showing only the merest effort at modeling and detail. Once again, the title of Lay's book is "AFRICAN EMANCIPATION." This print was also a direct copy from Kneass.

Yet another version of the picture, a lithograph, is signed "Sinclair, Lith."[48] It is closely modeled after the Dawkins print, down to the small details of the picture and the inscription (Fig. 9). Under the inscription is the legend, "Fac-Simile of an Old Engraving." The lithogra-

FIG. 8. *Benjamin Lay*. New York, *ca.* 1842. Etching; image, H. 3″, W. 3″. (Friends Historical Library of Swarthmore College.)

FIG. 9. Thomas S. (?) Sinclair, *Benjamin Lay*. New York or Philadelphia, 1830–1881. Lithograph; innermost border, H. 8½″, W. 7¼″. (Norris Scrapbook, Joseph Downs Manuscript and Microfilm Collection, Division of Libraries, Winterthur.)

---

and I hope will also prefix the Portrait which I remember Benj. West painting, and wch thee has considered generally as a caracature is certainly a faithful Resemblance of the Man" (Roberts Vaux MSS, HSP) .

Despite this rather surprising reference to Benjamin West, the letter obviously points to the Williams-Dawkins image on which Vaux's frontispiece was based and vouches for its descriptive accuracy. It is not unreasonable that Dillwyn should think of West as the painter. The portrait must have been painted before Lay's death in 1759. It was at about this time that West knew Williams in Philadelphia, and it is possible that Williams might even have allowed the young West to execute minor parts of the canvas. Since then, West had become one of the foremost painters of England, and the aging Dillwyn might have confused the two artists some sixty years after the event.

[45] A loose copy is in QCHC. It is printed on wove paper and its provenance is not known.

[46] Groce and Wallace, *Dictionary of Artists*, p. 485.

[47] American A. S. [Anti-Slavery] Society, *Memoir of Benjamin Lay: Compiled from Various Sources*, with an Introduction by L. Marie Child (New York: The society, 1842) . Copies of the book with frontispiece intact are in the LCRB and the FHL.

[48] Copies are in DMMC, HSP, QCHC, and FHL.

Fig. 10. *Benjamin Lay*. Place unknown, probably late nineteenth century. Wood engraving; border, H. 10¾″, W. 7⅜″. (Atwater Kent Museum.)

pher was probably Thomas S. Sinclair (*ca.* 1805–1881), a native of the Orkney Islands who arrived in America in 1830. He worked in Philadelphia and New York, and sometime after 1850 was assisted by his sons William and Thomas, Jr. The family business was sold in 1889.[49] This lithograph, like the Dawkins print, bears no mention of Lay's antislavery activity. If it dates from the 1830's, this need not be too surprising, since temperance and vegetarianism were also popular reform themes at that time.

Another version of the image occurs in an unsigned and undated wood engraving (Fig. 10).[50] The characteristic pose, with the walking stick and "African Emancipation" in the extended right hand, is embellished by the addition of a balance in Lay's raised left hand, presumably representing the Scales of Justice. The rendering is

flat and poorly articulated. Beneath the figure is a facsimile signature, "Benjamin Lay," which may have been copied from a genuine autograph (one of which was still in existence in Philadelphia as late as 1916 or 1917).[51] The whole is bordered by printer's flowers. The inscription reads:

"Do justly, love mercy, and to walk humbly with thy God." / Micah the Prophet, 6th Chap., 8th v. In due respects and profound reverence, by M. J. WILKERSON, to the above / name as the first and moving cause of the Emancipation of Slavery in the / Society of Friends, commonly called Quakers, &c.

Oh precious name that did first proclaim the loving cause of Emancipation; that truly / lived and preached the same in all of his land and nation. JOHN WOLMAN next that / adhered to the text, and did the Friends truly perplex, Until he made them truly know / that Slavery was an awful woe. At this the Friends warning took, and from their sinful / ways forsook.

This act of Emancipation took place in Philadelphia, Pa., about the year of / our Lord 1767. Amen.[52]

Common to each of these six portraits, and possibly to the painting from which they all descended, is a notable lack of those qualities for which a work of art is usually praised. Certainly the subject is not physically beautiful, nor are any of the renderings executed with finesse. But the absence of high artistry in this derivative series of pictures, produced over the span of a century, demonstrates that their merit lay in their message. Through these prints, Lay's image was repeatedly invoked in behalf of the growing reform spirit in American life. Whittier wrote of Lay's effect on the eighteenth-century Philadelphia Society of Friends, but he might have applied the same lines to his continuing presence in nineteenth-century America: "Such was the irrepressible prophet . . . clinging like a rough chestnut-burr to the skirts of its respectability and settling like a pertinacious gad-fly on the sore places of its conscience."[53]

[49] Groce and Wallace, *Dictionary of Artists*, p. 581.

[50] Copies are in QCHC and the Atwater Kent Museum, Philadelphia (where it is incorrectly catalogued as a portrait of "Benjamin Say"). The former is printed on wove paper; the latter could not be examined closely.

[51] See *Americana curiosa et Quakeriana*, Lot 190a.

[52] The last phrase probably refers to one of the decisions of the Philadelphia Yearly Meeting between 1758 and 1776, a period of growing abolitionist sentiment among Quakers. In 1758, partly due to John Woolman's urgings, the Yearly Meeting voted to bar slave-trading Friends from most church leadership positions. Other resolutions, increasingly strong, were passed in the following years, and in 1776 the Yearly Meeting directed local meetings to disown Quakers who refused to free their slaves. See Thomas Edward Drake, *Quakers and Slavery in America* (Gloucester, Mass.: Peter Smith, 1965), pp. 46, 61–72.

[53] Whittier, *Journal of Woolman*, p. 14.

After the Cloth Was Removed

Anna Wells Rutledge

A N INK and wash drawing, now at The Henry Francis du Pont Winterthur Museum, has been a source of amusement for over two hundred years in Charleston, South Carolina (Fig. 1).[1] Today the little drawing of the officers and gentlemen gathered at the Hon. Peter Manigault's house at "Steepbrook," [2] St. James, Goose Creek, is considered a document of social history. The provincial gathering, recorded by one of the guests, George Roupell, Esq., took place sometime between 1757 and 1760. From the *mise en scène,* one may conclude that the objects of decorative art shown here represent types of items in daily use in South Carolina in the mid-eighteenth century. Aided by letters, wills, inventories, and contemporary newspaper accounts, the drawing gives a vivid picture of the place and the people.

In the 1740's, Charles Town and South Carolina were described by Eliza Lucas, who knew both the Caribbean world and England as well as her new residence. She wrote:

I am now set down my Dear Brother to obey your commands and give you a short discription of the part of the world I now inhabit. So. Carolina then, is a large and Extensive Country near the Sea. . . . The Country abounds with wild fowl, Venison and fish, Beef, veal and mutton, are here in much greater perfection than in the Islands, tho' not equal to that in England—but their pork exceeds any I ever tasted anywhere. The Turkeys extreamly fine, especially the wild, and indeed all their poultry is exceeding good, and peaches, Nectrins, and mellons of all sorts extreamly fine and in profusion, and their Oranges exceed any I ever tasted in the West Indies or from Spain or Portugal.

The people in gen[l] hospitable and honest, and the better sort add to these a polite gentile behaviour. The poorer sort are the most indolent people in the world or they could never be wretched in so plentiful a country as this. . . .

C[rs] Town the Metropolis is a neat pretty place. The inhabitants polite and live in a very gentile manner. The streets and houses regularly built—the ladies and gentlemen gay in their dress, upon the whole you will find as many agreeable people of both sexes for the size of the place as almost any where.[3]

Dr. George Milligen, who had lived in South Carolina for fifteen years prior to 1763, wrote that *"Charles-town* is the Metropolis. . . . *Bay-Street* which fronts *Cooper-River* and the Ocean, is really handsome, and must delight the Stranger who approacheth it from the Sea." [4] He also found that the complexion of the people was

---

[1] This drawing was shown by the Carolina Art Association, Gibbes Art Gallery, Charleston, S.C., in its "Life in Charleston" exhibition in 1940. It appears in Anna Wells Rutledge, *Artists in the Life of Charleston through Colony and State from Restoration to Reconstruction* (Philadelphia: The American Philosophical Society, 1949), p. 173, Fig. 8; also in the *Art Quarterly,* XXVI, No. 4 (1963), 496. There are two mid-nineteenth-century copies, both by descendants of the artist and both privately owned; one was reproduced in Anthony Harrigan, "The Charleston Tradition," *American Heritage,* IX (Feb., 1958), 52.

[2] Henry A. M. Smith, "Goose Creek," *South Carolina Historical and Genealogical Magazine* (hereafter *SCH&G*), XXIX (Jan., 1928), 15–17; Charles Fraser, *A Charleston Sketchbook, 1796–1806,* with an introduction and notes by Alice R. Huger Smith (Charleston, S.C.: Carolina Art Association, 1940), p. 20. This drawing of "Steepbrook" was reproduced in Harrigan, *American Heritage,* IX, 53.

[3] Harriott Horry Ravenel, *Eliza Pinckney* (New York: Charles Scribner's Sons, 1906), pp. 17–19. Eliza Lucas (1723–1797), daughter of George Lucas (lieutenant governor of Antigua; d. 1747), came to South Carolina in 1737/38; in 1744, she married Chief Justice Charles Pinckney (1699–1758/59).

[4] George Milligen-Johnston, *A Short Description of the Province of South Carolina with an Account of the Air,*

little different from the Inhabitants of *Britain,* and they are generally of a good Stature and well-made, with lively and agreeable Countenances; sensible, spirited, and open-hearted, and exceed most People in Acts of Benevolence, Hospitality, and Charity. The Men and Women who have a Right to the Class of Gentry (who are more numerous here than in any other Colony in North America) dress with Elegance and Neatness: The personal Qualities of the Ladies are much to their Credit and Advantage.[5]

The first and most obvious point in the drawing of the dinner party is that those depicted were having a very good time. It might represent a dinner such as one reported in the *South-Carolina Gazette,* November 10, 1766:

The Anniversary of the glorious Revolution, by the landing of King William, and the nation's happy deliverance from a horrid Popish Plot, the same was observed here with suitable demonstrations of Joy. The hon. Peter Manigault, Esq; Speaker of the Commons House of Assembly, gave upon this occasion, an elegant entertainment to the Light Infantry Company, at his seat at Goose Creek, 14 miles from Charles Town, where the company arrived at 7 o'clock in the morning, spent the day most agreeably, and returned before 9 at night.

Of the eight gentlemen shown in the drawing, five served in one or another of the colonial military companies. The three others were the host, Peter Manigault (1731–1773); his neighbor, Isaac Godin (d. 1777) of "Fontainbleau," St. James, Goose Creek, a prosperous Charleston merchant and planter; and the artist, George Roupell (d. 1794) of Charleston and "Roupelmonde,"[6] Port Royal Island. Roupell, an amateur artist who held various civil appointments, shows himself seated at the foot of the table, to the right of the host. A Hogarthian effect possibly was intended: these individuals surely knew Hogarth's work and would appreciate a fellow guest's attempt at that manner.

Four of the five officers at this party are in uniform; one has a sword at his side and another wears a sword belt. The coats and waistcoats are long, and all coat cuffs are deep. Ruffles at the wrists are obvious on most of the figures, but the neckcloths are not differentiated clearly. Two of the officers have black neckbands. Because of the sketchiness of the work, it is not clear whether only one or all wear wigs—Godin's is on the end of the cane or crop of another guest. This jocund effort, and an officer rendering, "Hey to the Midnight Hark a-way, Hark a-way," shows that the tempo was not slow. One gathers, however, that they were *comme il faut:* they wear no hats, nor are pipes and tobacco boxes visible. Tobacco was not yet used in a private residence—in a club meeting, yes, for pipes and tobacco are in evidence in Dr. Alexander Hamilton's Tuesday Club sketches[7] and in John Greenwood's painting of carousing American captains in a tavern in Surinam.[8]

The small figure at the right is as pleasantly informal as the diners. The young Negro waiting boy is perhaps ten years old and is shown standing asleep, comfortably leaning on the window trim. His costume is neat: he wears shirt, collar, waistcoat, coat, and trousers. Apparently he is barefoot. A visitor to South Carolina early in the nineteenth century wrote: "In the opulent families, there is always a negro placed on the look-out, to announce the coming of any visitant; and the moment a carriage, or horseman, is descried, each negro changes his every day garb for a magnificent suit of livery. As the negroes wear no shirts, this is quickly effected; and in a few moments a ragged fellow is metamorphosed into a spruce footman."[9]

Crises in South Carolina, other parts of America, and the world must have been discussed at such dinner parties, but the immediate interest of the guests, of course, was the wine; thus one may first consider the bottles, decanters, and glasses on the table and what might have been in them.

Weather and Diseases, at Charles-Town (London: Printed for John Hinton, 1770), p. 31. This material was later published in *Colonial South Carolina: Two Contemporary Descriptions by Governor James Glen and Doctor George Milligen-Johnston,* ed. Chapman J. Milling (Columbia, S.C.: University of South Carolina Press, 1951).

[5] *Ibid.,* p. 24.

[6] Plat of Confiscated Estates (Port Royal Island Collection, South Carolina Archives Department, Columbia, S.C.).

[7] Alexander Hamilton, *Hamilton's Itinerarium,* ed. A. B. Hart (St. Louis: William K. Bixby, 1907); Anna Wells Rutledge, "Portraits in Varied Media in the Collections of the Maryland Historical Society," *Maryland Historical Magazine,* XLI (Dec., 1946), 283, 318; see also "The Tuesday Club of Annapolis," *Maryland Historical Magazine,* I (March, 1906), 59–65; and Robert R. Hare, "Electro Vitrifico in Annapolis: Mr. Franklin Visits the Tuesday Club," *Maryland Historical Magazine,* LVIII (March, 1963), 62–66.

[8] Reproduced in E. P. Richardson, *Painting in America: The Story of 450 Years* (New York: Thomas Y. Crowell Co., 1956), p. 62, Fig. 19.

[9] John Davis, *Travels of Four Years and a Half in the United States of America; During 1798, 1799, 1800, 1801, and 1802* (London: R. Edwards, 1803), p. 89.

FIG. 1. George Roupell, *Mr. Peter Manigault and His Friends.* St. James, Goose Creek, S.C., *ca.* 1760. Ink and wash drawing on paper; H. 10⅜6″, W. 12⅜6″. (Winterthur 63.73a.)

Glass was not made in South Carolina, and England was probably their source (unless they came off a captured foreign vessel and were acquired at vendue). They appear plain, and only one decanter is in a coaster, which apparently is not of silver. The bottles are dark in color and may have had the owner's initials on them, although none such of Manigault's are known to have survived. The wine glass was of an adequate size and on a tall stem. Eleven glasses are on the table; one with a broken stem lies before Peter Manigault. Glasses for syllabub, beer, wine, and jelly and tumblers, decanters, cruets, "glass tart panns," and bottles were listed in great number in inventories. Bottles were usually listed by the dozen, as a parcel, or as cases with bottles. In addition to bottles, decanters, and glasses for liquid refreshment in Charleston, glass and china bowls for punches were listed in inventories, and punch ladles were common. At least one silver monteith was owned in that city; and a silver punch urn or cup, with the strainer, was mentioned in the will of George Roupell's daughter.[10]

Approximately a decade before this dinner party, Manigault resided in England studying at the Temple and riding circuits. While on a continental tour, he wrote from Paris, "I am vastly pleased with the small Wines that they drink at

[10] Charleston Wills 1839–1845, Typed Book No. 43, p. 826 (Probate Court, Charleston, S.C., hereafter CPC).

Meals: They are much better than small Beer & Agree extremely well with me." [11] Dr. Milligen knew well of what he spoke when he said that, in Charleston, *"Madeira* Wine and Punch are the common Drinks of the Inhabitants; yet, few Gentlemen are without Claret, Port, Lisbon, and other Wines, of the *French, Spanish* or *Portugal* Vintages.—The Ladies, I mention it to their Credit, are extremely temperate, and generally drink Water." The Doctor added, "The *German Protestants* . . . industrious People distil a palatable Brandy from Peaches, which they have in great Plenty; likewise from Potatoes, *Indian* Corn, and Rye." [12]

Wine was sent to America in casks, pipes, and hogsheads. It was desirable that wine be aged on a voyage—shifting the liquid in its container improved it—and a wine that had made such a journey usually was named after its geographical origin, or the vessel on which the voyage had been made, which perhaps identified the year and vintage. For example, "East India" was a Madeira that had been on an India Company ship. An apparently fond father, giving both advice and a wedding present to his son, wrote, "I send you a pipe of wine for immediate use, 'tis nearly your own age. By importing a pipe every year and storing in your garrett you will always have a bottle to offer your friends." [13] In 1745, the governor of Antigua wrote to his daughter in Carolina saying, "I send by Cap[t] Cooper an Hhd of Clarett & a Hhd of Porter, & hope they will both prove good and worth y[r] Acceptance." [14] Later, writing to his son-in-law and contemporary about wine sold from vessels taken by Admiral Townsend, he complained that he "could not find a Drinkable Caske of Claret among them." [15]

In 1741, the inventory of Thomas Gadsden listed thirteen dozen and eleven bottles of Madeira wine, five bottles of claret, three bottles of cherry brandy, one bottle of Rhenish, sixteen dozen and eight bottles of vidonia wine, sixteen dozen and one bottle of ale, "19 pints 29 quarts and 2 pint bottles different sort of Liquor . . . 2 dozen 8 quarts & 1 pint madeira . . . 1 large Case 12 bottles rum (old)," one large and one small

case of twelve empty bottles, and fifteen dozen empty bottles.[16] The long inventory was taken and appraised on August 27, 1741, by John Rutledge, James Mathewes, and Jordan Roche. Three months later, Messrs. Hill and Guerard added: "The following Came to our Knowledge Since the foregoing Appraisement was taken and will be Accounted for by us / 1 horse Colt at Watboe Plantation / 1 hh[d] English Beer (part out) sent by M[r] Colleton / Rec[d] from Barbados, but we Apprehend the Estate is yet Indebted for 1 hh[d] Rum / 1 bb Clay'd Sugar / 1 d[o] Musvado D[o]." The inventory was recorded December 4, 1741. The 1773 will of the host in this drawing left his Madeira to his two sons, each to have half when reaching age twenty-one.[17] When Josiah Quincy, Jr., of Boston, was at the house of Miles Brewton in Charleston in 1773, he said that he had "Dined with considerable company. . . . By odds the richest wines I ever tasted." [18]

The "Steepbrook" table is lighted by three candles in silver candlesticks. The latter seem English baroque in style, with generous curves and pointed angles exaggerated. An embossed pattern extends from the baluster to the base.

It can be assumed that, although no parts of a dinner service are seen in the drawing, an excellent meal had been served. Great quantities of various types of ceramic dinnerware were listed in inventories; among them were earthen and enameled dishes, crockery ware, burnt china, stoneware, "delph" (possibly Bristol-made delft), china (blue-and-white, red-and-white, black-and-white), and "Queen's ware"; but factories were not named.

In addition to native game, turtles were considered a great delicacy by South Carolinians and their friends in England. Numbers at a time were sent to England from South Carolina, as were ducks and caged birds of various species. In a letter of 1758, Mrs. Eliza Pinckney asked that a business correspondent "give the person that takes care of them, a crown for every Turtle you receive alive, and whatever you think reasonable for each bird and Summer Duck, and send them free of

[11] Mabel L. Webber (ed.), "Peter Manigault's Letters," *SCH&G*, XXXII (April, 1931), 122.

[12] Milligen-Johnston, *Short Description*, pp. 29 and 28.

[13] Ravenel, *Eliza Pinckney*, p. 48.

[14] *Ibid.*, p. 123.

[15] *Ibid.*, p. 132.

[16] Charleston Inventories 1741–1743, Typed Book No. 73, pp. 97–109 (CPC).

[17] Charleston Wills 1774–1779, Typed Book No. 16, pp. 26–27 (CPC).

[18] "Journal of Josiah Quincy, Junior, 1773," *Proceedings of the Massachusetts Historical Society*, XLIX (June, 1916), 444–46.

expence to the persons they are designed for." She asked that a Mr. Morley please accept "all the rest of the birds, how many I can't say, there was a great many when I left town." [19] Mrs. Manigault frequently sent birds to her son Peter in London, who wrote her in 1750, "Mrs. Brailsford . . . brought the Red birds you were so kind to send me as far as Dover, but in coming up to London, the Poor creatures died in the Post Chaise." [20] American birds were still novelties abroad. Some of them were beautifully marked, such as nonpareils, cardinals, and bluebirds. The eighteenth-century household often had caged birds. Richard Waring's Charleston inventory in 1753 listed "An Hour Glass Bird cage and Slats," [21] and that of Cato Ash listed in 1776 "Birds & Bird Cages £20." [22] Josiah Quincy, Jr., wrote that in the dining room of the new and handsome Brewton house on King Street, Charleston, "A very fine bird kept familiarly playing over the room, under our chairs and the table, picking up the crumbs, etc., and perching on the window, side board and chairs: vastly pretty!" [23]

The dining-room chairs and the table depicted are plain and substantial. Although probably Carolina-made, chairs such as those represented, with the ten quatrefoil piercings in the splats, seem to be a type unknown today. Furniture was sent out from England, but there were extremely competent resident cabinetmakers who produced handsome pieces. Chairs that the cabinetmaker Richard McGrath mentioned in his 1772 advertisement must have been handsomer than those seen in the drawing: ". . . caned Chairs, of the newest fashion, splat Backs, with hollow slats and commode fronts, of the same Pattern as those imported by Peter Manigault." [24] The Manigaults may well have ordered those in the "newest fashion" for their new house, which was raised in 1770. [25]

South Carolina furniture was frequently made

of native woods—walnut, oak, cyprus, cedar, red bay, and pine. Sometimes old walnut, English oak, or white oak differentiated pieces in contemporary listings. Mahogany was the fashionable wood and was used for many furniture forms. It was so frequently employed that chairs and sets were sometimes classified in lists by types of seat covering; noted are calico bottom chairs, chintz and silk bottom, and "Russia Bottom'd" (probably leather seats). One 1754 inventory listed "false bottom chairs." [26] A rush bottom chair and a "Pa[l]meto Bottom Couch" simply used native grass and leaves. Sometimes Windsor chairs were specified, and "painted black chairs" mentioned in contemporary inventories were probably of that type. The plain dining-room table shown in the "Steepbrook" drawing may have been called "a flap table" at one time.

The tablecloth and napkins appear to have been removed before the wines were served, for no linen is seen in the drawing. In 1773, Josiah Quincy, Jr., noted that, before the sweets and the wine, "the upper cloth [was] removed." [27] Quantities of tablecloths, breakfast tablecloths, napkins, and tea napkins, made of damask, "diapert," huckaback, Russia, and Holland (linen), are listed in inventories. A 1753 list includes an embroidered tea cloth. In Charleston, as late as the 1750's, table carpets were noted, as well as rugs on tables and beds.

Carpets for floors, or floor coverings of any type, were mentioned less frequently. However, they were used, and were listed as painted floor cloths, woolen rugs, floor carpets, cotton carpets, woven carpets, India carpets, and Turkey carpets. No floor covering is seen here at "Steepbrook."

Also absent from the sketch is a curtain at the window. Window hangings appear infrequently in Charleston inventories, although in 1773 the great room of Miles Brewton's house was described as "The grandest hall I ever beheld, [with] azure blue satin window curtains." [28] When listed, curtains were usually with the bedstead and bed furniture, and they probably matched the bed curtains and covering. In 1776 Mary Hyrne Smith, wife of the second Landgrave Smith, left to her

[19] Ravenel, *Eliza Pinckney*, pp. 173–74.
[20] "Six Letters of Peter Manigault," *SCH&G*, XV (July, 1914), 115.
[21] Charleston Inventories 1753–1756, Typed Book No. 82A, p. 7 (CPC).
[22] Charleston Inventories 1776–1784, Typed Book No. 100, p. 17 (CPC).
[23] "Journal of Josiah Quincy," *Proceedings of the Massachusetts Historical Society*, XLIX, 446.
[24] E. Milby Burton, *Charleston Furniture, 1700–1825* (Charleston, S.C.: The Charleston Museum, 1955), p. 104.
[25] "Extracts from The Journal of Mrs. Ann Manigault 1754–1781," annotated by Mabel L. Webber, *SCH&G*, XXI (Jan., 1920), 18.

[26] Charleston Inventories 1753–1756, Typed Book No. 82A, p. 293 (CPC).
[27] "Journal of Josiah Quincy," *Proceedings of the Massachusetts Historical Society*, XLIX, 448.
[28] *Ibid.*, p. 444.

son Benjamin, "my worked curtains now in his possession." [29] With the belongings of James Ramsay in 1753 were "one Sett Bed and Window Curtain with Furniture"; [30] and to James Fowler "five setts Curtains" [31] were credited. The next year Mr. McKay's house had "a suit of window Courtains" valued at one pound,[32] although three pounds were noted after "a Compass, Curtain Bed Rod and 2 Window Rods" in the 1754 inventory of George Hamilton.[33] Henry Peronneau's inventory of the same year listed "1 Compleat Sett fine Stamp'd Cotton Curtains £30" and "4 Compleat Setts of Callicos D° £50." [34]

An advertisement in the *South-Carolina Gazette* of June 6, 1774, listed rather elegant furnishings:

Will be Sold By public Vendue, on Tuesday the 28th Day of June *Inst.* At TEN o'clock in the Forenoon, At the House of Sir Egerton Leigh, All his valuable Furniture, Books, Plate, Pictures, China and other Effects.— The Furniture consists of elegant white and Gold Cabriole Sophas and Chairs, covered with blue and white Silk, Window Curtains to match; one other Set of Sophas and Chairs, coverd with black and yellow Figures of Nuns Work in Silk, inlaid Commodes, Card Tables, several Suits of handsome Chintz Cotton Window Curtains lined and ornamented with Silk Fringe and Tassels, a complete Set of Chintz Cotton Bed Curtains, a curious and superb India Cabinet, a Rose Wood Desk and Book-Case with Chinese Paintings on Glass very masterly executed, Carpets, Beds, Bedsteads, Toutenag Grates, &c.

The lack of both a floor covering and curtains in the drawing may indicate a seasonal change or that "Steepbrook" was used simply as a change of air for a few days and, therefore, was not handsomely equipped. In South Carolina after the second quarter of the eighteenth century, visits were often made to see friends at different plantations purely for informal association, as well as for more festive gatherings.

There were balls and assemblies in Charles Town: Eliza Lucas wrote of one in 1742, "The

Gov[r] gave the Gent[n] a very gentile entertainment at noon, and a ball at night for the ladies on the Kings birthnight, at w[ch] was a Crowded Audience of Gent[n] and ladies. I danced a minuet." [35] In addition to balls, there were races, military musters, cards and billiards, planting, trading and speculating, hunting and fishing, and discussions of Indians, explorations, natural history, and politics. Conformist and nonconformist politics—local and international—occupied the colonists' time, as did church affairs. Miss Lucas' agreeable impression seems to have been general among visitors, for in 1740 the Rev. Mr. Whitefield noted that immediately on coming into South Carolina a visible change was observable in the manners of the people, and he could have thought, when in Charleston, he was among Londoners, both in respect to gaiety of dress and politeness of manners.[36]

Mrs. Manigault used the forms *Steepbrook* or *Steep Brook* interchangeably. The plantation was within easy riding or driving distance of Charleston, with the New Market racecourse on the way. The Manigaults' handsome furnishings must have been in the Charleston residence, where they made an effort to be *tout à fait à la mode.* "Steepbrook," their country residence, apparently was a "double house" (to use a Charleston expression), and is said to have been built by Peter Manigault, who bought the land with its large frontage on Goose Creek in 1757. The building may have been of brick with a wall thick enough to accommodate a window seat. The mantle wall has fielded paneling above the chimney opening, with no molding around it. There is a chair rail on the window wall, and the sashes have nine over nine glasses. A fire iron, apparently tongs, may be seen against the fireplace wall behind Captain Massey.

The host, Peter Manigault, Esq., was the third generation of this family to reside in Carolina. He was the only child of the eminent merchant Gabriel Manigault (1704–1781) and his wife Ann Ashby Manigault (d. 1782), who noted in a journal: "P.M. was born 10th. October 1731, sailed for England 22 April 1750, arrived from London 1st. Dec. 1754 and was married 8 June 1755." [37] On

[29] Charleston Wills 1774–1779, Typed Book No. 17, p. 472 (CPC); and Elizabeth Anne Poyas, *The Olden Time in Carolina* (Charleston, S.C.: S. G. Courteny & Co., 1855), p. 108.

[30] Charleston Inventories 1753–1756, Typed Book No. 82A, p. 70 (CPC).

[31] *Ibid.,* p. 101.

[32] *Ibid.,* p. 163.

[33] *Ibid.,* p. 357.

[34] *Ibid.,* p. 258.

[35] Ravenel, *Eliza Pinckney,* pp. 20–21.

[36] John Gillies, *Memoirs of the Life of The Rev. George Whitefield, M.A.* (London: E. & C. Dibly, 1772), p. 49.

[37] "Journal of Mrs. Manigault," *SCH&G,* XXI (July, 1920), 120. The *South-Carolina Gazette,* Feb. 22, 1773, reported: "On Friday last died, in the Prime of Life, Mrs.

May 16, 1773, nearly three months after the death of her daughter-in-law, she added, "My Son went over the Bar at 1 oClock on Sunday."[38] Over two weeks later the *South-Carolina Gazette* of May 17–24, 1773, noted that the Packet *Sandwich* had sailed and on board, "for the Recovery of his Health, [was] the Hon. *Peter Manigault, Esq;* late Speaker of several successive Commons Houses of Assembly." Mrs. Manigault recorded on September 9, 1773, "I heard of my Son's arrival in England"; and on January 13, 1774, "Heard of my Sons death."[39]

An able, well-educated, and agreeable man, Peter Manigault was also handsome, as shown in the portrait painted by Allan Ramsay in London in 1751.[40] Before that, he had written:

I have now been in England three Weeks, and in London, Seventeen Days, I have, in this short time, had an Opportunity of seeing some of the Diversions that this great City affords and if I did not confess it to be a much finer Place, than I have ever seen before, I should shew great Want of Skill, yet I see nothing in it, that would make me quit my Native Country. I find every thing in general much cheaper here than in Carolina, and it is well that it is so, for there are so many Ways of Spending Money that one never would have thought of, that if Things, were not in common very reasonable, it would be impossible for one to live here.[41]

South Carolinians in London, either for study,[42] on business, on leave, in port between voyages, or for any other reason, saw each other, exchanged news of births and deaths, fevers and smallpox, as well as gossip, and sent home presents such as "fanns," tippets, muffs, slides for the camera obscura, gloves, books, magazines, and plays. They enjoyed London, but some were homesick, and continued to "wish for the agreeable Society so prevalent in Carolina," as did young Peter in

1753.[43] The following year he wrote his "Mama" that her friend

Mrs. Wragg, after much Fatigue upon her Passage looked at first but poorly, but the Sight of her Friends, & a little Ease have brought her pretty well to herself again. They say her principal Errand to England was to take care that no strapping Irishman run away with her Daughters: An odd Business this when we consider that the young Ladies are very little, & not extremely handsome.[44]

Mrs. Wragg and her daughter, Elizabeth (Fig. 2),

[43] Webber, "Peter Manigault's Letters," *SCH&G*, XXXII (April, 1931), 118.

[44] *Ibid.*, XXXIII (April, 1932), 148; see also Rutledge, *Artists in Charleston*, p. 114 and p. 172, Fig. 4; and Margaret Simons Middleton, *Jeremiah Theus, Colonial Artist of Charles Town* (Columbia, S.C.: University of South Carolina Press, 1953), reproduced p. 87, pp. 146–47.

FIG. 2. Jeremiah Theus, *Mrs. Peter Manigault* (Elizabeth Wragg). Charleston, S.C., 1757. Oil on canvas; H. 50", W. 40". (Charleston Museum: photo, Frick Art Reference Library, 13882.)

Manigault, Wife of the Honourable Peter Manigault, late Speaker of the Commons House of Assembly of this Province—much regretted by all who knew her amiable Disposition and Accomplishments, in neither of which She was excelled."

[38] "Journal of Mrs. Manigault," *SCH&G*, XXI (April, 1920), 64.

[39] *Ibid.*, pp. 65 and 66.

[40] Webber, "Peter Manigault's Letters," *SCH&G*, XXXI (Oct., 1930), 277–78; and Rutledge, *Artists in Charleston*, p. 116 and p. 172, Fig. 5.

[41] "Six Letters of Peter Manigault," *SCH&G*, XV (July, 1914), 114.

[42] E. Alfred Jones, *American Members of the Inns of Court* (London: St. Catherine Press, 1924), pp. 153–54.

returned to South Carolina before young Manigault, who came back in 1754 after some months on the Continent. Mrs. Ann Manigault's journal recorded in 1755: "[June] 8. My son married to Miss Elizabeth Wragg. 9. Gentlemen to breakfast here. Dined at Mrs. Wragg's. . . . 21. My son and his wife drank tea here & rode out. . . . [July] 30. My son went to live at his own house. We supped there." [45]

"Steepbrook" contained over six hundred acres, and in Peter Manigault's will the "plantation or tract of land on the south west side of Goose Creek called Steepbrook bought by me of Isaac Godin containing . . . highland and marsh" was left to his son Gabriel Manigault.[46] From Charles Fraser's water-color sketch,[47] done early in the nineteenth century (Fig. 3), details of the construction of the house cannot be determined, but from Roupell's drawing it seems to have been comparatively large. The dimensions of the plain and well-proportioned paneling might be estimated from the fireplace in the dining room.

Manigault's untimely death early in his professional career (but after serving eighteen years in the Commons House of Assembly for the Parish of St. Thomas & St. Dennis) saved him from the grim decisions that faced his contemporaries, who had to decide on which side to stand in 1776. In 1884, his great-grandson, Louis Manigault (1828–1899), wrote that a contemporary of Peter Manigault's had said:

By his early death, at the age of forty-two he was exempted from all the buffetings of the Revolutionary Storm, to the raising of which he had largely contributed. He was an elegant classical scholar, an elegant public speaker, and possessed of an inexhaustible fund of wit. Many of his repartees and other effusions of a brilliant imagination are still remembered and often quoted by the few companions of his social hours.[48]

The *South-Carolina Gazette* of February 21, 1774, declared:

On Wednesday last arrived here, in the Brigt. Amity,

Capt. Ash, from London, and was the same Evening deposited in the family-Vault in the French Church Burying-Ground, the Body of *Hon. PETER MANIGAULT,* who went for England May last for the Recovery of his Health, but died in London on the 12th of November, aged 42 Years.—This Gentleman was a Native of this Town, and only Son of Gabriel Manigault, Esq; one of the most respectable Characters in this Province.—An excellent Understanding, improved by the most liberal Education, a benevolent Heart, a liberal Hand, and a most social Disposition, rendered him a very useful Member of the Community, and a most agreeable Companion. He was chosen Speaker of three successive Houses of Assembly of this Province, in which important Station his Talents so distinguished him that he always acquitted himself with Honour and to the entire Satisfaction of his Constituents and Countrymen: And he was one of those Gentlemen to whose liberal Support we owe the Establishment of Mr. Egan's Brewery in this Town, now in such a State, as to rival our Northern Neighbors, and retain in this Province near 20,000 £ a Year. We must not omit to mention, that many Unfortunates in particular, enjoyed his Friendship in an uncommon Degree, and will long deplore his Loss, with unaffected Grief.

The dinner party sketch is the work of an amateur artist, an educated man associating with other men of the world. George Roupell, Esq., was of a family that migrated to England with those who accompanied William and Mary.[49] James Glen of "Longcroft" came to America in December, 1743, as governor of South Carolina, and Roupell may have been with him. Glen was a Scot and Roupell had Edinburgh connections; as a refugee in Britain in 1777, he was a member of the "Old Revolution Club" there.[50] His appointment as searcher of the customs in Charleston became effective late in 1743.

Roupell was still in his customs post when he married. The *South-Carolina Gazette* of May 14, 1753, reported: "On Monday last, MR. GEORGE ROUPELL, (one of the Officers of his Majesty's Customs for this Port,) was married to Miss ELIZABETH PRIOLEAU, an agreeable young lady with a handsome Fortune and other amiable Accomplishments." [51] Apparently, three of the six Roupell children died young. Their second child,

---

[45] "Journal of Mrs. Manigault," *SCH&G,* XX (Jan., 1919), 60.

[46] Charleston Wills 1774–1779, Typed Book No. 16, p. 20 (CPC).

[47] From the Fraser water color and the drawing at the Museum of Early Southern Decorative Arts, Winston-Salem, one might say it was substantial and plain.

[48] A manuscript note, in the hand of Louis Manigault, on Henrietta Middleton Manigault's copy of the Roupell drawing of the dinner party (private collection).

[49] Roupell Family Papers (private collection).

[50] *Ibid.*

[51] See also "Records Kept by Col. Isaac Hayne," *SCH&G,* X (Oct., 1909), 232; and *Marriage Notices in the* South-Carolina Gazette *and Its Successors,* comp. and ed. by A. S. Salley, Jr. (Albany, N.Y.: Joel Munsell's Sons, 1902), p. 17.

FIG. 3. Charles Fraser, *Gabriel Manigault's Seat on Goose Creek* ["Steepbrook"]. St. James, Goose Creek, S.C., 1802. Water color on paper; H. 3¾₁₆″, W. 6⁷⁄₁₆″. (Collection of the Carolina Art Association, Gibbes Art Gallery, Charleston, S.C., gift of the late Alice Ravenel Huger Smith.)

Anne[52] (b. 1756), married Robert McCulloch and died at Carleton, England, in 1785; in 1762 George Boone Roupell[53] (later a distinguished

London advocate) was baptized; his sister Polly (Mary) probably was younger and was long remembered as having flirted with British officers.[54] The Roupells maintained a residence in Charleston. The house, torn down about 1875, was on Tradd Street at Friend (Legaré) Street.[55] In 1782, Mrs. Elizabeth L. Johnston was in Charleston and wrote that Roupell "lived very handsomely. I resided with my father's old friend Mr. McCulloch and his good wife (who was a Miss Roupell) about three weeks. We were very handsomely billeted in a fine house belonging to one of the rebel gentlemen who had left town."[56] As late as the

[52] *Register of St. Philips Parish, Charles Town or Charleston, S.C., 1754–1810,* ed. D. E. Huger Smith and A. S. Salley, Jr. (Charleston, S.C.: Society of the Colonial Dames of America, 1927), pp. 5 and 35; Elizabeth Lichtenstein Johnston, *Recollections of a Georgia Royalist* (New York and London: Bankside Press, 1901), p. 49. On Dec. 14, 1785, the *South-Carolina Gazette and Public Advertiser* reported: "Died. At Carleton, in England, Mrs. Ann McCulloch, lady of Robert McCulloch, Esq, and eldest daughter of George Roupell, Esq; of this State."

[53] Jones, *American Members,* p. 187; Smith and Salley, *Register of St. Philips Parish,* p. 51; William T. Whitley, *Artists and Their Friends in England, 1700–1799* (London and Boston: The Medici Society, 1928), II, 376; Algernon Graves, *The Royal Academy of Arts: A Complete Dictionary of Contributors and Their Works from Its Foundation in 1769 to 1904* (London: Henry Graves & Co. & George Bell & Sons, 1905), II, 159. When discussing recently identified subjects of portraits in Royal Academy exhibitions, Whitley noted that one by John Singleton Copley in the 1780 catalogue (No. 195, "Portrait of a Gentleman") had been "a fine whole length of Mr. Roupel, native of South Carolina. He stands in a graceful, easy attitude and the whole is well painted." This could imply that the portrait was of Deputy Postmaster-General Roupell, and was so interpreted in Rutledge, *Artists in Charleston,* pp. 118–19. However, after having had the privilege of seeing the Roupell Collection, the author found it to be a portrait of George Boone Roupell. See Anna Wells Rutledge, "Portraits

of American Interest in British Collections," *Connoisseur,* CXLI (May, 1958), 265, Fig. 10; and 270.

[54] Personal recollections of Miss Roupell's goddaughter, the late Mrs. William Mason Smith (Eliza Carolina Middleton Huger [1824–1919]), who was the great-grandmother of the author. The latter remembers Mrs. Smith's remarks and family conversations about Miss Roupell and her belongings. See also Harriott Horry Ravenel, *Charleston, The Place and the People* (New York: Macmillan Co., 1906), pp. 296–97, 393–94.

[55] The *Charleston Directory* for 1782 listed "Roupell, George Deputy Postmaster General / 45 Tradd Street." The 1782 *Directory* was reprinted by the Historical Commission of Charleston in 1951.

[56] Johnston, *Recollections,* p. 73.

mid-nineteenth century, people called that part of Tradd Street "Tory Row." [57]

Dr. Alexander Garden, a physician and botanist who accompanied Governor Glen on his expedition into the Cherokee lands in 1756, wrote that "one of our company was a very accurate drawer" and that he was having work done by "a very tolerable hand here" [58]—but did not identify the individual. On February 17, 1759, Dr. Garden asked the great naturalist John Ellis (d. 1776), of London, that he be sent "one of Mr. Ehret's draughts, such as he gives to the engraver. The gentleman who draws for me has begged me often to write to you for one, that he may regulate himself by the method he uses." [59] Later that year Ellis replied, "Mr. Roupel has shown an excellent genius in drawing. I am persuaded he has copied nature most exactly. When you get him to draw any more for you, the outlines will be sufficient, as in Plumier's American plants, and one blossom, leaf and fruit only, shaded. The rest can be finished here." [60]

The virtues of botanical plates were discussed, and as early as 1757 Garden had written, "Mr. Ehret's plates, they are indeed inimitable, and far exceed any thing which I could have imagined within the power of human art. What difference is there between them and Catesby!" [61] In January, 1760, Garden wrote Ellis to thank him for some plates

especially the original drawing of the *Halesia*. Mr. Roupel was struck with astonishment on seeing it, but he cannot yet well judge with what kind of pencil he (Mr. Ehret) does it, or can possibly do it so fine. . . . Both Mr. Roupel and I are very glad that you liked the drawing of the *Ellisia*. . . . Mr. Roupel is just now about draughts of five different species of the *Rhus*, which I intend to send to the Edinburgh Society.[62]

Botanical knowledge and international correspondence on the flora of the new continent were recorded with scientific exactness, the terminology of the savant being supplemented by the skill of the draftsman. On November 19, 1764, Garden

wrote Ellis, "I sent Mr. Roupel's draught and specimens, seeds and characters, to be forwarded to Linnaeus," and later in the summer he continued: "I shall be glad to hear of the fate of my new genera; what is your choice, and what has become of the former genus which I sent him, and of which you have Mr. Roupel's drawing. I have another species of the same, a still more elegant and beautiful plant, though its leaves are not quite so broad, but the flowers excel in beauty." [63]

Probably the most widely known plant about which Garden and Ellis corresponded, and in whose placing Mr. Roupell was involved, was the *Gardenia*. In January, 1761, Garden wrote, "In my last letter to Linnaeus, I sent him the characters of a shrub, which I took to be new, and which I imagined he was to call the *Gardenia,* if he found it so. . . . I now send you Mr. Roupel's draught of it, which I think is well done, and exactly copied from the life. If you think it worthwhile, pray have a print of it, or a copy, and send this to Linnaeus." [64]

In 1760, a personal rather than a scientific point came into the correspondence, and Garden asked Ellis to pardon him for requesting a favor at what might be an inconvenient moment; however, would Mr. Ellis mention to the Earl of Halifax that George Roupell, in Charleston, South Carolina, had applied for the position of comptroller of the customs or surveyor general of the customs there:

Honour, probity, uprightness, veracity, and noble generosity, are the distinguishing virtues that point him out a real gentleman, a worthy member of society, and a fit person for serving his King and country in such a trust.

He has served his Majesty as an Officer of the Customs, in this port, for I believe ten if not eleven years, but in a station far below his merit and capacity. In the office of Searcher he has borne an upright and unblemished character for that space of time.[65]

Ellis had to reply that he could not ask a favor of Lord Halifax, but that when the governor arrived in England he might venture to address him on the subject.

In 1765, the American Postal Service, under the Postmaster General in London, had been divided into a Northern and a Southern District. On

[57] Ravenel, *Charleston*, p. 172.

[58] Sir James Edward Smith, *A Selection of the Correspondence of Linnaeus, and Other Naturalists, from the Original Manuscripts* (London: Longman, Hurst, Rees, Orme, and Brown, 1821), p. 394.

[59] *Ibid.,* p. 432.

[60] *Ibid.,* p. 461.

[61] *Ibid.,* p. 395.

[62] *Ibid.,* pp. 465 and 467.

[63] *Ibid.,* pp. 522 and 534.

[64] *Ibid.,* p. 504.

[65] *Ibid.,* p. 487.

November 9, 1771, George Roupell was commissioned deputy postmaster general of the Southern District, holding office to the end of the colonial period.

Roupell was involved in unpleasant episodes resulting from the various parliamentary acts that inflamed both the Americans and the British. In South Carolina, the stand of the Court of Vice Admiralty and the moves of various officers were noted in the *South-Carolina Gazette* of June 18, 1772, which carried an extensive account of the contest between Roupell and Roger-Peter-Handasyde Hatley for collector of customs. Roupell took charge as well as he could, which involved taking possession of the legal forms, rooms, and the "Kings Chest." He cleared ships, and officers sent letters by him.

In the various troubles leading up to the outbreak of hostilities, Roupell, as an officer of the Crown, was not one of those making the decision for resistance. In 1777, in London, he wrote to the Lords Commissioners of the Treasury that he had been in Charleston, and

in the execution of his Office until . . . the breaking out the present rebellion . . . your memorialist hath suffered the same hardships and imprisonments that have been inflicted on the other Officers of the Crown, and hath also for upwards of Two years before his leaving Carolina been deprived of all benefit from the said office which used to produce him Yearly the sum of one hundred and eighty pounds sterling and upwards.

That your Memorialist hath been obliged to leave his fortune & all his family except his Son, whom he hath brought to England as well for his Education as to prevent his being persecuted by the Rebels . . . [please grant] such relief as in Your Wisdom you shall see fit.[66]

In London the last royal governor, Lord William Campbell, and the lieutenant governor, William Bull, in January, 1778, wrote on Roupell's behalf. Lord William said:

I do hereby Certify that George Roupell Esq'r hath for many years past been Searcher of the Customs of the Port of Charles Town in South Carolina, and was also Deputy Postmaster General for the Southern District of America, that he discharged the duties of his Offices with Assiduity and integrety, and was ever a faithful and Loyal subject to his Majesty, on which Account hath suffered great losses & long imprisonment, until he was finally compell'd to leave the Province and Family and Fortune for his refusal to take the Oath ap-

pointed to be taken by the Act of their assumed Legislature pass'd the 7th day of March last.[67]

Because of the movement of troops, the evacuation of Charleston, and the flights of refugees, costs had been very heavy, and there was great loss and distress for many. In 1776, Colonel Probart Howarth and Postmaster Roupell had been put on parole in Charleston.[68] In 1780 and 1781 their names were listed among "six setts of persons who refused to take an Oath of Allegiance to the State . . . and in Consequence thereof, [were] by Law obliged to depart the Same . . . their estates now Confiscated, and their Persons subject to Banishment."[69] The list mentioned the governor, the lieutenant governor, the attorney general, the chief justice, the secretary, the clerk of council, the collector, Colonel Probart Howarth, and other officials and holders of Crown appointments including a ship's carpenter and a blacksmith.

Yet, in 1774, the *South-Carolina Gazette* for March 21 had printed:

Friday last being the ANNIVERSARY of the REPEAL of the AMERICAN STAMP-ACT . . . the same was celebrated here. . . . The Review over, the whole Light Infantry Company repaired to Mrs. Swallow's Tavern, where an elegant Entertainment had been provided by the Officers, which was honoured with the Presence of the Lieutenant-Governor, many of the Members of the Commons House of Assembly, all the Officers of the Regiment of Militia, many civil Officers, several of the Clergy, and a great number of other Gentlemen. After Dinner, many loyal and constitutional Toasts were drank; the King, the Queen and Royal Family, the Governor and Province, respectively, succeeded by a Discharge of Cannon from Capt. Arthur's Ship. In the Evening, they went in a Body to the Theatre, where the Comedy of the *RECRUITING OFFICER,* with the *ORACLE,* were presented by particular Desire of the Officers: After the Play, they returned to Mrs. Swallow's to Supper, where they spent the Night in a Manner suitable to the Day, in loyal and harmonious Joy.

However, on June 6, 1774, the *South-Carolina Gazette* reported, with great indignation, the act blockading the port of Boston, closing the column with:

Saturday last being the King's Birth-Day, when His

---

[66] Roupell Family Papers.

[67] *Ibid.*

[68] "A Letter of John Laurens to His Uncle James Laurens," *SCH&G,* X (Jan., 1909), 52; see also the biographical note under Howarth (p. 60–61).

[69] "Josiah Smith's Diary, 1780–1781," annotated by Mable L. Webber, *SCH&G,* XXXIV (Oct., 1933), 198.

Majesty entered into the 36th Year of his Age, the same was observed here in the usual Way, *i.e.* The Bells were rung—Colours displayed—Guns at the Forts fired—the Militia were reviewed—and His Honour The Lieutenant-Governor had Company to dine with him in the Council-Chamber—but there was not a single House illuminated at Night, nor any other Demonstration of Joy; the People *lamenting* that so good a Prince should be beset by a Ministry who seem to have studied to *alienate* rather than preserve the Affections of his most loyal Subjects.

Savannah was occupied by British troops after December 28, 1778; Charleston, after a siege, surrendered and was occupied in May, 1780. In July, 1782, when Tories and officers had to leave Savannah, Roupell wrote, "what a horrid affair." [70] Undoubtedly, he would have described his leaving Charleston (which was surrendered to the Americans in December, 1782) in the same words, for his son in England heard in 1783 that a friend had seen George Roupell in St. Augustine: "He tells me that my father had been obliged to land his furniture & everything bulky that he had with him, on Anastatia Island that a violent gale of wind coming on, the Sea rose & the whole of it together with his Wine and Rum, was either stove to pieces or washed into the Sea & irrecoverably lost. How cruelly unlucky!" [71]

The senior Roupell owned land in Florida, and perhaps in Jamaica, but had returned to his wife and daughter in South Carolina by 1787 when his son in London wrote to him, "We could not help laughing at the mishap you made in sending a general Printed Powers—it must be a mistake from the words of conclusion—I am sure you never read it—it ends thus—and in the *Eleventh Year of the Independence of the United States of America*—you must on reflection conceive that such a Power could never be offered at the General P. O." [72]

Although his circumstances must have been considerably reduced, George Roupell apparently preferred life in South Carolina, growing indigo and cotton, to life in England. *The City Gazette and Daily Advertiser* for October 28, 1794, carried: "DIED. At his plantation near Beaufort, *George Roupell, Esq.* for many years deputy postmaster general of the southern department of

America. Few men have better deserved, or more happily obtained, the good opinion of their fellow citizens. His life was a life of honor, and his death, the subject of regret." [73]

Letters exchanged between Roupell's son in England and his daughter in America continued for decades. "Miss Polly" was asked to send to England a variety of Carolina-grown products such as rice, grits, and pickled peppers, as well as notes on business, planting, and financial problems.

The wills of both Mrs. Roupell and her daughter itemized personal belongings and made particular bequests.[74] That of "Miss Polly," proved in January, 1845, left to a family friend and legal adviser, Henry Alexander DeSaussure, "the Silver Punch cup or urn that was my Fathers, with the Strainer and also my two Silver bread or cake baskets." [75]

The life, the professional career, the interests, and the occupations of George Roupell were not unusual. During the eighteenth century, cosmopolitanism of style, taste, and fashion entered the modern pattern. The positions of executives in civil and military establishments, the careers of professional men, merchants, and planters, were already international in character. Theirs was a most practical outlook: they were intelligent men seeking both success and prosperity. No hard lines of class and caste existed, and one had a choice of interest and association (however, for the less influential, the choices were within small, rather changing groups in outlying places). One could enjoy the lighter aspects of life: horse racing, cock fighting, dancing, fencing, music, theater, cards, drawing, and painting. Some had serious intellectual interests: science, the arts, and religion—this was the period of The Enlightenment.

Alexander Gordon (d. 1754), musician, artist, and antiquarian in Scotland, Italy, and London, was a resident in South Carolina for over ten years; [76] and Jeremiah Theus occupied the position that might be styled "painter in ordinary"

---

[70] Roupell Family Papers.
[71] *Ibid.*
[72] *Ibid.*

[73] See also the *South-Carolina State Gazette and Timothy & Masons Daily Advertiser,* Oct. 29, 1794.
[74] Charleston Wills 1818–1826, Typed Book No. 34, pp. 93 ff.; and Charleston Wills 1839–1845, Typed Book No. 43, p. 824 (CPC).
[75] Charleston Wills 1839–1845, Typed Book No. 43, p. 826 (CPC).
[76] Anna Wells Rutledge, "A Cosmopolitan in Carolina," *William and Mary Quarterly,* 3rd ser., VI (Oct., 1949), 637 ff.; see also Rutledge, *Artists in Charleston,* p. 114.

from 1740 to 1774.[77] The talents, training, and interests of George Roupell were not of the caliber of these men. If we may judge from the few pieces now known, his drawings were useful in recording things of a serious nature as well as in depicting friends. Botanical drawings sent from America to England surely were completely and correctly anonymous in style, and George Roupell's small drawing of Isaac Mazyck (Fig. 4) is as accurate and factual as studies for botanists.[78] Undoubtedly Roupell could "catch a likeness" and endow each figure with a definite personality, but exaggeration was not the point in designs for botanical plates or in the likeness of Mazyck.

At the Manigault dinner party there is not a serious thought. Gaiety and diversion were needed by persons whose daily life was often "as of this moment" in the forest or on the sea. Wit and personal courage were of as much value as wealth, power, service, and one's professional and governmental responsibilities.

IDENTIFICATION OF FIGURES IN THE SKETCH

A legend inscribed on the linen backing of the drawing (Fig. 5) lists the subjects as follows: "1. P. Manigault / 2. Taylor, an officer / 3. Demaré, an officer / 4. Capt. Massey / 5. M.r Isaac Godin / 6. Coytmore, an officer / 7. Col. Probart Howarth / 8. M.r George Roupell, who made the within / Drawing—to represent the House of P. / Manigault.—"

Number 1. PETER MANIGAULT (1731–1773), the host.
"Your Tost Howarth." (Biographical material in text.)

Number 2. TAYLOR, an officer.
"Hey to the Midnight Hark a-way, Hark a-way."
Probably this represents Charles Taylor, who was in an Oglethorpe regiment in Georgia that was disbanded in 1749.[79] Many of the officers and

[77] Rutledge, *Artists in Charleston,* p. 114.
[78] The drawing of Mazyck by Roupell is inscribed on the back, "Isaac Mazyck / Drawn by Old Mr. Roupell / Before the Revolution / 1756"; and, in another hand, "Given me by Mr. Edward Mazyck / May 1866." Isaac Mazyck (1699–1770) was a Charleston merchant and landowner. Educated in Charleston and Trinity College, Dublin, he served for thirty-seven years in the South Carolina Commons House of Assembly.
[79] The extensive files in the library of the Fort Frederica National Monument, St. Simon's Island, Ga., have many notes on the personalities in the regiments.

FIG. 4. Roupell, *Isaac Mazyck.* Charleston, S.C., *ca.* 1756. Sepia drawing on paper; H. 5⅛", W. 3⅞". (Collection of the Carolina Art Association, Gibbes Art Gallery, gift of Colonel Alston Deas, U.S.A. Ret.)

men from this regiment later joined the South Carolina Independent Companies. Their uniforms were scarlet coats with blue or green facing and cuffs.

Number 3. RAYMOND OR PAUL DEMERE.
"Success to Caroline G-d dame"

The brothers Raymond and Paul Demere were French-born. The elder, Raymond, served with the British at Gibraltar for over ten years and then served in regiments in Georgia and South Carolina. Both were on the expedition that built Fort Loudon in 1756. When Raymond Demere retired from the fort, he was succeeded by his brother Paul, who lost his life in the massacre of 1760. Raymond Demere (d. 1766) was a member of various Charleston organizations, but had his main residence in later years at "Harrington Hall," near Frederica, Georgia.

Number 4. CAPTAIN MASSEY.
"This one bumper dear Isaac."

This may be either Captain John Massey or Captain William Massey.

Number 5. ISAAC GODIN (d. 1777).
"I shall be Drunk, I tell ye Massey"

Isaac Godin, of "Fontainbleau," St. James, Goose Creek, was of a family settled in that neighborhood since the beginning of the century.[80] Benjamin Godin, the father of "Squire Isaac," was a wealthy merchant and landowner whose progeny numbered eleven—nine daughters and two sons.[81] His will was proved in 1748 and mentioned, as well as his wife and children, a nephew in London and a niece in Rotterdam. He left a great deal of personal property and real estate, perhaps well over 12,000 acres. Isaac Godin kept some of the property, and left his wife the plantation in Goose Creek "where I most commonly reside."[82] This plantation was part of an aggregate owned by the Godin family from 1707 to 1784 and was on the west side of Public Road opposite "Steepbrook." "Fontainbleau" was a brick residence with a large number of outbuildings. Godin was a former owner of the "Steepbrook" property as well as a neighbor of Manigault's, and there probably was warm friendship between them.

Number 6. RICHARD COYTMORE (?).
"Whose Tost is it"

Because this figure is saying, "Whose Tost is it," and the host (No. 1) replies, "Your Tost Howarth," it seems possible that the identities of Nos. 6 and 7 have been reversed. Furthermore, No. 7 says, "Squire Isaac, You[r] Wig You Dog"—a remark more appropriate for a cheerful young man than for the ranking officer. The colonel was a nearby landowner whose visit was that of a familiar friend and neighbor; therefore, he would not be in uniform. Moreover, the face of No. 6 seems too old for a man who was killed when very young.

Richard Coytmore was an ensign in 1754 when Captain Raymond Demere wrote that "I find myself alone here with a young officer who although quite capable, is yet too young for such a command unassisted at this time."[83] Unfortunately, in 1760 Coytmore was left in charge of Fort Prince George on the Keowee River, several hundred miles northwest of Charleston. Disasters followed: the Cherokees killed fourteen men within a mile of the fort, and Coytmore was shot when he was leaving the fort for a conference. After his death, the garrison butchered their Indian hostages.

Coytmore's will was drawn at Fort Prince George, Cherokee Nation, on February 16, 1760, and proved in Charleston, January 9, 1761.[84] His lieutenant, Laughlin Shaw, was named executor. Shaw was to receive Coytmore's pay and arrears and "pay my Creditors that he thinks will stand in most Need." His bequest to Mrs. Shaw was "all my books." His gun, pistol, saddle, and furniture were left to Dr. William Rowan; while his servant, John Bell, was to receive his broad and small swords and his clothes in Charleston. His silver watch was left to Sergeant Daniels with fifty pounds South Carolina currency; all the clothes then in his home at Fort Prince George went to his servant John Ballentine. Coytmore apparently had not been able to buy land or to acquire it by marriage.

Number 7. COLONEL PROBART HOWARTH (d. 1796).
"Squire Isaac, You[r] Wig You Dog"
(The identity may be reversed with No. 6.)

[80] Smith, "Goose Creek," *SCH&G,* XXIX April, 1928), 71 ff.
[81] Charleston Wills 1747–1752, Typed Book No. 6, pp. 85 ff (CPC).
[82] Charleston Wills 1774–1779, Typed Book No. 17, p. 700 (CPC).

[83] Files in the library of the Fort Frederica National Monument (St. Simon's Island, Georgia).
[84] Charleston Wills 1760–1767A, Typed Book No. 9, p. 18 (CPC).

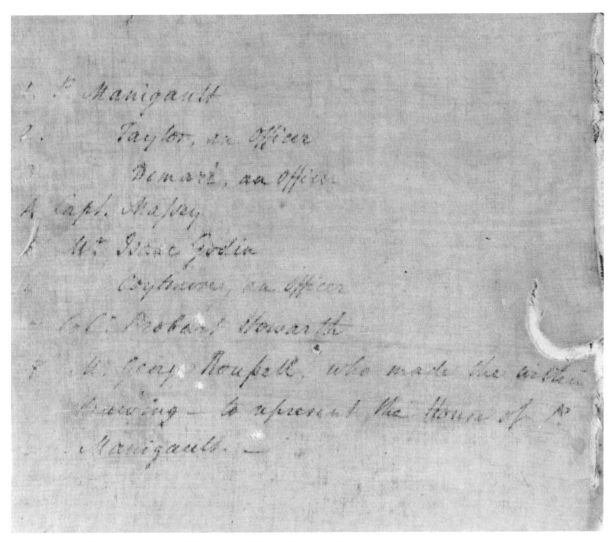

Fig. 5. Inscription on backing of Figure 1. (Winterthur 63.73b.)

From 1768 to 1775 Colonel Howarth was in command at Fort Johnson, James Island, controlling the entrance to Charleston Harbor. Before 1762 he married Anne, daughter of Childermas Croft who held land on Charleston Neck. The property, near the New Market Course,[85] was west of the Broad Path and fronted on the Ashley River [86] in the neighborhood of "Steepbrook." Howarth was interested in racing, and in February, 1769, his "Roan filly" ran in the Colt's Plate at New Market.[87] In 1767, under the will of Francis Kinlock, Howarth was left "any Saddle Horse he shall make choice of out of my Collection as also two hundred Gallons of the best London Porter, which Quantity of Porter shall be delivered to him yearly and every year as long as he lives in his House in Charles Town." [88]

On September 26, 1768, the *South-Carolina Gazette* said: "Last night died, M$^{rs.}$ Anne Howarth, the wife of Col. Probart Howarth, com-

[85] John B. Irving, *The South Carolina Jockey Club* (Charleston, S.C.: Russell & Jones, 1857), pp. 34–35.
[86] Henry A. M. Smith, "Charleston and Charleston Neck," *SCH&G*, XIX (Jan., 1918), 35.

[87] "Journal of Mrs. Manigault," *SCH&G*, XXI (Jan., 1920), pp. 12–13, n. 28½.
[88] Charleston Wills 1767–1771, Typed Book No. 11, p. 234 (CPC).

mander of Fort Johnson—as universally regretted *dead* as esteemed *living,* by all her friends and acquaintances." [89] Howarth's name appears in cabinetmaker Thomas Elfe's account book; and on October 28, 1774, he was charged £60 for "a Mahog^y Coffin full trimmd & lined for Miss Crofts." [90] An officer of the Crown, Howarth refused to take the Oath of Allegiance to the State; and in October, 1776, a letter from Charleston dated August 14 reported to refugees in London that the colonel and the collector were "at large

on their Parole." [91] After the capitulation of Charleston, he was in Florida and New York before he arrived in London in April, 1783. In London in 1786, he must have heard of the death of his daughter, Mrs. Hester Graham, whose husband James Graham held approximately 175 acres of Charleston Neck land; when the land was leased in 1794, the family vault was reserved.[92] In 1796 George Boone Roupell probated the will of Probart Howarth in London.

Number 8. GEORGE ROUPELL (d. 1794).
"Pray less noise Gen^{tn}" (Biographical material in text.)

[89] See also "Records Kept by Col. Isaac Hayne," *SCH&G,* X (July, 1909), 165.

[90] "The Thomas Elfe Account Book 1765–1775," contributed by Mabel L. Webber and copied by Elizabeth Jervey, *SCH&G,* XL (April, 1939), 61.

[91] "Letter of John Laurens," *SCH&G,* X (Jan., 1909), 52.

[92] Smith, "Charleston and Charleston Neck," *SCH&G,* XIX (Jan., 1918), 35–36.

The Albany of Magdalena Douw

Robert G. Wheeler

ON MAY 29, 1740, Magdalena Douw, daughter of Peter Jonas and Anna Douw of "Wolven Hoeck," married Harme Gansevoort, a merchant and brewer of Albany. The portrait of Magdalena, known familiarly as "The Girl with the Red Shoes," probably was painted close to the time of the wedding (Fig. 1).[1]

The importance of the portrait of Magdalena Douw, beyond its decorative quality and its unique place in the school of New York Hudson Valley patroon paintings, is in the nature and the background of the subject. Magdalena, in the 1730's, was a resident of a community that was beginning the transition from Dutch to English culture. She personified the prevailing Dutch customs, habits, and practices still surviving strongly but becoming diluted in a province long under English government and control. Her portrait is, in fact, a social document and helps to reveal the conditions under which an entire school of art developed and flowered.

Beginning with the first decade of the eighteenth century American painters were at work in the Hudson Valley. Their portraits—known generally as the "patroon portraits"—and their religious subjects represent "the earliest significant development of native-born talent in American painting."[2] These portrait subjects included members of the leading families of the Hudson Valley: Beekmans, Van Cortlandts, Van Schaicks, De Peysters, Schuylers, Wendels, and Van Rensselaers.

The basic painting style of these artists was broad, flat, and decorative. Background features, as in the portraits of the three Van Cortlandt boys and Ariaantje Coeymans (Fig. 2), often were borrowed from English mezzotint engravings.[3] While the patroon artists of the Hudson Valley (none of whom, with the possible exception of Pieter Vanderlyn, have been identified as yet) painted with imagination and an occasional gay verve, they achieved firm statements of mood and character. They generally portrayed individuals of Dutch background who typified the strength of body and soul necessary to settle a wilderness, flourish, and retain the Dutch traits of tolerance, thrift, and forthrightness for over a century. The painting of Magdalena Douw comes near the close of this school of early Hudson Valley portraiture. By the 1750's a "new wave of migrants" and a "new generation of native-born talents" were expressing the character of the American scene with increasing technical skill.[4]

Magdalena Douw, in the second quarter of the eighteenth century, obviously differed from the

---

[1] This painting is now in The Henry Francis du Pont Winterthur Museum. Mrs. Edgar Morris Griffiths (Maude Ten Eyck Gansevoort Griffiths), the last private owner of the portrait, has provided data on the line of descent of the painting which tend to document its identification. The portrait appears to have passed from Magdalena Douw Gansevoort to her sixth child and second surviving son, Leonard (1751–1810), who married Hester Cuyler in 1770. The portrait apparently passed next to their daughter Magdalena (1777–1863), who married Jacob Ten Eyck (d. 1862) of Albany in 1795. According to family tradition the portrait was hung at "Whitehall," the family home, where Jacob and Magdalena Ten Eyck moved in 1800. It survived the burning of "Whitehall" in 1883 and later came into the possession of Mrs. Griffiths, a descendant of Magdalena Douw.

[2] E. P. Richardson, *Painting in America, The Story of 450 Years* (New York: Thomas Y. Crowell, 1956), p. 40.

[3] *Hudson Valley Paintings, 1700–1750* (Cogswell Fund Series, Publications No. 1; Albany: Albany Institute of History and Art, 1959), p. 22.

[4] Richardson, *Painting in America*, p. 48.

FIG. 1. *Magdalena Douw* (Mrs. Harme Gansevoort). Albany County, N.Y., *ca.* 1740. Oil on canvas; H. 51¹⁄₁₆″, W. 33″. (Winterthur 63.852.)

majority of her Albany contemporaries in a most important manner: she was attractive, if her likeness is reasonably accurate. Dr. Alexander Hamilton visited Albany in 1744 and noted that the women of this community "in general, both old and young, are the hardest favoured ever I beheld. Their old women wear a comical head-dress, large pendants, short petticoats, and they stare upon one like witches." [5] Hamilton was not alone in his judgment of Albany womanhood of that day, nor was he exhibiting a personal prejudice in his remarks. Existing Albany portraits of the 1720's and 1730's confirm his opinions: *Ariaantje Coeymans* (*ca.* 1717); *Margarita van Vechten* (1719); *Anna Cuyler* (1720); *The Girl of the Ten Eyck Family* (1720/21); *Magdalena Bogardus; Jane Goelet* (*ca.* 1733)—all evidence more straightforward character than delicate beauty. [6]

Magdalena Douw was a proper Albany Dutchwoman, whose great-grandfather, Volckert Janse Douw (son of Jan Douw of Leeuwarden, Friesland), was in Albany (Rensselaerswyck) by April 27, 1642. A farmer, trader, and brewer, he married Dorothe Janse van Breestede in 1650. In 1683 their son Captain Jonas Volckert Douw (d. 1736) married Magdalena, daughter of Pieter and Maritje Quackenbush. [7] Peter (Petrus) Jonas Douw (1692–1775), son of Captain Jonas, married, in 1717, Anna, the daughter of Hendrick and Catherine van Bruggen van Rensselaer. Magdalena Douw, born August 1, 1718, was the first child of this union. Her brother, Volckert Petrus Douw, born two years later, was followed by seven more children. All lived to reach maturity. [8]

Had it been in her power to do so, Magdalena could not have chosen a more proper Hudson Valley lineage. Her maternal great-grandmother was Maria van Cortlandt, sister of the Lord of the Manor of Cortlandt and wife of Jeremias van Rensselaer, the patroon's agent in America. Further, Maria was the sister-in-law of Gertrude Schuyler, of the Albany Schuylers, and of Frederick Philipse, First Lord of the Manor of Philipsburg. She was an aunt by marriage of Stephen De

Lancey, Catherine De Peyster, Colonel Henry Beekman, and Samuel Bayard. In addition, she had marriage ties with the Livingstons of the Manor of Livingston. [9] Thus, through her mother's line, Magdalena was connected in some degree to all of the great landholding and merchant families of the Hudson Valley—a social and economic factor of no little worth. This background of position and means could not help but shape young Magdalena's life.

Albanians of the mid-eighteenth century were termed "rustic and unpolished." [10] It is probable, indeed, that many were, since they had a local reputation for plain and frugal living. Invariably, however, there were exceptions to the rules of conformity. There did exist people of fashion.

Jeremias van Rensselaer may be said to have begun this individual trend when, in the 1650's, he ordered a coat from Amsterdam to be made up "according to fashion," and later a cloak "of the latest color and fashion." [11] Magdalena Douw was obviously cut from the same pattern as her great-grandfather. The gown in which she was painted has been tentatively identified as being of harrateen, a fine English wool moire. [12] This fabric was figured and was also described as "flowered." One of the newest fabrics of the mid-eighteenth century, it was first advertised for sale in the *Boston Gazette* of 1737. [13] If it can be assumed, because of her physical development, that Magdalena's portrait was painted about 1740, she is garbed in a new and most fashionable material. Her gown is obviously a country variation on the form known as the Watteau sacque, a style popular in America from 1720 to 1776. Her bright red shoes, with their upturned, pointed toes, could well be of a group noted in 1740 newspaper advertisements offering "Red Morocco" and "red everlasting" shoes. [14]

The details in this portrait—the apparent age

[5] Alexander Hamilton, *Hamilton's Itinerarium*, ed. A. B. Hart (St. Louis: William K. Bixby, 1907), p. 89.

[6] *Hudson Valley Paintings*, pp. 22, 25, 27, 28, 30, 31.

[7] Cuyler Reynolds, *Genealogical and Family History of Southern New York and the Hudson River Valley* (New York: Lewis Historical Publishing Co., 1914), III, 1118.

[8] Sebastian V. Talcott, *Genealogical Notes of New York and New England Families* (Albany: Weed, Parsons and Co., 1883), p. 69.

[9] See Appendix to this article.

[10] Hamilton, *Itinerarium*, p. 88.

[11] *Correspondence of Jeremias van Rensselaer, 1651–1674*, trans. and ed. A. J. F. van Laer (Albany: University of the State of New York, 1932), pp. 110 and 241.

[12] Information supplied by Milo M. Naeve, assistant director, Department of Collections, Colonial Williamsburg, through conversation with Mrs. Charles F. Montgomery, assistant curator, Winterthur Museum. It is possible that the gown could have been made of silk.

[13] Anna Brightman, "Woolen Window Curtains," *Antiques*, LXXXVI (Dec., 1964), 722–27.

[14] Alice Morse Earle, *Two Centuries of Costume in America* (New York: Macmillan Co., 1903), I, 384.

FIG. 2. *Mrs. David Ver Planck* (Ariaantje Coeymans) . Albany County, N.Y., *ca.* 1717.
Oil on canvas; H. 79⅝″, W. 47½″. (Albany Institute of History and Art.)

of the subject, the style and the probable fabric of her gown, the boldly turned table suggestive of the Queen Anne style, and even the shoes—strongly hint that this painting was done close to the time of her marriage in 1740. At this point in Albany history the town was still Dutch in many of the details of daily living, and Dutch influences were still predominant.

Magdalena Douw, logically, could be gowned in what appears to be an English cloth while wearing the traditional Dutch choker, a necklace form worn proudly to this day in many areas of the Netherlands. Her clothing and accessories represent a current mode of the day rather than a specific Dutch or English fashion.

There is nothing incongruous in a Dutch citizen of Albany wearing English cloth and standing beside a table that might be said to be a distortion of the English Queen Anne style. The Dutch, in the Old World and the New, were a people of trade. The colony of New Netherland (New York) was explored and settled by the New Netherland Company (1613/14–1617) and the Dutch West India Company, organized in 1620, with an eye to the fur trade and the natural resources of this new land. Although the agricultural colonization of the Hudson Valley began under the patroon system (and especially the patroonship of the first Kiliaen van Rensselaer) through the 1629 Charter of Freedoms and Exemptions, the major agricultural products of corn, wheat, and timber were viewed as items for an expanding provincial commerce.

The leading families of the colony were traders and merchants first, and landholders second. By the 1680's and 1690's New York ships were sailing to the towns on the Atlantic seacoast, to the islands of the Caribbean, and to English, continental European, and African ports. Merchandise from the East Indies was available through transshipment.

Proper Hudson Valley Dutchmen found nothing strange in maintaining their Dutch identity while prospering through world trade and using desirable goods from their far-flung commercial activities within their personal households. Trade, more than any other feature in the seventeenth and eighteenth centuries, modified the prevailing Dutch culture of this area. The Dutch have always been known for their love of substantial possessions of both local and foreign origin.

Magdalena apparently wears no rings upon her fingers. Madam Knight, in her 1704 visit to New York, found the ladies of that place had "their fingers hoop't with Rings, some with large stones in them of many Coullers." [15] Portraits of married women, such as those done of Mrs. Anthony van Schaick (1720) and of Mrs. Kiliaen van Rensselaer (first half of the eighteenth century), show subjects wearing traditional wedding bands on their left hands. At the same time, however, girls, such as Jane Goelet and Magdalena Bogardus, are portrayed without finger ornaments. [16] This variation suggests that girls, before marriage, did not wear rings. It seems possible that Magdalena was still a maiden.

A special feature of Magdalena's portrait is the architectural detail. The windows, with their Italianate flavor, were obviously borrowed from print sources. Similar windows and Romanesque door arches are common in the Albany religious paintings: *The Marriage at Cana* (Fig. 3), *Christ at Emmaus, Isaac Blessing Jacob, Crowning of King Jereboam,* and *Belshazzar's Feast*. [17] Probable sources for the religious subject matter were the Bibles, common in the Albany area, printed in the Netherlands and illustrated with engravings that suggest a familiarity with the Italian scene. [18]

A rare detail in the portrait is the horizontal board wainscoting that extends from the floor to the base of the window sills. No similar wainscoting is known to exist in any surviving Hudson Valley house of the first half of the eighteenth century, although it was used in Connecticut during this period. [19]

In the Albany area the Hudson River is

---

[15] Sarah Kemble Knight, *The Journal of Madam Knight* (Boston: Small, Maynard & Co., 1920), p. 55.

[16] *Hudson Valley Paintings*, pp. 25, 29–31.

[17] *Ibid.*, pp. 39–40, 44, 45, 47.

[18] *Ibid.*, p. 45.

[19] "After plaster had come into common use, wainscot persisted until 1750 or even later, in a much diminished form, beneath the chair rail of the exterior walls. The joints of such wainscot are always horizontal, unless, as in some instances, a regular system of panelling was installed, with rails, stiles, and raised or bevelled panels. The height of such horizontal wainscot above the floor was evidently determined by the height of the window sills above the floor; for the chair rail, or wainscot cap, is generally formed by a continuation of the window stool and of the mouldings beneath it" (J. Frederick Kelly, *The Early Domestic Architecture of Connecticut* [New Haven: Yale University Press, 1924], pp. 146–47 and p. 148, Fig. 160, Philo Bishop House [Guilford, Conn.]).

bounded on both sides by low, flat shores extending several hundred yards from the stream. The land then rises sharply to wide plateaus of fertile, rolling countryside. To the west of the river this plateau region terminates in the rugged Helderbergs; eastward it extends to the foothills of the Berkshires in Massachusetts and the Green Mountains of Vermont.

Magdalena's home was built on the river flats. The view from any of the windows of this structure would have shown hills such as those in the portrait. Undoubtedly, this view is to the west. A frequent sunset light in the Hudson Valley combines the rosy pinks and blue so often captured by the patroon painters in their portrait backgrounds.

Of the more than seventy-five existing Albany area portraits painted between *ca.* 1715 and 1743, the portrait of Magdalena Douw stands apart. It does not appear to be related to the main body of portraits of the period and area. At the same time, however, there seems to exist a stylistic relationship between the portrait of Magdalena and certain of the early eighteenth-century religious subjects of the upper Hudson area. Both Dr. Alexander Hamilton and Mrs. Anne Grant commented on these Albany religious paintings. In 1744 Dr. Hamilton observed that the residents of Albany were fond of pictures, particularly scenes from Biblical history, with which they adorned their rooms.[20] Mrs. Grant reported that about 1760 the Schuyler family at their home, "The Flatts," north of Albany on the Saratoga Road, had some fine scriptural paintings in their eating room. She specifically described Esau coming to demand the blessing of Isaac.[21]

Christ at Emmaus, Isaac Blessing Jacob, and *The Marriage at Cana* all utilize the concept of double penetration into space, a particular characteristic of the portrait of Magdalena Douw. In the painting of Magdalena, the arch on the right opens to a middle distance, while that on the left exposes a far distant view. In *Christ at Emmaus* the left arch opens into a middle interior vista and the right arch shows a further interior distance.

Among the portrait subjects, Magdalena's face is unique in its two-dimensional quality. Presumably, before early cleaning and restoration, her features might have shown considerable evidence of modeling. It has been suggested that the left foot of the subject was repainted in a distorted manner, that the subject's skirt has been overpainted to some extent, and that architectural elements such as the window frames and details of the foreground table have been altered.[22] One of the table legs may well have been added after the portrait was completed. Moreover, the drawing of this table presumably is not exact, since no prototype for the double cyma legs with sharp knees has yet been found. However crudely this table may be represented, it still has the flavor of the Queen Anne style. The history of this painting must be kept in mind at all times for general viewing and for comparative studies. The portrait has required considerable repairs over the years. Not the least of the damages it has suffered was some charring, which probably occurred during the burning of "Whitehall," where it hung in 1883.

In 1749 Peter Kalm noted, "The greater part of the merchants at *Albany* have extensive estates in the country," [23] and Peter Jonas Douw was no exception. Magdalena grew up at "Wolven Hoeck," the house built by her father in 1724 on the east bank of the Hudson, across the river from Albany. Her family connections determined the place of her upbringing.

In 1715 "Wolven Hoeck" or Wolves' Point, land located on the Manor of Rensselaer, was conveyed by the Lord of the Manor, Kiliaen van Rensselaer, to his brother Hendrick, Magdalena's grandfather. Hendrick lived here at "Crailo," the great brick house which presumably dates from the seventeenth century and which still stands in Rensselaer, New York.

Peter and Anna van Rensselaer Douw established themselves on this Van Rensselaer property close to the Hudson River and just to the south of "Crailo." [24] Their brick house, "Wolven Hoeck," was typical of its day. A surviving painting shows it to have been a story and a half in height, with a

[20] Hamilton, *Itinerarium,* p. 87.

[21] Anne Grant, *Memoirs of an American Lady* (Boston: W. Wells, Thomas B. Wait and Co. and Hastings, Etheridge, and Bliss, 1809), I, 90.

[22] Microscopic and Xray examinations at Winterthur Museum have, in fact, revealed many of these changes. It is quite possible that they were the result of the artist's striving for a particular effect.

[23] Peter Kalm, *Travels in North America,* trans. John Reinhold Forster (London: T. Lowndes, 1772), II, 100.

[24] Helen Wilkinson Reynolds, *Dutch Houses in the Hudson Valley before 1776* (New York: Dover Publications, 1965), pp. 113–15.

FIG. 3. *The Marriage at Cana.* Albany County, N.Y., 1725–1750. Oil on canvas; H. 31¼″, W. 39¾″. (Albany Institute of History and Art.)

roof of steep, single pitch. There were end chimneys, portholes in the gables, and board shutters.[25] Although this pleasant country house was demolished between 1835 and 1840, counterparts still stand: the house of Leendert Bronck, built in 1738 in West Coxsackie, New York, and the 1737 Van Alen house in Kinderhook, New York.[26]

From the doorway of "Wolven Hoeck" Albany could easily be seen to the north, across the tidal waters of the Hudson. The town sprawled up the steep hillside west of the river. Although Magdalena lived outside the city proper, her family was intimately associated with this community by blood, social contacts, business, and religion.

In the early 1740's Albany, with a population

approaching four thousand, was still a fortified town surrounded by a wall of wooden palisadoes, or trunks of pine trees rammed into the ground close together. Each tree trunk, pointed at the top, was about ten feet high and one foot thick.[27] The town consisted of three principal streets, two of which were parallel to the river and cut at right angles by the third, which extended up the hill to the fort.[28]

The fort, a stone breastwork about two hundred feet square, had a bastion at each corner, on which were mounted eight or ten guns. Within the fort were two large brick houses to lodge officials, officers, and soldiers. The fort was badly situated, because the high hills on the west permit-

[25] *Ibid.,* pp. 78–79.
[26] *Ibid.,* p. 134, Plate 17, and p. 158, Plate 41.

[27] Hamilton, *Itinerarium,* p. 87.
[28] *Ibid.,* p. 86.

ted an observer to see all that went on within the fortification.[29]

The community had but three major public buildings. The Dutch Church (Fig. 4), with a steeple, bell, and weather vane, was near the foot of the street leading to the fort. The steepleless, stone English Church stood just below the fort. The Town Hall or Stadt-Huis (Fig. 5), a three-story stone structure, with a steeple, bell, and weather vane, was located near the river to the south of the Dutch Church. The majority of the private dwellings in Albany were of stone or brick covered with shingles of white pine. Most of them were built in the old style, with the gable end toward the street. To prevent the walls from being damaged by rain, the gutters from the houses ran almost to the middle of the streets. Although most of the houses had wells, the water had an acid taste, so water for tea, brewing, and washing was commonly drawn from the river.[30] Within this semirural town every householder had a garden and kept a cow, which, in season, was milked daily in the dooryard.[31]

An element of Albany social life was the *stoep* or porch. The street entrance was generally in the center of the façade with a small *stoep*. Benches were customarily placed on both sides of this low wooden entrance platform, and during fair and warm weather the older citizens, women, and girls spent most of the day on these porches—especially those shaded by the houses. In the evening the benches were filled with people of both sexes. Peter Kalm found this quite troublesome, since "those who pass by are obliged to greet every body, unless they will shock the politeness of the inhabitants of this town." [32]

A perhaps apocryphal story concerning mid-eighteenth-century Dutch Albany, related by a contemporary New Englander, said that the Albanians kept their houses cleaner than their bodies, their bodies cleaner than their souls. Certainly, visitors to the city found the houses very neat and clean, both inside and out. The chambers and rooms, described as large and handsome, were floored with rough planks which through constant rubbing and scrubbing became extremely smooth and white. Beds were generally placed in alcoves,

or were built into them. One could literally go through a house and never see a bed at all.[33]

The cabinet shelves in Albany were filled with decorative china: delft, yellow glaze comb ware from the Staffordshire area, and salt glaze. Kitchens were especially clean; and earthen and delft plates were hung around the walls like paintings by means of loops of ribbon put through holes drilled in their edges.[34]

The climate of Albany can be extreme: hot and humid in the summer, bitterly cold in the

Fig. 4. Henry W. Snyder, *A View of the Late Protestant Dutch Church in the City of Albany.* New York, 1806. Engraving after drawing by Philip Hooker, published by John Low; plate: H. 11½", W. 10¼". (Albany Institute of History and Art.)

winter. The early householders are said to have been unacquainted with stoves, although it has been reported that their chimneys were so wide above the great fireplaces a driver could take a cart and horses through them.[35] Obviously, the "cart and horses" phrase is a figure of speech. Still, surviving hooded Hudson Valley fireplaces are so large that it would take a horse to pull the great logs into position for burning.[36] Dr. Hamilton, in 1744, was fascinated by this quality of cold. At

[29] Kalm, *Travels,* II, 98.
[30] *Ibid.,* pp. 96, 97, and 95.
[31] Grant, *Memoirs,* I, 30–31.
[32] Kalm, *Travels,* II, 97.

[33] Hamilton, *Itinerarium,* p. 87.
[34] *Ibid.,* pp. 87–88.
[35] Arthur James Weise, *The History of the City of Albany* (Albany: E. H. Bender, 1884), p. 305.
[36] For example, see the fireplace in the Hasbrouck House, Washington's Headquarters, Newburgh, N.Y., built before 1747 and now a New York State Historic Site.

that time he wrote that the residents of Albany were

a healthy, long-lived people, many in this city being in age near or above 100 years, and eighty is a very common age. They are subject to rotten teeth and scorbutic gums, which, I suppose, is caused by the cold air, and their constant diet of salt provisions in the winter; for in that season they are obliged to lay in, as for a sea voyage, there being no stirring out of doors then for fear of never stirring again.[37]

This, briefly, was the town that Magdalena knew as a girl and as a young matron—a town still definitely Dutch in architecture, in customs, and in language. In reality, there had been little or no

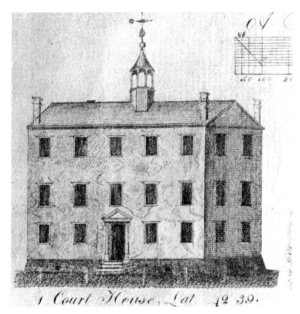

FIG. 5. Isaac Hutton, *Court House* (Stadt-Huis). Albany, N.Y., 1794. Engraving, detail from *A Plan of the City of Albany;* H. 20″, W. 15½″. (Albany Institute of History and Art.)

change in the social customs and amusements of Albany between the mid-seventeenth century—when the young Jeremias van Rensselaer wrote of hunting, racing his horse and sleigh on the frozen Hudson River, or passing long winter evenings at singing psalms set to music [38]—and the mid-eighteenth century of Magdalena Douw.

Later, in the 1760's, Mrs. Grant chronicled a town where the girls were still taught to knit stockings, make clothes for their family members, and manage intricate household details. Boys

found their main relaxation in hunting and fishing. Group activities consisted of picnicking, gathering wild fruits and nuts, and sledding down the hilly Albany streets in the winter.[39]

Breakfast was an early meal in every Albany house. Dinner was served between noon and 1 o'clock, followed by an early tea and, finally, supper. Game, poultry, or shellfish in season were favored dinner foods. A variety of pastries was usually served with tea.[40]

Entertaining was very simple and, to the visitor from afar, somewhat disconcerting. A rather sophisticated gentleman from Baltimore wrote in disgust, "I now began to be quite tired of this place, where there was no variety or choice, either of company or conversation, and one's ears perpetually invaded and molested with volleys of rough-sounding Dutch, which is the language most in use here." [41] This man had the good fortune of having been introduced into more than twenty of the more important Albany homes. At each, he complained, he went through the farce of kissing most of the women, "a manner of salutation which is expected from strangers. . . . This might almost pass for a penance." [42]

There are constant references throughout the mid-eighteenth century, and even toward the end of the century, to the prevalence of the Dutch language in Albany. Dr. Timothy Dwight (the eminent divine, and future president of Yale) visited Albany in 1792. At this late date, 128 years after the English had taken over the political control of the Dutch colony of New Netherland and almost a decade after the close of the Revolution, he found the community still exhibiting strong Dutch traces. He noted, "Until within a few years, the inhabitants have been, almost without an exception, descendants from the original settlers. From this fact it has derived its whole aspect, and character." [43] He found, however, that English customs were gradually taking hold. So definite was this movement that he fully expected even "the humblest classes of the Dutch must, within a short period, adopt the English language and manners." [44]

[37] Hamilton, *Itinerarium,* p. 89.
[38] *Correspondence of van Rensselaer,* pp. 160 and 231.

[39] Grant, *Memoirs,* I, 39–40, 58–60.
[40] *Ibid.,* pp. 54–55.
[41] Hamilton, *Itinerarium,* p. 84.
[42] *Ibid.,* p. 75.
[43] Timothy Dwight, *Travels in New-England and New-York* (New Haven: The author, 1821–1822), II, 491.
[44] *Ibid.,* p. 493.

From the surviving evidence it is apparent that Magdalena spoke Dutch at home and in social conversation. At the Dutch Church she heard sermons preached in Dutch. Her dominie, the Rev. Theodorus Frelinghuysen, wrote on the affairs of the local churches to the Classis of Amsterdam in 1748. He reviewed the fact that, since Albany was on the frontier and near the enemy, men were sent from other places to guard the town. Because most of these men were English rather than Dutch, and because the English Church had no preacher at this time, "I have undertaken by their request to preach for them in the English language, and this I have now done for some time . . . on the Lord's Day, after having preached twice in the Dutch language."[45]

The strongest evidence as to Magdalena's customary use of the Dutch language is found in a reference to her brother Volckert Petrus Douw. On boarding a sloop at Albany on July 2, 1744, to return to New York City, Dr. Hamilton found that his fellow passenger was young Volckert.

I flattered myself I should not be quite alone, but enjoy some conversation; but I was mistaken. . . . I never was so destitute of conversation in my life as in this voyage. I heard nothing but Dutch spoke all the way. My fellow passenger Volkert Douw could speak some English, but had as little in him to enliven conversation as any young fellow ever I knew that looked like a gentleman. Whoever had the care of his education had foundered him by instilling into him enthusiastic religious notions.[46]

Sloops like that used by Hamilton and Volckert Douw were important elements in sustaining trade, the lifeblood of Albany. Although a law had been passed in 1703 providing for the building of roads to connect New York and Albany on both sides of the Hudson,[47] it was not until 1785 that a stage line was chartered to run regularly on the east shore of the river between the two cities.[48] Throughout the eighteenth century the Hudson River was the highway north and south. Travelers, traders, and merchandise were carried on the broad-beamed, shallow-draft Albany sloops. Because of its location near the junction of the Hud-

son and the Mohawk rivers, Albany was the gateway to Canada and the West. It was a reasonably easy water passage northward, via the Hudson, to Lake Champlain and the St. Lawrence. The Mohawk was the passage to the Susquehanna Valley, the Great Lakes, and to even more remote areas. Cadwallader Colden wrote in 1738, "By means of these lakes [the Great Lakes] & the Rivers which fall into them, Commerce may be carried from New York, through a vast Tract of Land, more easily than from any other Maritime Town in North America."[49]

Writers of the day noted that, with the exception of the Hudson's Bay settlement, there was no place in all the British colonies where such quantities of furs and skins were bought from the Indians as at Albany. Even the French merchants of Canada sent furs by their Indians to Albany. These Indians, in turn, bought cloth and other goods there at a lower rate than they could obtain in the French provinces.[50]

Magdalena, therefore, was accustomed to the sight of Indians near her home. She knew at first hand the value of liquor and beer in trading for furs and was aware of the trade items laid in by the Albany merchants for their dealings with the savages. Her husband, Harme, as an Albany merchant, would have stocked such standard items as muskets, shot, and musket balls; white cloth and blue or red cloth for petticoats; shirts and shifts of linen; hatchets and knives; scissors and needles; steel to strike sparks; kettles of copper and brass; vermilion and verdigris to paint the body; looking glasses; earrings and beads; brass and steel wire; and brandy. These were the chief goods in the Indian fur trade.[51]

The pattern of Hudson River trade worked to the advantage of such fashionable young ladies as Magdalena Douw. The Albany sloops, during the season of navigation on the Hudson, sailed to New York City with cargoes of fur, timber, flour, and peas.[52] On their return trips they carried the merchandise required by their owners, by friends of their owners, and also by the local merchants and traders.

[45] *Ecclesiastical Records, State of New York,* ed. Edward T. Corwin (Albany: J. B. Lyon, 1902), IV, 3018.

[46] Hamilton, *Itinerarium,* pp. 85–86, 96.

[47] *The Colonial Laws of New York* (Albany: James B. Lyon, 1894), I, 532–38.

[48] *Laws of the State of New York* (Albany: Weed, Parsons and Co., 1886), II, 99.

[49] John Romeyn Brodhead (comp.), *Documents Relative to the Colonial History of the State of New-York: Procured in Holland, England and France,* ed. E. B. O'Callaghan (Albany: Weed, Parsons and Co., 1855), VI, 122.

[50] Kalm, *Travels,* II, 98.

[51] *Ibid.,* pp. 391–95.

[52] *Ibid.,* p. 98.

Life for the inhabitants of the Albany frontier undoubtedly was harsh and demanding much of the time. Still, as evidenced by the portrait of Magdalena Douw and by the daily rhythm of the city she knew, there were sufficient creature comforts and pleasures to compensate for the privations.

Dr. Hamilton recorded that in Albany "The young men here call their sweethearts *luffees,* and a young fellow of eighteen is reckoned a simpleton if he has not a *luffee.*" [53] Magdalena Douw became the *luffee* of Harme Gansevoort in the 1730's.

Harme Gansevoort could trace his American roots to his grandfather Harme van Ganzvort, who settled at Catskill in 1660. His father, Leonard Gansevoort, born in Albany in 1681, married Catherine De Wandelaer, of a New York and Albany merchant family, in 1712. By occupation Leonard Gansevoort was primarily a brewer.[54] Harme, the first child of Leonard and Catherine Gansevoort, was born in 1712. With the exception of a brief political career, between 1750 and 1760, when he served as clerk of the County Court, clerk of the Court of Common Pleas, and clerk of Peace

and of the Sessions, Harme was quite inconspicuous in the life of his community. After he established himself as a merchant, he inherited the brewery of his father.[55] The Gansevoort house and brewery were located in Albany at the present junction of Broadway and Maiden Lane, and it was to this property that the young Harme and Magdalena moved after their marriage in 1740. Family genealogical notes reveal that their son Peter was born in this residence in 1749.[56] Colonel (later General) Peter Gansevoort distinguished himself as commander during the successful defense of Fort Stanwix against St. Leger in 1777.[57]

It is difficult to conceive of the charming girl with the red shoes aging, since she is the embodiment of all that is youthful, fresh, and innocent. She did, however, and the adult life of Magdalena Douw Gansevoort proved to be a period of comfortable serenity. She gave birth to nine children —four girls and five boys—and at least four of these children lived to maturity. Magdalena died in 1796, five years before the death of her husband.[58]

[53] Hamilton, *Itinerarium,* p. 90.
[54] Reynolds, *Genealogical and Family History,* I, 139–40.

[55] *Ibid.,* p. 140.
[56] *Ibid.,* p. 141.
[57] *Ibid.*
[58] *Ibid.,* p. 140.

Appendix

Family Alliances of Magdalena Douw Gansevoort

First Generation

Oloff Stevense van Cortlandt (*ca.* 1600–1683/84), came to America 1638, md. 1642 Annetje Loockermans (–1684)

Second Generation

Children of Oloff Stevense van Cortlandt and Annetje Loockermans

Stephanus van Cortlandt (1643–1700), md. 1671 Gertrude Schuyler (1654–1719)
Maria van Cortlandt (1645–1689), md. 1662 Jeremias van Rensselaer (1632–1674)
Catherine van Cortlandt (1652–1730), md. 1675 John Dervall and 1692 Frederick Philipse (1626–1702)
Johannes van Cortlandt
Sophia van Cortlandt
Cornelia van Cortlandt
Jacobus van Cortlandt

Third Generation

Children of Stephanus van Cortlandt and Gertrude Schuyler

Johannes van Cortlandt, md. Anna van Schaick
Margaret van Cortlandt, md. Samuel Bayard and Stephen Kemble
Anne van Cortlandt, md. Stephen De Lancey
Oliver van Cortlandt
Maria van Cortlandt, md. Kiliaen van Rensselaer and John Miller
Gertrude van Cortlandt
Philip van Cortlandt, md. Catherine De Peyster
Stephanus van Cortlandt, md. Catalina Staats
Gertrude van Cortlandt, md. Henry Beekman
Gysbert van Cortlandt
Elizabeth van Cortlandt, md. Rev. William Skinner
Catherine van Cortlandt, md. Andrew Johnston
Cornelia van Cortlandt, md. John Schuyler, Jr.

Children of Maria van Cortlandt and Jeremias van Rensselaer

Kiliaen van Rensselaer (1663–1719), md. 1701 Maria van Cortlandt (1680–)
Hendrick van Rensselaer (1667–1740), md. 1689 Catherine van Bruggen
Others

Fourth Generation
Children of Hendrick van Rensselaer and Catherine van Bruggen

Johannes van Rensselaer, md. 1734 Angelica Livingston
Anna van Rensselaer (–1756), md. 1717 Peter Jonas Douw (1692–1775)

Fifth Generation
Children of Anna van Rensselaer and Peter Jonas Douw

Magdalena Douw (1718–1796), md. 1740 Harme Gansevoort (1712–1801)
Volckert Petrus Douw (1720–1801)
Hendrick Douw (1722–1756)

Catrina Douw (1724–1811)
Maria Douw (1725–1759)
Margarita Douw (b. 1729)
Anna Douw (1732–)
Elizabeth Douw (1733–)
Rageltie Douw (1736–1806)

Sixth Generation
Children of Magdalena Douw and Harme Gansevoort

Sarah Gansevoort (1741–), md. John Ten Broeck
Peter Gansevoort (1742–1743)
Anna Gansevoort (1744–1794), md. Cornelius Wyncoop
Catherine Gansevoort (1747–1749)
Peter Gansevoort (1749–1812), md. Catherine van Schaick
Leonard Gansevoort (1751–1810), md. Hester Cuyler
Henry Gansevoort (1753–1755)
Hendrick Gansevoort (1757–)
Catrina Gansevoort (–1761)

The Cassin Medal

Edgar P. Richardson

WHEN Benvenuto Cellini designed medals and jewelry as well as monumental sculpture or Peter Paul Rubens (an ardent collector of coins and medals) wished to publish a book on antique cameos, there was no dividing line among men of taste between sculpture large and sculpture small. In modern times, the history of sculpture is usually written without including glyptic and medallic art, and it is thereby the poorer. In the early days of our Republic, the design of medals was a keen interest among men of high intelligence such as Franklin and Jefferson; it engaged the services of talented artists such as Joseph Wright and Thomas Sully and formed a significant element among the arts. It is gratifying that The Henry Francis du Pont Winterthur Museum—notable for showing the ensemble of the arts in which large and small, the grand and the intimate, all find their place—should acquire an outstanding piece of American medallic art. This object is the original gold medal (Fig. 1) awarded by resolution of Congress, October 20, 1814, to Lieutenant Stephen Cassin, who six weeks earlier had commanded a ship in Macdonough's squadron that won (according to the resolution) "the decisive and splendid victory gained on Lake Champlain, on the eleventh of September, in the year one thousand eight hundred and fourteen, over a British squadron of superior force." [1] Characteristically, this medal is interesting both as history and as art. It adds value to the Winterthur collection already so rich in the imagery of the War of 1812.

Stephen Cassin was born in Philadelphia on February 16, 1783. His father, John Cassin, a captain in the merchant service, was appointed lieutenant in the navy, November 13, 1799, and rose to the rank of commodore. In the War of 1812 Cassin senior commanded the naval forces in the Delaware for the protection of Philadelphia. The son, Stephen, entered the navy as a midshipman on February 21, 1800, in his seventeenth year. His first cruise in 1801 was under Commodore Stephen Decatur, father of the more famous son of the same name, on the frigate *Philadelphia*. After a cruise of nearly two years under the elder Decatur, the command of the *Philadelphia* was given to Captain Samuel Barron. Shortly thereafter, Midshipman Cassin was transferred to the schooner *Nautilus*, serving under Lieutenant Richard Somers; then, in April, 1804, he became its master. The following month, Commodore Edward Preble promoted him to lieutenant. He returned to America in November, 1805, at the end of the Tripolitan War, on the *John Adams*.

From that time until the War of 1812, there

[1] Thomas Wyatt, *Memoirs of the Generals, Commodores and other Commanders who distinguished themselves in the American Army and Navy during the Wars of the Revolution and 1812 and who were presented with medals by Congress for their gallant services* (Philadelphia: Carey & Hart, 1848), pp. 281–84, Plate 13, Fig. 37. See also James Ross Snowden, *A Description of the Medals of Washington; of National and Miscellaneous Medals; and of Other Objects of Interest in the Museum of the Mint* (Philadelphia: J. B. Lippincott & Co., 1861), p. 86, No. 43; Joseph F. Loubat, *The Medallic History of the United States of America, 1776–1876* (New York: The author, 1878); T. L. Comparette (ed.), *Catalogue of Coins, Tokens and Medals in the Numismatic Collection of the Mint of the United States at Philadelphia, Pa.* (Washington: Government Printing Office, 1912); and Georgia S. Chamberlain, *American Medals and Medallists* (Annandale, Va.: Turnpike Press, 1963). Loubat published the resolutions of Congress and Macdonough's reports on the action.

FIG. 1. Moritz Fürst, The Cassin Medal, obverse. Philadelphia, 1814. Gold; dia. 2½″, size 80. (Winterthur 64.145.)

was little opportunity for young officers in the United States Navy. Cassin took several furloughs to sail in the merchant service. On one of these merchant voyages to the Pacific, he is said to have been captured by the Spaniards and detained nearly two years; but this has not been verified.[2] His opportunity to see action in the War of 1812 came when he was ordered, in February, 1814, to the squadron being built for service on Lake Champlain under the command of Captain Thomas Macdonough.

The Lake Champlain–Hudson corridor between Canada and the United States, which had been a battleground in all previous wars on the continent, was of little importance in this war until 1814; the earlier fighting for control of the Great Lakes occurred farther west. Napoleon's abdication in April of that year enabled the British

to send forces to Canada to carry the war into the United States. By mid-August an army of some 10,000 veteran troops was encamped near Montreal, under the command of Sir George Prevost, ready to march south along the old route of Montcalm and Burgoyne. It was a strong, well-equipped veteran force, more formidable in every way than the American land forces facing it. Most of the American regular army was defending the Niagara frontier. General Alexander Macomb had only 1,500 regulars, supplemented by several thousand militia, to face Prevost. A good engineer, Macomb built a strong line of defenses along the south bank of the Saranac River, which empties into Lake Champlain at Plattsburg, and there his army had its best chance to make a stand; but the prospect on land was bleak. The issue was, however, decided by the fleets, which were hastily built to contest the control of the great waterway.

The naval battle of Lake Champlain was re-

[2] Wyatt, *Memoirs of Generals*, p. 282.

markable in many ways. The two fleets were rushed to completion in the spring and summer. The Americans got theirs into the water first, although the brig *Eagle,* their second largest vessel, was launched only thirty days before the battle. The largest British warship had been in the water only sixteen days when it went into action. It was a frigate mounting thirty-seven guns, being thus as heavily armed as the strongest vessels of the American Navy, the *Constitution* or the *United States.* Each squadron in the battle consisted of four large vessels supported by galleys, or gunboats, mounting one or two guns. The American squadron contained ten of these galleys, while the British fleet boasted twelve. Because of greater weight of armament, the British had every reason to expect to win control of the lake, and the name of their biggest vessel, the *Confiance,* seemed justified. But by skill, courage, and good fortune Macdonough won the victory (Fig. 2) .

It was impossible for the two fleets to cruise in the long, narrow lake. Macdonough brought his squadron north to Plattsburg Bay and anchored offshore from Macomb's position, a little south of the mouth of the Saranac. He arranged his four larger ships in line, about two miles offshore, with the *Eagle* at the north, under Captain Robert Henley; the *Saratoga,* Macdonough's flagship, next; the *Ticonderoga,* under Lieutenant Cassin, next; and the sloop *Preble,* fourth. The head of his formation was protected by the shore of the bay to the north, and its foot by a shoal to the south. Thus, his line could not be bypassed at either end; it would have to be broken. The galleys, propelled by sweeps, formed a second line inshore, supporting the larger ships.

The British squadron came down the lake protecting the march of Prevost's army. On the eleventh of September, Prevost's force was drawn up facing Macomb's defenses along the Saranac. Early that morning the British fleet appeared around Cumberland Head, which formed the northern extremity of Plattsburg Bay. Their four ships, with their galleys in support, swung into the bay and dropped anchor abreast of the American line. The battle, fought at anchor and at short range, was a contest of courage, endurance, and gunnery. The decisive moment came when the *Confiance* had silenced all the starboard guns of the American flagship *Saratoga* and killed a fifth of her crew. Captain Macdonough "wound ship"

(turned the *Saratoga* around while at anchor) and brought her port battery into action. The *Confiance* attempted unsuccessfully to perform the same manoeuvre, became disabled, and, two hours and a quarter after the beginning of the action, was forced to haul down her flag.

The rear of the American line was its weakest point. The little *Preble* was attacked so fiercely by the British galleys that she was forced out of the line and out of action. The galleys then concentrated on Cassin, but the *Ticonderoga,* says James Fenimore Cooper in his history of the navy,

was very nobly fought. Her spirited commander, Cassin, walked the taffrail, where he could watch the movements of the enemy's galleys, amidst showers of cannister and grape, directing discharges of bags of musket balls, and other light missiles that had the effect of keeping the British effectually at bay. Several times the English galleys, of which many were very gallantly fought, closed quite near, with an evident intent to board, but the great steadiness on board the *Ticonderoga* beat them back, and completely covered the rear of the line for the remainder of the day.[3]

The *Ticonderoga's* fire was so rapid that once or twice the nearest vessels thought her in flame.

The victory of the American squadron was complete. All four large vessels forming the British line of battle were disabled and surrendered. Only their galleys escaped up the lake, the American galleys being so shattered that Macdonough had to order the men to the pumps instead of in pursuit. "I could only look at the enemy's galleys going off in a shattered condition, for there was not a mast in either squadron that could stand to make sail on," he said in his report to the Secretary of the Navy dated September 13, 1814.[4]

While the naval battle was in progress, the British land forces were testing out the American defenses along the Saranac; but Sir George Prevost was so discouraged by the loss of his fleet that he made no further effort and withdrew to Canada. The American army on the Niagara frontier, meanwhile, had retrieved itself by the hard fights at Chippawa and Lundy's Lane in July, ending

[3] James Fenimore Cooper, *History of the Navy of the United States of America* (Philadelphia: Lea & Blanchard, 1839) , II, 435.
[4] *American State Papers: Naval Affairs, 1794–1823* (Washington: Gates and Seaton, 1834) , I, 310. Also quoted in Loubat, *Medallic History,* pp. 191–92.

the threat of invasion in the west. The war on the Canadian frontier came to a successful end.

Congress voted a series of gold medals to the military officers who brought the war to a gallant close. Among the officers receiving the gold medals were the commanders of the three vessels that survived in the battle line at Plattsburg: Macdonough of the *Saratoga,* Henley of the *Eagle,* and Cassin. Each of the other commissioned officers of the navy and army serving on board (infantry were serving as marines) received a silver medal; a sword was given to each of the midshipmen and sailing masters; and three months' extra pay went to all other ranks.

Thomas Sully provided the likenesses for most of these medals, making small drawings which, in some instances, he enlarged to profiles in monochrome, painted in oil. The portrait heads of Stephen Decatur, Jacob Jones, and Charles Stewart,

painted for these medals, are now in the United States Naval Academy at Annapolis. Curiously enough, Sully did not do the likenesses of two Philadelphians—Captain James Biddle, who was awarded a medal for the capture by the U.S.S. *Hornet* of the British ship *Penguin* off the island of Tristan da Cunha, and Cassin. The source of these two likenesses is unknown.

The medals were the work of the engraver and diesinker, Moritz Fürst, who was born about 1782 at Boesing, a small town near Pressburg, Hungary (now Pesinok, near Bratislava, in Czechoslovakia), and had been trained at the Austrian imperial mints in Vienna and Milan. He came to America in 1807 with letters from Thomas Appleton, consul for the United States at Leghorn, to President Jefferson. Appleton, according to Fürst's claim, had engaged him at a salary of $2,000 a year as engraver and diesinker at the United States

FIG. 2. Benjamin Tanner, *MacDonough's Victory on Lake Champlain.* Philadelphia, 1816. Engraving after painting by H. Reinagle; H. 19¹⁄₁₆″, W. 25⅝″. (Winterthur 60.115a.)

Mint in Philadelphia. Fürst arrived in this country, where, he supposed, "the gold grows on trees," [5] to find that, while Appleton was talking to him in Leghorn, the new director of the mint, Robert Patterson, had engaged a Bavarian named John Reich as assistant engraver and diesinker at $600 a year. Fürst received neither the position of engraver nor the salary (nor, it may be added, did Reich); but he set up in business in Philadelphia as a seal engraver, diesinker, and steel engraver. Employed by the mint as a free-lance engraver, he did a beautiful series of Indian peace medals, as well as the medals awarded by Congress to eleven

army and twelve naval officers in the War of 1812 and three given by the state of Pennsylvania.

The medal awarded Lieutenant Stephen Cassin is a good example of Fürst's skill. The obverse presents a bust of Lieutenant Cassin, in uniform, facing right, with the inscription: "STEP. CASSIN TICONDEROGA PRAEFECT. QUAE REGIO IN TERRIS NOS. NON PLENA LAB. [6] [*Stephanus Cassin,* Ticonderoga *praefectus. Quae regio in terris nostri non plena laboris:* Stephen Cassin, commander of the *Ticonderoga*. What region of the earth is not full of our toils.] FURST.F[*ecit*]." (Fig. 1). The reverse shows

---

[5] Most of our information about Fürst's career comes from a printed pamphlet, apparently prepared as evidence to be submitted to the Court of Claims when Fürst, for the last time, tried to get the position that he said had been promised him by Appleton. It was reprinted in the *American Journal of Numismatics,* XLIII, No. 2 (1908–1909), 45–50. Fürst's remark about gold growing on the trees appears on p. 49.

[6] This is a graceful adaptation of one of the famous passages in Virgil's *Aeneid,* Book I, lines 459–60, "*Quis iam locus, inquit, Achate, quae regio in terris nostri non plena laboris? En Priamus. Sunt hic etiam sua praemia laudi; sunt lacrimae rerum et mentem mortalia tangunt.*" Aeneas, however, was speaking more of the troubles of the Trojan refugees rather than their deeds of valor. "What spot is there now, Achates, what region of earth is not full of our toils?"

Fig. 3. Fürst, The Cassin Medal, reverse of Figure 1. (Winterthur 64.145.)

naval action on Lake Champlain between the United States fleet, carrying eighty-six guns, under the command of Captain Macdonough, and the British fleet, with ninety-five guns, commanded by Commodore Downie (Fig. 3). To the right, the town of Plattsburg is in flames. The inscription reads: "UNO LATERE PERCUSSO. ALTE-RUM IMPAVIDE VERTIT [Struck hard on one side, he fearlessly turns the other]." The exergue has: "INTER CLASS. AMERI. ET BRIT. DIE XI SEPT. MDCCCXIIII [*inter classim Americanam et Britannicam, die XI Septembris, MDCCCXIIII:* Between the American and British fleets, September 11, 1814]." On the platform is "FÜRST.F[*ecit*]."

The process by which medals were produced at the United States Mint, before the introduction of the reducing pantograph in 1836 revolutionized it, began with the now-forgotten art of the engraver or diesinker, who cut the design into a steel die blank. As in the engraving of semiprecious stones, the engraving of a medal might be either cut into the metal (which would be called "intaglio" in a jewel) or carved in relief (called "cameo" in a jewel). The engraver either carved his design in relief on a steel blank, using this relief to make a matrix from which the impressions of the medal were struck, or, more commonly, he carved his design in intaglio in the steel die and used this as the matrix to strike the impression.[7]

American technology was in its infancy when Fürst arrived in Philadelphia. The mint itself was only fifteen years old and was still struggling to master its problems. According to Don Taxay's admirable history of the United States Mint,[8] the process adopted in Philadelphia was as follows: The diesinker cut first, in a blank of fairly soft steel, a master die that contained only the device or central part of the design. The original die was then hardened and used to raise a hub (a duplicate of itself in relief); it was never used to strike the coin or medal. Fixed in a large screw press, the original die was brought down with great force on the blank hub. The blank had to be struck a number of times, with several annealings, to raise a perfect impression. The hub was next hand-finished by the diesinker to add the details more

easily executed in relief. It was then hardened and used to sink a number of intaglio working dies. At this stage the lesser parts of the design—wreaths, stars, letters, numerals—were added, either by individual punches or by the graver. This explains why an ornamental detail on an 1812 medal may re-appear thirty-five years later on another medal supporting an entirely different device. Taxay suggests that the reason for the adoption of such a cumbrous method, instead of sinking a complete master die at the beginning, was the difficulty encountered by the new mint in obtaining good steel and a desire to preserve the life of its master dies.

There is a description of the use of the screw press (Fig. 4), operated by hand, in the first United States Mint, at Seventh and Filbert Streets in Philadelphia, which is worth quoting. It is from the reminiscences of George Escol Sellers (grandson of Charles Willson Peale and thus a member of the clan that contributed so much artistic skill and mechanical ingenuity to the tradition of Philadelphia), who grew up in a house next door to the mint:

In the rear room, facing on the alley, with a large low-down window opening into it, a fly press stood, that is a screw-coining press mostly used for coining the old copper cents. Through this window the passerby in going up and down the alley could readily see the bare-armed vigorous men swinging the heavy end-weighted balanced lever that drove the screw with sufficient force so that by the momentum of the weighted ends this quick-threaded screw had the power to impress the blank and thus coin each piece. They could see the rebound or recoil of those end-weights as they struck a heavy wooden spring beam, driving the lever back to the man that worked it; they could hear the clanking of the chain that checked it at the right point to prevent its striking the man, all framing a picture very likely to leave a lasting impression, and there are no doubt still living many in Philadelphia who can recollect from this brief notice the first mint.[9]

The mint continued to derive its power entirely from the muscles of men and horses until a steam engine was purchased from Oliver Evans in 1816 to drive the machines for rolling and drawing the strips of metal. But a screw press operated by hand was used to strike the dies as late as 1860; and the mint director's report for 1893 mentions

---

[7] Charles Blanc, *Grammaire des arts du dessin* (Paris: Renouard, 1886), p. 471.

[8] Don Taxay, *The U.S. Mint and Coinage, An Illustrated History from 1776 to the Present* (New York: Arco Publishing Co., 1966).

[9] George Escol Sellers, "Early Engineering Reminiscences," *American Machinist*, XVI (May 4, 1893), 12–13; also quoted in Taxay, *U.S. Mint*, p. 96.

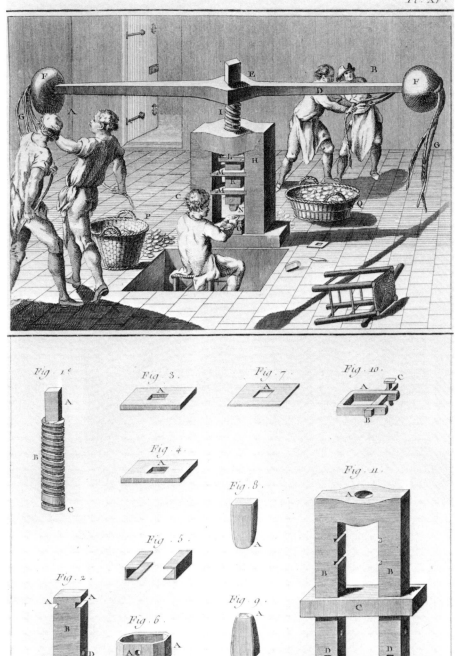

Monnoyage, Balancier.

FIG. 4. Hand-operated screw press, of a more primitive type than that described by Sellers. Engraving from D. Diderot, *L'Encyclopédie; ou, Dictionnaire raisonné des sciences, des arts et des métiers: Recueil de planches, sur les sciences et les arts,* VIII (Paris: Briasson, 1771), *Monnayage,* Plate XV; H. 15″, W. 8⅞″. (Photo, Winterthur.)

the purchase of a hydraulic press to replace the large screw press used until then to strike medals.[10]

Medals, both original and plaster casts, were collected throughout the western world in the eighteenth century. Du Simitière mentioned in his notes several collectors of medals in Colonial America before the Revolution.[11] In the early Republic, medals were of lively interest as portrait likenesses and works of art; they also appealed to the intense feeling for history characteristic of the age. They were used even as decoration of rooms. The Rev. Manasseh Cutler, visiting the home of Sir John Temple, British consul-general in New York City in 1787, remarked on the spacious and richly furnished formal rooms of the second story. "The paintings are principally historical, and executed by the greatest masters of Europe. The Parlor is ornamented chiefly with medals and small busts of the principal characters now living in Europe, made in plaster of Paris or white wax."[12] When Cutler later called upon Benjamin Franklin in Philadelphia, he found the mantel in Franklin's house a mass of portrait medals. The collections at Winterthur evidence the extraordinary popularity of the medal-sized portrait likeness in the taste of the early Republic. Patriotic portraits appear at Winterthur in countless and unexpected places, upon doorknobs and curtain holders, teacups and pitchers, clocks and stoves.

The diesinker's art, now forgotten, was central to this taste. William Dunlap speaks of it as "in many respects so distinct from the other arts of

design that I hoped to give a sketch of its history, and an account of the process by which such beautiful works are produced," and records his disappointment at being unable to do so.[13] It was a skill closely allied to that of the engraver, as shown by the fact that William Kneass, diesinker at the mint from 1824 until 1840, and his successors, Christian Gobrecht, mint engraver from 1840 to 1844, and James Barton Longacre, 1844–1869, were all book engravers before taking positions at the mint. The diesinker's and engraver's tools, and the skill, patience, and control needed for both crafts, must have been the same. The diesinker's work was not only highly skilled but time-consuming and costly. It was abandoned in the 1840's for a simpler process by which the medal was first modeled in clay or wax, then cast in plaster; a casting in fine iron was then made from the plaster; and from this casting, or a reduced facsimile, a die was produced by means of a portrait lathe. Each step in this process, except the original modeling in clay or wax, was done by machine; thus, the diesinker's art was eliminated.

Moritz Fürst was an outstanding figure in this field in the United States for nearly thirty years, but he was never given a regular post at the mint. Reich retired as assistant engraver in 1817 and was not replaced until 1824, when the position of engraver was given to William Kneass, an engraver of plates for books and banknotes. Fürst at this time laid claim to the position of engraver and diesinker for which he said he had been brought to America in 1807. The Court of Claims decided there was no evidence that Appleton had been authorized to hire him, and the claim was denied.[14] Sometime before November, 1841, he returned to Europe, where he died. William Dunlap wrote of him in 1834, "I fear his emoluments from his profession have not been equal to his skill or his deserts."[15]

[10] Taxay, *U.S. Mint*, p. 152, n. 4.

[11] The Hon. John Smith of Burlington, N.J., had a collection of silver coins and medals, acquired from du Simitière, that eventually was sold through Joseph Richardson, a goldsmith, to William Logan (Society Misc., du Simitière, 1771, Historical Society of Pennsylvania; hereafter HSP). In 1778 Col. John Montresor gave du Simitière his collection of bronze medals by the seventeenth-century medalist Jean Dassier, of Geneva (John William Potts, in *Pennsylvania Magazine of History and Biography*, XIII, No. 3 [1889], 341–63). A collection of coins in the possession of Major James, in New York, is described by du Simitière in a letter to John Smith, Aug. 6, 1767 (Etting Papers, Artists, p. 21, HSP). Du Simitière himself was continually collecting: "Coins and medals I have a collection of; but nowadays these are become scarce, notwithstanding I meet with some now and then" (Stauffer Collection, XXX, 2340, HSP). He apparently was also a *marchand amateur*, for in the "du Simitière Scraps" (no call number, du Simitière Papers, HSP), there are several lists of Roman coins, ancient and modern gold medals, and other coins that belonged to him at various times.

[12] William Parker Cutler and Julia Perkins Cutler, *Life, Journals and Correspondence of Rev. Manasseh Cutler, LL.D. by His Grandchildren* (Cincinnati: R. Clarke & Co., 1888), I, 235.

[13] William Dunlap, *The History of the Rise and Progress of the Arts of Design in the United States* (New York: G. P. Scott and Co., 1834), II, 220.

[14] *American Journal of Numismatics*, XLIII, No. 2 (1908–1909), 45–50. A letter in the records of the American Consulate at Leghorn (Record Group 84) was discovered and brought to my attention by Mark G. Eckhoff, assistant director of the Diplomatic, Legal and Fiscal, Records Division of the National Archives and Records Service. It is a letter, dated June 10, 1807, from Appleton to President Jefferson, which confirms that the consul encouraged Fürst and another engraver to emigrate to America and recommended them to Jefferson, but without making reference to any position or salary in the mint.

[15] Dunlap, *History of Arts of Design*, II, 221.

The Doolittle Engravings
of the Battle of Lexington and Concord

Ian M. G. Quimby

THE four engravings by Amos Doolittle (1754–1832) of the Battle of Lexington and Concord are among the rarest American historical prints. Complete sets are in The Connecticut Historical Society and The New York Public Library, and at least one complete set exists in the private collection of Mr. and Mrs. J. William Middendorf, II. Partial sets may be found in other institutions, including three plates at the New Haven Colony Historical Society, and two at The Henry Francis du Pont Winterthur Museum. Charles E. Goodspeed, Boston antiquarian bookseller, considered it (speaking of the set as one print) one of the five most important engravings of early American events. During his entire career he handled only a few individual plates and but one complete set.[1]

Strictly speaking, the first engraved views of the battle were published in London, before Doolittle offered his series of prints in December, 1775. The first print was a cartoon issued by the Whig press to taunt Lord North's government. It is entitled *The Retreat From Concord to Lexington of the Army of Wild Irish Asses Defeated by the Brave American Militia* (Fig. 1). Published June 19, 1775, two months to the day after the battle, it is crudely drawn and full of misinformation. Three houses, not four, were burned by the British; and one of them belonged to Deacon Loring, not two houses belonging to "Mr. Deacon" and "Mr. Loeings." Of course, the purpose was to influence public opinion, not to provide a factual visual account, and in this sense it is very effective. Much more useful for the purpose of this study is

A Plan of the Town and Harbour of Boston and the Country adjacent with the Road from Boston to Concord (Fig. 2). It was published July 29, only forty-two days after the Battle of Bunker Hill, which it mentions. In addition, it shows the encampments of the American troops that besieged Boston. As a contemporary map of the area, it will prove useful in the detailed discussion to follow.

We are fortunate to have Doolittle's honest presentation of one of the most significant events in American history, for in their crude simplicity we have documents of inestimable value to the historian. Crude as they are, Doolittle's prints of the battle are the best pictorial record—indeed, the only pictorial record by a contemporary American—of the events of April 19, 1775. They are the only representations of the battle with a genuine claim to authenticity. The historians who have gone over all the verbal evidence of the battle concur that, except for relatively minor details, Doolittle's engravings provide us with an accurate and detailed visual account. Unaware of prevailing canons of art, Doolittle gave us a realistic version of the events totally outside the heroic tradition that dominated historical painting at the time. John Trumbull's paintings of various battles of the Revolution are examples of accepted academic treatment of similar events. They convey an idea of heroism as exemplified by the posture and gestures of a few individuals—all rendered in theatrical terms. Such a treatment of historical events contributes more to the mythology of nationalism than to an understanding of what actually happened. The battle of Lexington and Concord was given the "heroic" treatment over the years.

[1] Charles E. Goodspeed, *Yankee Bookseller* (Boston: Houghton Mifflin Co., 1937), p. 111.

The plates are a series numbered from one to four and entitled: *The Battle of Lexington, April 19th 1775, A View of the Town of Concord, The Engagement at the North Bridge in Concord,* and *A View of the South Part of Lexington.* Important buildings, individuals, or groups of people are keyed to a legend that explains what is happening. Doolittle made absolutely sure that the viewer of the prints would have the essential facts to support the visual narrative. It is indeed a very literal rendition, and one must conclude that Doolittle intended the prints to be informative in the same sense that a photograph in a modern newspaper is informative. Nevertheless, the prints by themselves are not a self-contained explanation of the entire series of events. They presuppose a general knowledge, not only of the ill-fated British expedition to Concord, but of prior tensions and incidents and of subsequent battles and preparation for battles up to the time of their publication in December, 1775. Americans had not yet severed their legal ties with Great Britain, but there was widespread realization that in Lexington and Concord a Rubicon had been crossed. We take it

for granted today, but it was a momentous fact in 1775. Amos Doolittle realized this and shared it with the citizens of New Haven.

PART I

To fit the Doolittle prints into the context of events, it is necessary to review briefly the state of affairs on the eighteenth of April, the curious and almost comic movements by both sides that night, and, of course, the climactic events of the following day. A great deal of ink has been spilled on this subject, and much of the literature is appallingly repetitious. Nineteenth-century American writers found it difficult to be objective, with the result that most of their accounts of the battle are one-sided. Three twentieth-century historians, Harold Murdock, Allen French, and Arthur B. Tourtellot, have examined the subject with refreshing candor, and it is difficult to see how any more can be said unless new information is discovered.[2] The following summary is dependent largely on the work of these three authors.

[2] Harold Murdock, *The Nineteenth of April, 1775* (Boston: Houghton Mifflin Co., 1923); Allen French, *The Day*

FIG. 1. *The Retreat From Concord to Lexington of the Army of Wild Irish Asses Defeated by the Brave American Militia.* London, June 19, 1775. Engraving; H. 6%₂″, W. 11⅛″. (The John Carter Brown Library, Brown University.)

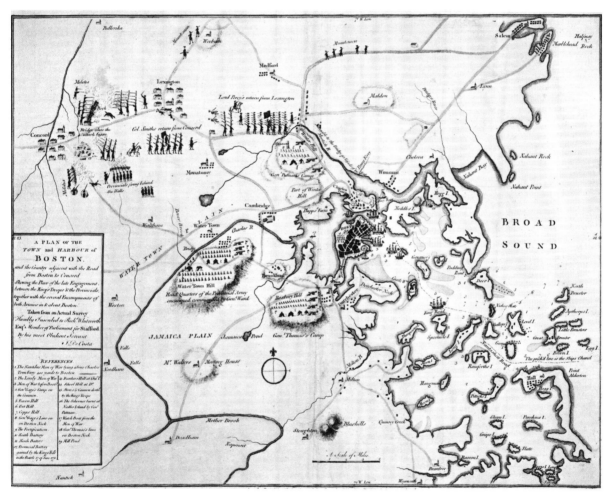

FIG. 2. J. De Costa, *A Plan of the Town and Harbour of Boston*. London, July 29, 1775. Engraving; H. 14³⁄₁₆″, W. 19″. (The John Carter Brown Library, Brown University.)

The state of affairs in Massachusetts in the spring of 1775 was serious, if not critical. The Coercive Acts of the preceding year had repealed the charter, closed the port of Boston, and installed General Gage as governor. By the Restraining Acts of early 1775, Massachusetts Bay was declared to be in a state of rebellion, and the ministry encouraged Gage to use force to restore Crown control over the recalcitrant province. When the Assembly was dissolved by Gage, it reconvened as the Provincial Congress and met in Concord intermittently from October to March. By April, 1775, Massachusetts was governed by the Provincial Congress and the local Committees of Public Safety. Gage, legally the chief executive for the entire province, was in fact only the military governor of the town of Boston. He was a reluctant oppressor and exercised the utmost restraint to prevent incidents, the consequences of which he could readily imagine. The memory of the Boston Massacre, and the way it had been used by patriot propagandists, was all too vividly present. Nevertheless, the pressures on Gage were mounting. The ministry in London had a low opinion of the military capability of the provincials and thought that a show of British military muscle would put things right. The Boston Tories criticized Gage for temporizing, and his own troops deeply resented the restraints he imposed on them while tolerating the most outrageous taunts and insults from the populace. On April 14, Gage received a letter from the Secretary of State, Lord Dartmouth, that was strongly critical of his handling of the situation. Dartmouth demanded action, specifically the arrest of John Hancock and Samuel Adams and the destruction of provincial military stores. Gage had long been contemplating the latter course—full information on the nature and exact location of the military stores in Concord was available to him through an informer—but even this sharp rebuke from his superior did not convince him of the wisdom of making martyrs of Hancock and Adams.

Saturday night, April 15, military preparations began with the launching of small boats from the transports and an order relieving the light infantry and grenadiers from regular duty. Paul Revere and Dr. Joseph Warren quickly got wind of these preparations and correctly guessed Gage's intention. In addition, they supposed that Hancock and Adams, residing for the moment with the Rev. Jonas Clarke in Lexington, were to be arrested and returned to Boston. Accordingly, the next day, Sunday, April 16, two days prior to his celebrated ride, Revere made a less heralded journey to Lexington to inform the two leaders of the suspicious activities among the British garrison. Hancock sent a messenger to Concord instructing the townsmen either to hide or disperse the military stores, and the word went out to all the surrounding towns to be prepared for a possible encounter with His Majesty's forces. The only thing the provincials did not know was when the British would make their move.

To succeed, the expedition had to be launched in secrecy and carried out with dispatch, so that the provincial forces would have no time to organize resistance. As it happened, the plans were public knowledge by the afternoon of the eighteenth, some eight hours before Lieutenant Colonel Smith, the commander of the expedition, knew what his destination was to be. Revere and William Dawes merely waited for the troop movement to begin before setting off to alarm the countryside. There were two possible routes to Concord: one crossing the Charles River ("by sea") to Charlestown, and the other going over Boston Neck ("by land") to Roxbury and Brookline and using the bridge across the Charles at Cambridge (Fig. 2). The sea route to Concord was sixteen miles and the land route about twenty-one miles. Advance knowledge of which route the British forces were taking not only would be useful to the towns along the way, but would enable the people in Lexington to know when they might expect the British to appear. To be certain that this information would get to its destination, Revere devised his famous set of signals. The two lanterns in the North Church tower were seen in Charlestown, from whence a messenger was sent on his way to Lexington. Then Revere went by the sea route and Dawes took the land route.

General Gage had anticipated just such an attempt by the patriots to send one or more messengers. That afternoon he had posted nine mounted officers on the road between Charlestown and Lexington. Their job was to intercept any

---

of Concord and Lexington (Boston: Little, Brown & Co., 1925); and Arthur B. Tourtellot, *William Diamond's Drum* (New York: Doubleday & Co., 1959). The Tourtellot work was reissued in paperback as *Lexington and Concord* (New York: W. W. Norton & Co., 1963).

suspicious rider to prevent news of the expedition from getting through. The subsequent interceptions, captures, and releases make a story that is almost unbelievably farcical. Revere and Dawes both got to Lexington, but Revere was captured by British officers on his way to Concord. Unaccountably, he was released, as were three Lexington minutemen, after being told by the officers that several regiments of regulars were on their way. Throughout the night the roads of Middlesex County were alive with riders dashing to and fro, either carrying information or in search of it. In short, whatever hopes the British had entertained for surprising the provincials were completely dashed.

Meanwhile, the expedition got off to a bad start because of a series of delays. The rendezvous on the banks of the Charles was scheduled for ten o'clock, but several officers and units were late, including Colonel Smith. It took four more hours to get the troops and supplies moved across the river and ready to march. By two o'clock in the morning the expedition had advanced only one-quarter mile from its starting point. After all the standing and waiting, the seven hundred soldiers could look forward to thirty-two miles of marching (to Concord and back), which, even without a battle, is a fairly arduous day's work.

On the march to Lexington, reports came to Colonel Smith in rapid succession that the countryside was alarmed and that from five hundred to a thousand minutemen were waiting for him in Lexington. He decided that the situation was deteriorating and sent a messenger back to Boston asking General Gage for reinforcements. As it turned out, this was a fortunate decision, even though the reports that prompted it were gross exaggerations. When at sunrise the advance guard of five companies of light infantry, under the command of Major John Pitcairn of the Royal Marines (and second in command of the expedition), marched up to Lexington Common, there were only about forty minutemen lined up to face them, with a group of unarmed fellow townsmen standing around. Apparently, Captain Parker, commanding the Lexington minutemen, did not expect his forty farmers to stand against seven hundred regulars. As the British troops moved across the common toward his two thin ranks, he gave the order to disperse and not to fire. Almost at the same time, Major Pitcairn ordered his sol-

diers not to fire but to surround and disarm the rebels. This could have been the end of it, and Lexington might never have gained a niche in history.

It was not an end but a beginning. Just who fired the first shot has been the subject of debate ever since. At this crucial moment, the light infantry rushed on the Americans, shooting at random and disregarding completely the commands of their officers. A few minutemen returned the fire—so few, in fact, that whether or not any did was disputed in later years. Colonel Smith, arriving late on the scene, recovered control of his troops by having the drummer beat to arms. Eight Americans were killed and nine wounded. One British soldier was nicked in the leg. It was more a massacre than a battle.

The first print in Doolittle's series depicts the scene just described (Figs. 3 and 4). The only major discrepancy appears to be the well-ordered ranks of the soldiers, for accounts of the affair by men on both sides tell how disorderly the troops became. The structures on the left are Buckman Tavern and its outbuildings, actually situated across the road from the common. The meeting house is in the center and the belfry is on the right; both structures were on the common. The long shadows suggest the early morning sun, an added detail that lends credibility to the visual account. A mistake in the caption identifies the soldiers engaged in battle as "the Regular Grenadiers." Actually, the grenadiers are somewhere in the background, and the light infantry is in the foreground. The Lexington militia is also in the foreground, in the act of dispersing. It should be noted that not a single minuteman is firing at the British. Doolittle saw no need to embroider the account by showing the outnumbered Americans making a glorious stand; it served better to depict a vastly superior military force slaughtering American farmers on their home ground. The propaganda value of the engagement was not lost on the canny Sam Adams, who said, when he heard the first shots, "Oh, what a glorious morning is this." [3]

Colonel Smith assembled his small army on Lexington Common. The only Americans in sight were the dead and wounded. The dramatic events of the past few moments should have convinced

---

[3] Tourtellot, *Lexington and Concord*, p. 139.

FIG. 3. Amos Doolittle, *The Battle of Lexington, April 19th 1775*. New Haven, Conn., 1775. Colored engraving; H. 13¾″, W. 19″. (Winterthur 65.23.)

FIG. 4. Sidney L. Smith, *The Battle of Lexington, April 19th 1775*. Re-engraved, after original by Amos Doolittle, for Charles E. Goodspeed, Boston, 1903. Colored engraving; H. 15″, W. 18¾″. (Boston Athenaeum: photo, George M. Cushing.)

him of the foolhardiness of pursuing his original mission. Perhaps the ease with which his troops had dispatched the Lexington minutemen lulled him into a false sense of security. Maybe it was simply a case of the military mind following orders without exercising the commander's prerogative of adapting to a new situation. Whatever the reasons, Colonel Smith regrouped his forces, lectured the men for disobeying orders, allowed them the three traditional victory cheers, and marched them toward Concord—deeper into what was now hostile territory.

Doctor Samuel Prescott, a Concord physician, was courting Lydia Mulliken in Lexington on the night of April 18 when he found himself pressed into service as a courier to carry the news of approaching British troops to his fellow townsmen. On the way, he was joined by Revere and Dawes, and all three were captured by the British officers sent out to intercept such couriers. Prescott escaped almost immediately by making a run for it across familiar fields and arrived in Concord with the news by one o'clock. Revere and Dawes never reached Concord. Shortly after dawn, a report of firing on Lexington Common was received. About 250 minutemen, consisting of two companies from Concord and one from nearby Lincoln, assembled in response to the news. In the words of Amos Barrett, "We thought we would go and meet the British."[4] Just what they hoped to accomplish by this display of aggressiveness is not certain.

About a mile and a half down the Lexington road, the British forces came into sight. The minutemen stopped and waited while the regulars closed the gap between them. It must have been a tense moment. When the British were about a hundred rods away and still coming, the Americans did an about-face and began marching back to Concord. Fifes and drums in both armies lent an almost festive atmosphere to the occasion, and, to quote Amos Barrett again, "We had grand music."[5] The militia marched back through Concord and retired across the North Bridge to a ridge from which they could observe the British. The regulars marched into Concord center at about nine o'clock that morning, having reached their objective eleven hours after starting.

Colonel Smith and Major Pitcairn climbed the ridge overlooking Concord center. Standing

among the gravestones of the ancestors of the men who had escorted them into town, the two officers oriented themselves on the map of Concord furnished by Gage and observed the movement of the minutemen. It is this moment which Doolittle shows in Plate II of his series (Figs. 5 and 6). On the left is the three-story Concord meeting house used for meetings of the Provincial Congress; in the center, Wright's Tavern where, later that morning, Smith, Pitcairn, and other officers would refresh themselves; and on the far right the small, steepled courthouse. Doolittle telescoped time somewhat in this print by showing a detachment of troops throwing military stores into the millpond and at the same time showing the troops entering Concord. It is a rare and fascinating view of an eighteenth-century New England town. Henry David Thoreau found it so in the 1850's, as will be shown later.

One company of light infantry was sent to guard the South Bridge, and seven were sent to guard the North Bridge. The grenadiers stayed in town to conduct the search for military stores. Gage's instructions were quite specific:

You will seize and destroy all the artillery, ammunition provisions, tents, small arms and all military stores whatever. But you will take care that the soldiers do not plunder the inhabitants or hurt private property.

You have a draught of Concord, on which is marked the houses, barns, etc., which contain the above military stores. You will order a trunnion to be knocked off each gun, but if it is found impracticable on any, they must be spiked, and the carriages destroyed. The powder and flower must be shook out of the barrels into the river, the tents burnt, pork or beef destroyed in the best way you can devise. And the men may put balls or lead in their pockets, throwing them by degrees into ponds, ditches, etc., but no quantity together so that they may be recovered afterwards.

If you meet with any brass artillery, you will order their muzzles to be beat in, so as to render them useless.[6]

Apparently the grenadiers who carried out the search had been thoroughly briefed, for they were careful not to injure persons or property. Indeed, they were so circumspect they were fooled in several instances into bypassing rooms containing supplies for the provincial army. Food and drink were dutifully paid for, and altogether this

---

[4] *Ibid.,* p. 152.
[5] *Ibid.*

[6] *Ibid.,* p. 103.

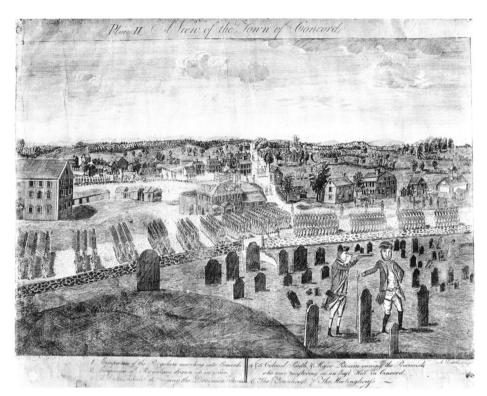

FIG. 5. Doolittle, *A View of the Town of Concord.* New Haven, Conn., 1775. Colored engraving; H. 11⅝″, W. 17⁹⁄₁₆″. (The New York Public Library, Prints Division, I. N. Phelps Stokes Collection.)

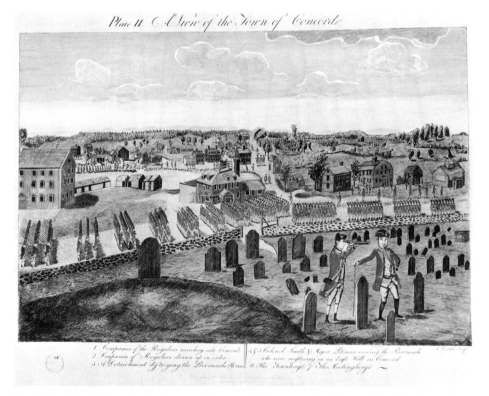

FIG. 6. Smith, *A View of the Town of Concord.* Re-engraved, after original by Amos Doolittle, for Charles E. Goodspeed, Boston, 1903. Colored engraving; H. 15″, W. 18¾″. (Boston Athenaeum: photo, George M. Cushing.)

phase of the mission went off rather well. If not very efficient, it was at least peaceful.

When violence finally erupted it was the result of a miscalculation. The grenadiers ended their activities by burning some gun carriages and wooden tools. Smoke from the fires was seen by the minutemen, whose ranks had now swelled to about four hundred by new arrivals from neighboring towns. They mistakenly concluded that the British were burning the town and felt they had no choice but to save their homes and families. First, they had to cross the North Bridge, which was guarded by a single company of light infantry consisting of about thirty-five men. When the provincial forces moved toward the bridge, Captain Laurie, the senior British officer, found himself in a desperate situation. Of the seven companies assigned to the North Bridge, four had been sent to destroy provincial supplies at Colonel Barrett's farm, some two miles beyond the bridge. Two of the remaining three companies had been deployed on some low hills about a quarter mile beyond the bridge. The bridge had to be held until all these troops returned. As the minutemen advanced, the two companies of light infantry retreated to the bridge. All three companies moved hastily across the bridge and began forming on the east bank of the river, but it was too late. Four hundred Americans were almost upon the British detachment of about one hundred soldiers. It was Lexington Common with the shoe on the other foot. Someone fired. Again it is not certain who, but probably one of the British soldiers. After a brief exchange, the detachment fled back to Concord to rejoin the grenadiers. There were dead and wounded on both sides.

Doolittle's representation of this scene is Plate III, entitled *The Engagement at the North Bridge in Concord* (Figs. 7 and 8). The view is from the Old Manse looking north. The minutemen are on the far side of the Concord River firing at the British troops on the town side. The latter are shown retreating toward the town, with one rank acting as a rear guard by firing at the Americans. As in the previous print, a simultaneity of events is depicted, a form of artistic license in order to tell the story. The prominent house in the background belonged to Major John Buttrick, second in command of the Concord militia.

After the smoke of battle had cleared, intelligence was received that indicated the British were not burning the town after all. The American force dispersed for the moment, but all the while a watchful eye was kept on the British in Concord. American strength was increasing by the hour as minutemen continued to arrive on the scene. Colonel Smith waited for the reinforcements requested earlier in the day, but they did not arrive. After biding his time for about two hours after the engagement at the bridge, Smith gave the order to march back to Boston. Miraculously, the four companies sent to Colonel Barrett's farm returned without incident, the provincials having deserted the bridge.

For a while all went well. Anticipating trouble, Smith spread out his light infantry in the fields on both sides of the road to protect his flanks. Given the situation, it was a sound tactic. About a mile out of Concord, however, at a crossroads known as Merriam's Corner, the terrain required the flanking troops to pull onto the road to cross a bridge over a small stream. The provincial militia lay in wait behind stone walls, barns, trees, and rocks. They opened fire, and thus began the last and most costly phase of the day's operations.

Conventional military tactics called for massed squads and volley firing, an effective technique when enemy forces are similarly massed, but fatal when applied against scattered snipers who are careful to keep themselves hidden. The Americans enjoyed another advantage. An almost continuous supply of fresh minutemen kept arriving on the scene, while the British troops were near exhaustion after having been on the move for over fourteen hours. For the regulars, it was a matter of running a gantlet of constant musket fire, an ambush not concentrated but continuous. This one-sided war of attrition went on for about two hours. As the bedraggled column neared Lexington, discipline gave way to panic and the retreat became a rout. Colonel Smith's expedition was in danger of annihilation.

But this was not to be. As Smith's exhausted and harassed soldiers passed Lexington Common, the scene of the first bloodshed of the day, they were greeted by the sound of artillery, which they recognized as their own. The long-awaited reinforcements had arrived in the form of the First Brigade, commanded by the Right Honorable Hugh, Earl Percy, consisting of three regiments of foot, a battalion of marines, and a detachment of artillery. The rescuing force was about twice the

FIG. 7. Doolittle, *The Engagement at the North Bridge in Concord.* New Haven, Conn., 1775. Colored engraving; H. 13½″, W. 18½″. (Winterthur 65.24.)

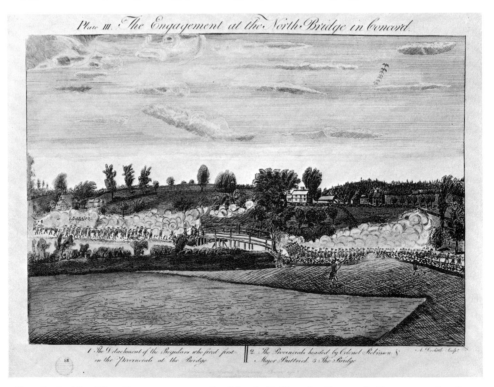

FIG. 8. Smith, *The Engagement at the North Bridge in Concord.* Re-engraved, after original by Amos Doolittle, for Charles E. Goodspeed, Boston, 1903. Colored engraving; H. 15″, W. 18¾″. (Boston Athenaeum: photo, George M. Cushing.)

size of Smith's expedition, which meant that Gage had now committed half his army of four thousand troops.

Lord Percy formed a large, square defense perimeter around Munroe Tavern, about a half mile southeast of Lexington Common. He had placed a cannon on each of two hills flanking the road, giving an effective field of fire that took in Lexington Common. A few well-placed rounds scattered the rebels who ventured into the area. After learning from Colonel Smith that the provincials used roadside houses as snipers' nests, Percy ordered three houses in his defense perimeter put to the torch. They could have been, and probably would have been, used by the minutemen to snipe at Percy's rear guard once his forces took to the road again. The three houses belonged to the Widow Mulliken (whose daughter Dr. Prescott had courted the night before), Joshua Bond, saddler and harness maker, and Deacon Joseph Loring. Regarded as vandalism by the Americans, this act was of much propaganda value later. The Whig press in England seized on it and included it in a political cartoon that appeared later in the year (Fig. 1).

Doolittle made the burning of the houses a principal feature of his fourth engraving entitled *A View of the South Part of Lexington* (Figs. 9 and 10). Once again, he telescoped time to get as many events as possible into one picture. The view is toward the southwest looking across the Lexington-Arlington road. Colonel Smith's detachment is shown entering the scene from the right. Lord Percy's First Brigade, well into the picture, had come from the opposite direction. Percy and Smith are shown meeting on horseback between their respective forces, while Percy's flank guards appear in the fields on both sides of the road. One of his fieldpieces is seen on a wooded knoll pointed toward Lexington; the provincial militia is firing at the British forces from behind a stone wall in the foreground; and the three houses are emitting great quantities of flame and smoke. First-hand reports by British officers verify the story as outlined earlier. The incidents related in the print did not all happen concurrently. Again, Doolittle tried to pack as much as he could into the one picture to enhance its journalistic quality. It should also be recalled that all Doolittle's information was derived second hand several weeks after the event.

Lord Percy took command of the combined

forces, and, after allowing Smith's men a brief rest, ordered the march to resume. Offensive operations were out of the question. Only one solution remained—to get His Majesty's forces back to Boston with the least possible number of casualties. By judicious use of the flanking troops and occasional rounds from his artillery, Percy edged his forces onward. Near Arlington, seven minutemen from Danvers were shot from behind when flankers came upon them from the rear. But while American casualties mounted, the cost was even greater for the British, who, in their scarlet uniforms and exposed positions, were inviting and easy targets. Discipline was lost for a time, and some of the regulars vented their frustration on the provincials by looting houses adjacent to the road.

Percy had brought the First Brigade out over Boston Neck and across the Charles River at Cambridge, but realizing that he would probably have trouble recrossing the bridge at Cambridge, he elected to march directly to Charlestown, where his men would be under the protection of the guns of the man-of-war *Somerset* (Fig. 2). This proved a wise decision, because the planks of the bridge had been removed and stacked on the south side of the river. The beleaguered army finally achieved the safety of Charlestown Heights about eight o'clock in the evening. In the words of Lieutenant Barker:

> Thus ended this Expedition, which from beginning to end was as ill planned and ill executed as it was possible to be. . . . For a few trifling stores the Grenadiers and Light Infantry had a march of about fifty miles (going and returning) through an enemy's country, and in all human probability must every man have been cut off if the brigade had not fortunately come to their assistance.[7]

British casualties for the day's action totaled 273 (73 killed, 174 wounded, and 26 missing); American casualties were 93 (49 killed, 39 wounded, 5 missing). It was a stunning military defeat for the British, who were lucky that their entire force was not wiped out. Only lack of leadership and organization in the American forces permitted the regulars to escape at all. The military significance of the day was painfully evident. The Tory charge that the provincials were cowards who would never fight was disproved once and for all. More disturbing from the British

[7] *Ibid.*, p. 203.

FIG. 9. Doolittle *A View of the South Part of Lexington*. New Haven, Conn., 1775. Colored engraving; H. 11¹¹⁄₁₆″, W. 17½″. (The New York Public Library, Prints Division, I. N. Phelps Stokes Collection.)

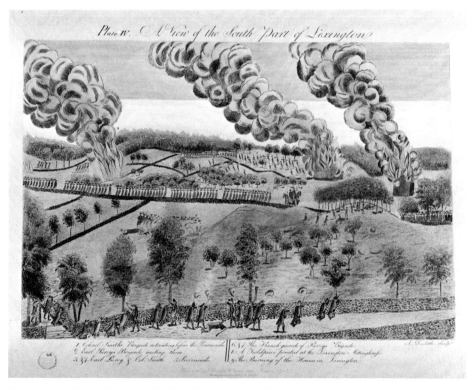

FIG. 10. Smith, *A View of the South Part of Lexington*. Re-engraved, after original by Amos Doolittle, for Charles E. Goodspeed, Boston, 1903. Colored engraving; H. 15″, W. 18¾″. (Boston Athenaeum: photo, George M. Cushing.)

point of view was the effectiveness of the relatively untrained militia against professional soldiers. The immediate consequence of the battle was that Gage and his army of four thousand found themselves confined to Boston, and within forty-eight hours they were besieged by 20,000 enemy troops. Minutemen from all over New England dropped the tools of their trades, grabbed their muskets, and ran to join their compatriots at Roxbury and Cambridge. Yet, three days after the battle, General Gage wrote in a letter to Lord Barrington: "I have now nothing to trouble your Lordship with, but of an affair that happened here on the 19th instant." [8]

PART II

News of the battle reached New Haven late Friday, April 21.[9] At a town meeting held on the twenty-second, the Tories carried the day, and it was decided that New Haven would not send troops to Cambridge. Captain Benedict Arnold disagreed with this decision. He called out his company of militia, known as the Governor's Second Company of Guards, and asked for volunteers to accompany him to Cambridge. Among the forty or so who elected to go was Amos Doolittle, one of the founding members of the company.[10] The Second Company departed Sunday, April 23, after Arnold threatened to use force if the selectmen did not give him the keys to the powder magazine. Arnold got his powder. The company arrived in Cambridge April 29 and returned home three or four weeks later. Within that time, probably sometime in May, 1775, Amos Doolittle traveled to Lexington and Concord and acquired the sketches and information required to make the four engravings. Levi Harrington, an eyewitness of the battle on Lexington Common, wrote years later:

After peace had been declared a stranger from Connecticut came here to take a sketch of the village as it appeared on the 19th of April 1775. Dan'l & Levi Harrington gave him an account of the stirring events of that day and he afterwards published a series of copper plate engravings illustrating the affair.[11]

This is the only known direct reference by a contemporary to Doolittle's presence in Lexington or Concord. While an undated document containing the handed-down reminiscences of an old man does not constitute ironclad proof, it is plausible and perhaps significant, as later discussion will attempt to show.

Presumably because it was his maiden effort in the art, Doolittle spent several months working on the four engravings. Finally, the following advertisement appeared in the *Connecticut Journal* for December 13, 1775:

THIS DAY PUBLISHED,
And to be SOLD at the STORE of
Mr. JAMES LOCKWOOD, near the College, in
NEW-HAVEN,
Four different Views of the BATTLES of
LEXINGTON, CONCORD, &c.
on the 19th of April, 1775.

Plate I. The Battle of Lexington.
Plate II. A View of the Town of Concord, with the Ministerial Troops destroying the Stores.
Plate III. The Battle at the North Bridge in Concord.
Plate IV. The South Part of Lexington where the first Detachment were join'd by Lord Piercy.
The above Four Plates are neatly engraven on Copper, from original Paintings taken on the Spot.
Price Six Shillings per Set for the plain ones, or Eight Shillings coloured.[12]

The advertisement is interesting on two counts. It does not bear Doolittle's name, although there is no doubt it describes the prints that he made. It mentions "original Paintings taken on the Spot," but does not say by whom. The anonymity of the artist (or artists) is wonderfully preserved by this advertisement which relies for its sales appeal entirely on the events depicted in the prints themselves.

If any recognition was accorded to Doolittle by

[8] *Ibid.*, p. 236.
[9] See alarm schedule for Connecticut in Henry Steele Commager and Richard B. Morris (eds.), *The Spirit of 'Seventy-Six* (New York: Bobbs-Merrill Co., 1958), I, 91. For the reaction in New Haven see Rollin G. Osterweis, *Three Centuries of New Haven, 1638–1938* (New Haven: Yale University Press, 1953), chaps. xiii–xv; Albert E. van Dusen, *Connecticut* (New York: Random House, 1961), chap. ix; and Franklin B. Dexter (ed.), *The Literary Diary of Ezra Stiles* (New York: Charles Scribner's Sons, 1901), I, 540. Stiles's chronology is accepted here.
[10] *Second Company Governor's Foot Guards; Souvenir History 150th Anniversary, 1775–1925* [New Haven: Tuttle, Morehouse & Taylor Co., 1925], opposite p. 8.

[11] Unpublished typescript in "Historical Papers," Vol. IV (Cary Memorial Library, Lexington Historical Society, Lexington, Mass.). The typescript is from an account by Levi to his son Bowen.
[12] The advertisement also appeared Dec. 20 and 27 in the *Connecticut Journal*.

his contemporaries for producing the first series of historical prints in the United States, there is little evidence of it. A search of the published writings of the major figures of the day reveals no mention of the engravings, although this need not mean that in the papers of some Revolutionary War figure there might not be a reference to their existence. Imitation is, however, a form of recognition as well as flattery. St. John Honeywood (1763–1798),[13] later a student and friend of Ezra Stiles at Yale College, copied the Doolittle engravings in water color (Fig. 11). He painted them in 1777 or 1778, when he was only fourteen years old.[14] Although crude, they possess a curious attention to detail and felicity in handling the human figure that is lacking in the Doolittle prints. In the view of Concord, Colonel Smith is shown as the fat man we know him to have been, standing in a pose familiar from the "conversation pieces" of the day. This is in marked contrast with Doolittle's treatment of the same figure, which is a mere caricature of a man. There are substantial alterations in the buildings of Concord as rendered by Honeywood, both in their relation to each other and in architectural details, the latter drawn with greater care than are Doolittle's. Unfortunately, Honeywood's version of Wright's Tavern is a disaster, so the only prominent building left standing cannot be used as a standard for the accuracy of both representations. Three of the four water colors are badly water stained; only *The ever Memorable Batle of Lexington* approximates its original condition. The water colors are owned by the Bangor (Maine) Historical Society and are housed in the Bangor Public Library.

The first significant public recognition of Doolittle for his engravings of the Battle of Lexington and Concord was accorded to him in the 1830's by John Warner Barber (1798–1885), the New Haven engraver, historian, and moralist. Barber tells how the engravings in question came to be produced, and in two of his books reproduces *The Battle of Lexington* in reduced size.[15] According-

ing to Barber, who claims to have been personally acquainted with Doolittle, "Mr. Earl, a portrait painter," produced the drawings from which Doolittle made the engravings.[16] As if to reassure his readers, Barber says he "conversed with him [Doolittle] repeatedly upon the subject of these drawings."[17] As Barber tells it, Earl was also a member of the Governor's Guards and accompanied Doolittle when Arnold's company went to Cambridge.

According to the statement of Mr. Doolittle, he acted as a kind of model for Mr. Earl to make his drawings, so that when he wished to represent one of the Provincials as loading his gun, crouching behind a stone wall when firing on the enemy, he would require Mr. D. to put himself in such a position.[18]

Barber is famous for his own engraved views of New England towns and states with authority:

Being familiar with these engravings, and having visited the places of which they are a representation, the author would state that these plates, though rude in execution, and defective in point of perspective, are from drawings *taken on the spot* [Barber's italics], giving a faithful representation of the houses, &c., as they appeared at that time.[19]

The reduced version of the *Battle of Lexington* is inscribed "Drawn by Earl & engraved by A. Doolittle in 1775 // Re-Engraved by A. Doolittle and J. W. Barber in 1832" (Fig. 12).[20] By a curious twist of fate, Doolittle worked on this re-engraving on the last day on which he was able to work before his death in 1832. It is, of course, the same view which had been his first attempt at engraving more than fifty years earlier. The re-engraving is a much neater performance, displaying a knowledge of perspective and some feeling for drawing the human figure. In the original version much of the common is vacant, and the scattered

[13] *Dictionary of American Biography* (hereafter cited as *DAB*) and William L. Warren, "St. John Honeywood, 1763–1798," *Connecticut Historical Society Bulletin*, XXV (July, 1960), 89–96.

[14] His *View of the Town of Concord* is inscribed "J. Honeywood pinx^t. AEtat 14."

[15] John W. Barber and Lemuel S. Punderson, *History and Antiquities of New Haven, Conn.* (New Haven: The authors, 1856), facing p. 157 (expanded edition of a book

by Barber first published in 1831); and John Warner Barber, *Connecticut Historical Collections* (New Haven: Durrie & Peck and the author, [1856–1857]), facing p. 568 (first published in 1836).

[16] Barber and Punderson, *New Haven*, p. 157, and Barber, *Connecticut*, p. 568.

[17] John Warner Barber, *Historical Collections of Massachusetts* (Worcester: Door, Howland & Co., 1839), pp. 398–99.

[18] Barber and Punderson, *New Haven*, p. 157.

[19] Barber, *Massachusetts*, p. 399.

[20] In Barber, *Connecticut*, facing p. 568, this plate appears with the following caption over the picture: "First published in 1775:–the First engraved Print published in Connecticut."

FIG. 11. St. John Honeywood, *The ever Memorable Battle of Lexington.* New Haven, Conn., *ca.* 1777. Water color on paper; H. 20½″, W. 19¾″. (The Bangor [Maine] Historical Society.)

militia is represented by grotesque figures who are smaller in the foreground than in the background. In the re-engraving the buildings are moved closer and the participants are drawn to scale, giving the entire scene a greater presence than in the earlier version. Whether these "improvements" can be credited to Doolittle is questionable. The re-en-

graving partakes of the same character as Barber's other efforts, and the joint credit may have been accorded out of deference to the older man. Doolittle was capable of a more sophisticated performance than is evident in the original prints. His technical skills improved over the years, as we know from his other engraved works, but this is not to claim very much for this self-taught engraver who remained essentially a primitive. Barber's interest in Doolittle was based on the subject of the engravings, not on the skill with which they were executed.

The story of the cooperation between Earl and Doolittle to produce the engravings of the Battle of Lexington and Concord has been accepted since

FIG. 12. Amos Doolittle and John W. Barber, *Battle of Lexington*. New Haven, Conn., 1832. Colored, engraved plate in John W. Barber, *Connecticut Historical Collections* (1856–1857); H. 4⅜", W. 7". (Winterthur Libraries.)

Barber first reported it. The most recent study of Ralph Earl, that by the late Laurence B. Goodrich, does not question the story.[21] Neither did William A. Beardsley in his useful essay on Doolittle.[22] Yet an examination of the lives and works of each man raises some questions which cast doubt on the report. Unfortunately, too little is known about both men. Ralph Earl is too important a figure not to have a full-length study. Goodrich's work is a small picture book with a brief essay, and, while useful, it is no substitute for the major effort which is required. The best work on Earl so far is William and Susan Sawitzky's excellent article examining his English period.[23] Doolittle has received even less attention, for no attempt to cope with his career has been made since Beardsley's article, published in 1914. Our lack of

knowledge renders it foolhardy, perhaps, to question the one story that purportedly explains the origin of the four engravings. Nevertheless, it is time Barber's hoary tale was examined in the light of other evidence.

Amos Doolittle was born in Cheshire, Connecticut, near New Haven, in 1754 (Fig. 13).[24] He learned the trade of a silversmith and moved to New Haven at an early age. The Battle of Lexington and Concord occurred shortly before his twenty-first birthday, and if the four engravings were indeed his first attempt at engraving on copper, the event also marked a turning point in his career. Like so many early American craftsmen, Doolittle earned his livelihood in a variety of ways. A small quantity of silver (bearing the mark "AD" in a rectangle) survives to testify to Doolittle's continued, if occasional, dependence on his original trade.[25] Newspaper advertisements indicate that he practiced varnishing and enameling as well as making metal eagles. He is known to have done a portrait in gold leaf of General Thomas Moore of South Carolina which Edward Hooker (1785–1846) called "a tolerable likeness."[26] Primarily, he is known to us as an engraver whose work includes book illustrations, bookplates, music, maps, diplomas, portraits, money, and such hard-to-classify prints as the well-known *A New Display of the United States* featuring a portrait of the President surrounded by the coats of arms of the states.

Doolittle's advocacy of the American cause is established by his signature on a petition, March 2, 1775, to the General Assembly of Connecticut to establish an independent military company.[27] The result of the petition was the Governor's Second Company of Guards, which marched to Cambridge and provided Doolittle with the opportunity of visiting Lexington and Concord. This excursion might have proved the sum of his military

---

[21] Laurence B. Goodrich, *Ralph Earl, Recorder for an Era* ([n.p.]: State University of New York, 1967).

[22] William A. Beardsley, "An Old New Haven Engraver and His Work: Amos Doolittle," *Papers of the New Haven Colony Historical Society*, III (1914), 132–50.

[23] William and Susan Sawitzky, "Two Letters from Ralph Earl with Notes on His English Period," *Worcester Art Museum Annual*, VIII (1960), 8–41.

[24] For the life of Amos Doolittle, see *DAB*; Beardsley, *Papers of the New Haven Colony Historical Society*, III, 132–50; and William F. Doolittle, *The Doolittle Family in America* (Cleveland: [Press of National Printing Co.], 1901–1908).

[25] *An Exhibition of Early Silver by New Haven Silversmiths* (New Haven: The New Haven Colony Historical Society, 1967), Nos. 68–71.

[26] J. Franklin Jameson (ed.), "Diary of Edward Hooker, 1805–1808," in *Annual Report of the American Historical Association for the Year 1896* (Washington: The association, 1897), p. 899.

[27] The petition is reproduced in *Second Company Governor's Foot Guards*, opposite p. 8.

Fig. 13. Artist unknown, Portrait of Amos Doolittle. Connecticut, *ca.* 1790. Pastel on paper; H. 12″, W. 16″. (New Haven Colony Historical Society.)

experience had it not been for the British raid on New Haven in July, 1779. The purpose of the raid was probably punitive, since New Haven was home port for some of the privateers who were harassing the British. The local militia resisted enemy penetration of the town, but they were outnumbered and soon dispersed. Doolittle's role on that occasion is described by Barber:

> Our informant, Mr. Amos Doolittle, who was one of the party who resisted the enemy at Hotchkisstown, states, that when obliged to leave there, his wife being sick, he returned to his house, which was near the College, and, after throwing his gun and equipment under the bed, awaited the coming of the enemy with anxiety. As soon as they arrived [in] front of his house, an English lady, who resided with him, stepped to the door, and addressing one of the officers, requested a guard for the house. The officer asked her, with an oath, who she was; she informed him that she was an English woman, and then had a son in his majesty's service; upon which the officer, addressing a Highlander, ordered him to guard the house, and not to allow the

least injury to be done to its inmates. It was owing to the address of this lady that Mr. D. was not carried to New York by the enemy; for some of the soldiers, entering the house by the back door, and discovering the gun under the bed, inquired the purpose of it. The lady, with great presence of mind, answered, that the law obliged every man to have a gun in his house, adding, that the owner of it was as great a friend to *King George* as themselves. A store near his house, having been broken open by the soldiers, one of them advised Mr. D. to go and provide himself with whatever he wanted, adding, that he was perfectly welcome; but, not wishing to take advantage of his neighbor's distress, the offer was, of course, declined.[28]

The account does not mention the loss or destruction of any of Doolittle's property, but the British invasion of New Haven must have been the occasion for his later claim of war losses in the amount of £11.6.6½.[29] The Assembly granted Western Reserve lands for the relief of such sufferers.

Unlike Doolittle, who spent most of his life in New Haven, Ralph Earl was almost continuously on the move. Born in Shrewsbury or Leicester, Massachusetts (his birth is recorded in both towns), May 11, 1751, he probably spent his early years in the Worcester County area.[30] The important facts of where and how he learned to paint are unknown. Since both he and his brother James became painters, it seems likely that they were exposed to the influence of a practicing painter at an early age, and perhaps served an apprenticeship to a New England limner. In 1774, he was painting portraits in New Haven and presumably became acquainted with Amos Doolittle, with whom he is said to have made the journey to Cambridge the following year. One of Earl's most famous paintings, the portrait of Roger Sherman, is thought to have been done at about this time.[31] The next three years were destined to be difficult for him. He chose to remain loyal to his king, and we have his own word for the consequences in the form of a petition submitted to the Lords Commissioners of the Treasury in 1779.[32] If the facts of

[28] Barber, *New Haven*, p. 129.
[29] *The Public Records of the State of Connecticut* (Hartford: Published by the State, 1948), VII, 462.
[30] Sawitzky, *Worcester Art Museum Annual*, VIII, 8.
[31] Goodrich, *Ralph Earl*, p. 14; illus. Fig. 2. opp. p. 14.
[32] The petition was reprinted in its entirety by John Marshall Phillips in "Ralph Earl, Loyalist," *Art in America*, XXXVII (Oct., 1949), 187–89. The original is in American Loyalist Claims Series II, A.O. 13, Bundle 41 (Public Records Office, London).

the petition are accurate (there may well have been some exaggeration), then the situation was as follows:

First, he claimed that having refused a commission in his father's regiment (his father being "a Colonel in the Rebel Service") he was deprived of "a very genteel Maintenance which he enjoyed under his Father," as well as forfeiting his inheritance. Second, he was called before the New Haven Committee of Safety in October, 1776, and offered a commission which he refused. For this act of defiance he was given the choice of prison or banishment. Rather than leave Connecticut he made himself scarce for a time by going to "a remote part of the Province" to stay with Tory friends. Third, Earl and five other Tories gave British forces on Long Island warning of an impending attack by the Americans during March, 1777. One month later Earl was once again brought before the Committee of Safety because of his suspected contact with British officers. He believed that he escaped the death sentence only out of deference to his father, and instead was offered the same choice as before—prison or banishment. This time he took the sentence seriously and went to Rhode Island with the intention of ultimately going to England. His sudden departure resulted in the loss of property "to a considerable amount," he claimed. Having befriended Captain John Money, Quartermaster General of the Northern Army (under the command of General John Burgoyne), Earl was taken from Providence to Newport under a flag of truce disguised as Money's servant. In the spring of 1778, Earl and Money sailed for England. Earl is not clear about the sequence of events between the time he departed Connecticut and the time he embarked for England, but it would appear that he was in Rhode Island for about a year. Probably this is where he met Captain Money. It should be recalled that Burgoyne's surrender to Gates occurred in October, 1777, and Money may have been part of the exchange of prisoners arranged by the Saratoga Convention. All of which is to say that it is highly unlikely that a Loyalist of such strong convictions joined the Connecticut militia at Cambridge, Doolittle and Barber notwithstanding.

Earl remained in England for seven years, and in terms of stylistic development it was a profitable sojourn. It is from his English period that we have the first documented paintings.[33] The severity of his early portraits gave way to the prevailing elegance as exemplified in the portraiture of West, Romney, and Reynolds. Earl probably studied with Benjamin West; at least it is certain that he was personally acquainted with him.[34] His petiton of 1779 suggests financial difficulties during his first year in England, but thereafter he did not lack patrons, and by 1783 he exhibited at the Royal Academy. Earl's marital affairs have proved difficult to sort out, with the result that he has been accused of desertion, adultery, and bigamy.[35] It seems that his first marriage, to Sarah Gates of Worcester, Massachusetts, in 1774, was short-lived and broke up before he left the country. It is not known whether there was a formal divorce. About 1784, Earl married Ann Whiteside of Norwich, England, whose portrait by her husband hangs at Amherst College. The portrait includes a globe which is turned prophetically to show North America. In the spring of 1785, Earl and his bride, in the company of Joseph Trumbull, the young apothecary-doctor from Worcester, sailed for the United States aboard the *Neptune*.[36] They arrived in Boston May 23, 1785. Earl's second American career was about to begin.

After a few months in Massachusetts, Earl journeyed to New York City where he announced himself as ready "to enter upon his profession in this City."[37] Whether from lack of patronage or from a taste for luxury acquired during his English period, Earl soon found himself in debtors' prison. The situation was partly relieved by the patronage of Mrs. Alexander Hamilton and a few of her friends. By the end of 1788, Earl was painting portraits in Connecticut, where, in spite of the difficulties he had endured earlier, he was destined to have his greatest artistic success. His portraits of

[33] The portraits of Mary Ann and William Carpenter, signed and dated, were painted in 1779 in England. They are now in the Worcester Art Museum.

[34] See the letter written by Earl to Joseph Trumbull, Sept., 1784, as reproduced and discussed by the Sawitzkys in *Worcester Art Museum Annual*, VIII, 9 ff.

[35] Albert Ten Eyck Gardner and Stuart P. Feld, *American Paintings I* (New York: The Metropolitan Museum of Art, 1965), p. 70.

[36] The *Salem Gazette* of May 24, 1785, and *Thomas' Massachusetts Spy* of May 26, 1785, noted the ship's arrival and published the passenger list, which is reprinted in Sawitzky, *Worcester Art Museum Annual*, VIII, 35 and 37.

[37] *Independent Journal; or, The General Advertiser* (New York), Nov. 2, 1785.

Daniel and Elijah Boardman of New Milford are typical examples of a style in portraiture that appealed to the Federalist gentry, and provided posterity with an unparalleled record of the men and women who were building the young Republic. By introducing real landscapes and interiors, Earl has also provided us with a record of the material culture of the time. Adapting himself to the rural and village-oriented society, he became an itinerant painter traveling to Litchfield, Hartford, Sharon, Fairfield, and Windsor. He enjoyed about ten years of success, but late in the 1790's there was a deterioration in his painting. He died August 16, 1801, at the age of fifty, in Bolton, Connecticut, at the home of Dr. Samuel Colby, who attributed the artist's death to "intemperance." [38]

In his later years Earl showed an increasing interest in landscape painting, but it was probably not so much an esthetic interest as an attempt to improve his sagging fortunes that took him to Niagara Falls in November, 1799.[39] The following June, an advertisement appeared in the *Connecticut Journal* that is of particular interest because it is the only documentation (aside from the Barber-Doolittle story) of an association between Doolittle and Earl.

PERSPECTIVE VIEW OF THE
FALLS OF NIAGARA,

One of the greatest Natural Curiosities in the known world, painted on the spot by the celebrated Ralph Earl, will be exhibited to view, THIS DAY, between the hours of 8 in the morning and 6 in the evening, at the house of AMOS DOOLITTLE, College street—This Painting is 27 feet long and 14 wide, and will afford the spectator as just an idea of this stupendous Cataract as can be represented on canvass. Price of admittance, 9d.

New-Haven, June 25, 1800

One undocumented comment refers to this painting as having been exhibited in a number of American cities, afterward being sent to England.[40] Cuthbert Lee referred to it in 1929 as among Earl's preserved efforts but did not say where it

was.[41] With the whereabouts of this huge painting unknown, perhaps we can get some idea of what it looked like from the insert view of Niagara Falls on *A Map of the United States and British Provinces of Upper and Lower Canada* engraved by Amos Doolittle and Thomas Kensett in 1816, a print of which is in the Connecticut Historical Society. One can only speculate on how such an enormous canvas could be exhibited, especially in a private home, or how it could travel. Presumably, it was rolled in the manner of panorama paintings, and only a part was revealed at any one time. Even so, there is the fourteen-foot dimension to consider, which suggests that Doolittle may have had a house of ambitious proportions. However, this incident does not solve anything so far as this study is concerned. It merely shows that on at least one occasion Doolittle and Earl co-operated in a business venture, and it may or may not mean that their acquaintanceship was of long standing.

At this point it might be well to summarize the pertinent facts on Doolittle and Earl and to draw some conclusions. The engraver's role in creating the prints seems plausible for the most part. On two occasions he took up arms against the British and thereby established his allegiance to the American cause. If the engravings of Lexington and Concord were his first efforts, and on the basis of the skill with which they were executed it is easy to believe they were, he at least went on to produce more engravings consistent with his political leanings. It is Earl's role which does not square with the available facts. Levi Harrington's recollection of "a stranger from Connecticut," while not the most reliable evidence, did not mention two men but one, the one who produced the engravings. By 1775 Earl had acquired a reasonably competent style. His modeling may have been two-dimensional and his figures awkward and stiff, but it is the supreme test of our credulity to believe that he is responsible for the childlike drawing in the four engravings. Even St. John Honeywood at the age of fourteen could do as well. It is simply not consistent with any of the known works of Ralph Earl. Neither is it likely that so much distortion would occur in transferring the sketches to copper. Some semblance of perspective

---

[38] Much of the foregoing is derived from Laurence B. Goodrich, *Ralph Earl.*

[39] *Litchfield* (Conn.) *Monitor*, Nov., 1799.

[40] *National Cyclopedia of American Biography* (New York: James T. White, 1901), XI, 147.

[41] Cuthbert Lee, *Early American Portrait Painters* (New Haven: Yale University Press, 1929), p. 215.

or more sophisticated composition would reveal itself, even if the unsteady hand of the neophyte engraver botched individual figures. The drawing could be Doolittle's and it probably is. It has been noted before that Earl's name does not appear on the prints—only Doolittle's—and neither is he mentioned in the advertisement. Most important of all, of course, is Earl's demonstrated loyalty to the Crown. Why would such a determined Tory accompany Arnold's troops, who went to Cambridge prepared to fight the British? He risked life and property to avoid just such a commitment, and this reason alone is enough to cast serious doubt on his alleged role in the creation of the engravings.

It is easier to raise questions than it is to find satisfactory answers. The implication is that Doolittle lied to Barber, a serious accusation that the author of this paper is not prepared to make categorically. Yet it cannot be eliminated as a possibility in any consideration of the problem. Why would Doolittle make Earl coauthor of the prints if it were not so? Earl had been dead for thirty years or more before the claim was made, and so were most of their contemporaries of 1775 who might have verified or denied it. Doolittle may have been capitalizing on Earl's reputation, or, possibly, shifting responsibility for the wretched drawing to the deceased. He must not have been very proud of the prints, else the re-engraving of the Battle of Lexington in 1832 would not have been altered so much. It might be that Earl greatly exaggerated his Tory sympathies and may have gone to England for nonpolitical reasons such as a shrewish wife or unpaid debts. His marriage was breaking up at about that time, and he was prone to overindulgence. It is remotely possible that Earl could have gone to Cambridge in the capacity of an observer rather than a combatant. Perhaps he did not want his name attached to the engravings, knowing what an amateurish performance would result from Doolittle's untutored hand. All this is speculation, and a thorough examination of the careers of both men might unravel the skein.

The web becomes even more tangled with the contributions of scholarship in our own century. Since the advertisement referred to "original paintings taken on the spot," the obvious thing to do is to look around for four paintings which resemble the engravings. In 1935, William Sa-

witzky claimed to have found one of the long-lost original paintings by Earl.[42] The painting corresponds to Plate II, *A View of the Town of Concord,* and, appropriately, was found in Concord (Fig. 14). Because the painting had a family history going back to the Revolutionary War, Sawitzky was certain of his find and was even convinced of stylistic similarities between this painting and details of landscapes in known Earl paintings. So sure was he that he said: "The rediscovery, so to speak, of at least one of Earl's historical paintings puts at rest all doubts concerning the veracity of Doolittle's statement, as recorded by Barber.[43]

Sawitzky may have been right. The gambrel-roof house in the right center is not unlike the houses which can be found in the landscape backgrounds of Earl's portraits during his second American period. The spatial relationships and the drawing are much better than they are in the engraving. The difficulty is that there is no other Earl landscape contemporary with this view of Concord, and comparisons with his later work do not reveal, to this writer at least, the similarities in style seen by Sawitzky. The most obvious explanation for the existence of the painting is that it was copied from the engraving by a local artist who improved on the Doolittle view. Sawitzky did not even consider this as a possibility. In the light of prior evidence presented in this paper, the burden of proof rests on those who try to make a case for Ralph Earl as the painter of this charming but basically primitive view of Concord.

There are other differences between the painting and the engraving in addition to the spatial arrangement and the degree of drawing skill. In the painting, the stone wall is carefully delineated with large stones and thin interstices, whereas in the engraving, the wall is practically all mortar with black spots, representing stones, which look like so many tracks in the snow. The engraver was careful to show shadows that are nonexistent in the painting, and the painter added some stylized plants to the mound in the left foreground which is barren in the engraving. The rather large, bulbous cloud mass in the painting is reduced in the engraving to several smaller clouds presented in a

[42] William Sawitzky, "Ralph Earl's Historical Painting, 'A View of the Town of Concord,'" *Antiques,* XXVIII (Sept., 1935), 98–100 and frontispiece.
[43] *Ibid.,* p. 100.

FIG. 14. Artist unknown, *A View of the Town of Concord.* Probably Massachusetts, 1775–1825. Oil on canvas; H. 29½″, W. 38½″. (The Concord [Mass.] Antiquarian Society: photo, Frick Art Reference Library.)

crude but conventional stylization traditionally used by engravers. There are numerous discrepancies between the profile of the horizon in the two versions, but it is presented with greater authority in the painting. As pointed out earlier, if Doolittle had such a painting to work from, even his shaky graver should have performed better. It seems probable that he did not have this painting at hand.

The very existence of the painting calls for an explanation. The painting has a long history in Concord, having been owned by the same family throughout most, if not all, of its existence. Now on exhibit at the Concord Antiquarian Society, it was left to the Society by Mrs. Stedman Buttrick, Sr., who inherited it from her father, George Merrick Brooks (1824–1893). Judge Brooks, as he was

known, inherited the painting from his father, Nathan Brooks (1785–1863), but the descent to Nathan is unclear. One tradition states that the first owner of the painting was Tilly Merrick, Jr., whose daughter Mary married Nathan Brooks.[44] According to the story told by Judge Brooks, it was painted on the spot by a distant relative of Tilly Merrick four days after the battle.[45] Unfor-

[44] Colonial Society of Massachusetts, *Transactions: 1927–1930,* XXVII, 158. The painting was exhibited to the society Feb. 28, 1929, by Percival Merritt, whose remarks appear on pp. 157–60.

[45] Sawitzky suggests that it is more likely that the painting descended to Nathan Brooks from his father Joshua Brooks. The latter spent all his life in Concord, while Tilly Merrick, Jr., went to England shortly after his graduation from Harvard in 1773 and remained throughout the Revolution. He lived in South Carolina several years before returning to Concord.

tunately, a search of the wills and inventories of Middlesex County proved singularly unfruitful in establishing the descent of the painting.

Judge Brooks was so proud of the painting he invited friends from Boston to come see it. It is not surprising to find such a local attraction the subject of extensive comment by Henry David Thoreau, who wrote in his journal October 24, 1855:

Looked at the old picture of Concord at Mrs. Brook's— she says by a Minott, an uncle (or grand-uncle?) of hers. There are the British marching into town in front of the meeting-house and facing about in front of where the tavern now stands, scattered Britons going up Main Street and about the town, and two officers on the Burying hill looking west with a spy-glass.[46]

The Minots were a local family related to the Merricks through the marriage of Mary Minot to Tilly Merrick, Sr.[47] The distant relative of Tilly Merrick, Jr., referred to earlier, may have been the Minot mentioned by Mrs. Brooks as the painter. The only other reference to a painter of that name is in the will of Judge Brooks, who bequeathed to his daughter Mary (Mrs. Stedman Buttrick) "my Minot portraits."[48] Of course, the painting of Concord also came to Mrs. Buttrick from her father. The discovery of paintings identifiable as the work of the elusive Minot might prove interesting, for it is entirely plausible that a local painter during the years immediately following the famous battle would reproduce Doolittle's engraving in oil. He would have the advantage of familiarity with the town and would thus be in a position to give a more accurate depiction. That the view of the town is quite accurate, we have the word of Thoreau, whose comments are so precise that the remainder of his entry for October 24, 1855, is reproduced below.

The meeting-house stands as I remember it, but with three stories of windows, door in front toward Common, and no porches or spire; horse-sheds and noon (?) house behind and one side. The Jarvis house; then Wright's Tavern very plain; a bevel-roofed house end-

wise to the road where the Middlesex House is, which Mrs. B. calls Dr. Minott's house; then a little hut; then the old court-house about where the brick schoolhouse is (this the extreme right). Left of the bevel-roofed house is a small house where the stable and sheds are, —some say Betty Hartshorne's; then a small building on the Mill-Dam; then the old mill; the Vose house, plain, three stories; another house *just* beyond and apparently in front of it; E. Hubbard's plain, and small house back and towards the Vose house, and a dozen or fifteen provincials there; then some houses, probably Peter Wheeler's three or four storehouses, whence redcoats are rolling barrels into the pond,—and maybe partly from E. Hubbard's; and perhaps that is the Timothy, and after Peter, Wheeler house seen a little further east, where N. Stow's house is now. A large house apparently where the brick house is, and a row seen behind it up the street; Dr. Hurd's house. But we see no further up *in* the street than where N. Brooks now lives. Beyond, the town appears well wooded. Lee's Hill also on this side. Great and Little Wachusett are seen in the horizon, and Nobscot.[49]

Two years later, while enjoying "the raspberry air of Maine," Thoreau visited a Mr. Thatcher, near Bangor, who owned "four rude pictures which belonged to Reuben Brown, on which is printed, 'A. Doolittle sculpt.' "[50] He then lists each plate by number and title, adding, "Plate II is like that at Mr. Brooks's." He is referring, of course, to the painting. Reuben Brown had been a resident of Concord from about 1770 until his death in 1832. A chaise had been stolen from his shop by the British on the day of the battle, and sometime in the succeeding years he acquired a set of the Doolittle engravings to remind him of the great day. Two of his sons are known to have moved to Bangor, Maine, and it is presumably from one of them that the prints came into the hands of Thatcher.[51] The entry establishes the presence of a set of the engravings in Concord at a time when they would have been available to a copyist, possibly the unknown Minot.

The painting of Concord remains a fascinating puzzle that may yet yield a solution. At some point in its history it was relined, so the back of the old canvas is no longer visible. An Xray

[46] *The Writings of Henry David Thoreau*, ed. Bradford Torrey (Boston and New York: Houghton Mifflin Co., 1906), XIII, 515–16 (from Vol. VII of Thoreau's original journals; 39 vols., Pierpont Morgan Library, New York City).

[47] Will of Timothy Minot, Concord, 1778 (Middlesex County Registry of Probate, Cambridge, Mass.).

[48] Will of George Merrick Brooks, Concord, 1893, No. 35672 (Middlesex County Registry of Probate).

[49] Torrey, *Thoreau*, XIII, 515–16.

[50] Torrey, *Thoreau*, XV, 502 (from Vol. IX of Thoreau's original journals, under date of Aug. 5, 1857).

[51] See Lemuel Shattuck, *A History of the Town of Concord* (Boston: Russell, Odiorne, and Co.; Concord: John Stacy, 1835), p. 114; and Edward Jarvis, "Houses and People in Concord 1810 to 1820" (unpublished manuscript, dated 1882, in Concord Public Library), pp. 141 and 463.

photograph may show an inscription, or an analysis of pigments might tell us something useful. It is hoped that the present owners of the painting will see fit to undertake these examinations. The painting is outlined by a strip of yellow paint about a quarter inch wide, a feature which is not included in the photographs of the painting and which may be significant if related works are discovered. A good cleaning to remove the heavy layer of varnish would, if nothing else, improve its appearance.

To further confuse the situation, a copy of the painting was made for John S. Keyes, of Concord, prior to 1858, "by a skillful convict in the Middlesex House of Correction," who also did a painting of the first Concord monument.[52] The present whereabouts of the copy is unknown, as is the name of the copyist. Perhaps it will be recognized for what it is should it ever surface on the art market again. There is no reason to suspect the painting now in the Concord Antiquarian Society of being the elusive copy, although it may well be a copy from the engraving—but that is quite a different thing. The family history, as partially confirmed by Thoreau, is good. What remains to be discovered is some early written reference to the painting that will shed light on its actual origin.

PART III

An analysis of the Doolittle engravings of the Battle of Lexington and Concord would not be complete without some mention of the later prints which were based on them or of the latter-day copies. Doolittle's primacy as the pictorial historian of the battle was recognized by those who, in subsequent years, wanted to re-create the events or places for their own generations. Barber's role in popularizing the image of the Battle of Lexington has been mentioned. He was not the first, however, for in 1794 *The Massachusetts Magazine* published two new engravings by Samuel Hill entitled *A View of the Green in Lexington where the British Troops first fired on the Americans in 1775* (Fig. 15) and *A View of Concord, taken in 1776* (Fig. 16).[53] The former corresponds to Doolittle's Plate I (cf. Figs. 3 and 15), and the latter is

FIG. 15. Samuel Hill, *A View of the Green in Lexington where the British Troops first fired on the Americans in 1775*. Boston, Mass., 1794. Engraved plate from *Massachusetts Magazine*, 1794; H. 4⅞", W. 6⅞". (Winterthur Libraries.)

obviously based on his Plate II (cf. Figs. 5 and 16). The Hill engravings follow Doolittle in almost every detail except that all human figures have been removed. The drawing and perspective have been improved, and the careful delineation of the horizon in the view of Concord suggests

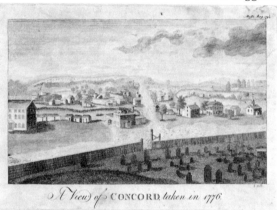

FIG. 16. Hill, *A View of Concord, taken in 1776*. Boston, Mass., 1794. Engraved plate from *Massachusetts Magazine*, 1794; H. 4¼", W. 6⅝". (Collection of Dr. Frank H. Sommer III: photo, Winterthur.)

that while the draughtsman obviously had Doolittle's views at hand he may also have taken the trouble to visit the site. The view of Lexington was published in the January issue as an illustration for an article entitled "Account of the Battle of Lexington," which is the story of the battle by Jonas Clarke, who had sheltered Hancock and

---

[52] Louis A. Surette, *By-Laws of Corinthian Lodge of Ancient, Free and Accepted Masons of Concord, Mass.* (Concord: Printed by Benjamin Tolman, 1859), p. 181. I am indebted to George T. Goodspeed for this reference.

[53] Since the Doolittle prints were published in Dec.,

1775, and were undated, it is easy to see how Hill made a mistake in dating his second plate.

Adams. The view of Concord appeared in the July issue along with "A Short Account of the Town of Concord," based on a description of the town by Williams Jones, a law student. In neither the articles nor the prints is there any formal recognition of Doolittle.

A rather fanciful version of the Battle of Lexington was published in the same decade, and it is worth noting because it is a complete departure from Doolittle, both in content and in manner of execution (Fig. 17). Engraved and published in 1798 by Cornelius Tiebout (1777–1832) after a design by Elkanah Tisdale (1771–?), it is an attempt to render the battle in heroic terms. The sky is completely obscured by the smoke of battle, and gaunt, scarred trees lend an air of battlefield desolation. What is depicted here is not the one-sided skirmish on Lexington Common, but the disastrous retreat of the British expedition. A small group of minutemen is shown firing, or in various stages of preparation to fire, across a stone wall at a column of regulars. The leader of this group, shown highlighted against the smoke of battle, is dramatically posed looking back toward his men with his arm raised to point out the enemy. On the right, a man explains to his kneeling wife the necessity for him to leave her and join the battle, while behind them a woman and a boy run for safety. A man fires from the doorway of a house on the extreme right. The whole print is quite literary, with the use of a variety of conventional poses to signify states of mind. The technical quality of the engraving is good—very good compared with Doolittle's prints—and reflects Tiebout's three years of study and work in London. As a work of art perhaps it deserves William Dunlap's caustic remark that "it is a feeble affair," [54] but as an American engraving of the late eighteenth century it is a fairly sophisticated performance and features a charmingly eclectic use of the stock devices of history painting.

In the 1820's and 1830's, a controversy erupted between Lexington and Concord over the issue of where the first stand was made against British aggression. Doolittle's engraving of the Battle of Lexington shows the minutemen in retreat while being fired upon by the British. No one on the American side is firing. The Lexingtonians wished

to make the point that their gallant forebears had, indeed, returned the fire of the British, and that, therefore, the first military resistance to British oppression had occurred at Lexington rather than at Concord. The people of Concord were not about to let Lexington steal their thunder and, of course, denied the allegation vigorously. Depositions were taken from surviving veterans of the battle on Lexington Green to prove that some shots had actually been fired at the British. The new evidence was recorded by Elias Phinney and published in 1825 in a small booklet called *The History of the Battle of Lexington.* Two years later the rebuttal appeared in the form of Ezra Ripley's *History of the Fight at Concord on the Nineteenth of April, 1775.* The Lexington version of the story gained some pictorial support by the publication, about 1830, of a lithographic version of the Battle of Lexington by John and William Pendleton, after a design by Moses Swett.[55] The new print showed most of the minutemen firing at the British, and only three actually running away. Lemuel Shattuck, the historian of Concord, spoke caustically of the new pictorial rendition. In recalling the Doolittle version he said:

As this would be rather an awkward representation of a *battle,* the editors, as is sometimes the practice of historians, thought fit to improve the original to suit their views of what the engagement should have been. From this picture wood cuts have been prepared, which appear in some school books to perpetuate error.[56]

The revisionist view of the Battle of Lexington gained ascendancy as the nineteenth century wore on. Hudson's *History of Lexington,* published in 1868, carried a drawing by Hammatt Billings of the affair, and it shows no one in retreat.[57] In 1886 the Lexington Historical Society paid Henry Sandham four thousand dollars for a painting in which any similarity to the Doolittle version is lost completely.[58] The transition from factual report-

[54] William Dunlap, *A History of the Rise and Progress of the Arts of Design in the United States* (New York: G. P. Scott and Co., 1834), II, 45.

[55] Murdock, *Nineteenth of April,* illus. opp. p. 8.

[56] Shattuck, *History of Concord,* p. 335.

[57] Charles Hudson, *History of the Town of Lexington, Massachusetts* (Boston: Wiggin & Lunt, 1868); revised and reprinted in two volumes by the Lexington Historical Society (Boston and New York: Houghton Mifflin Co., 1913). Illustration appears opposite p. 183 in the former and as the frontispiece in the latter.

[58] Murdock, *Nineteenth of April,* illus. opp. p. 38. For the purchase of Sandham's painting entitled *The Dawn of Liberty,* see *Proceedings of the Lexington Historical Society* (Lexington: The society, 1889), I, viii, xii.

FIG. 17. Cornelius Tiebout, *Battle of Lexington* after design by Elkanah Tisdale. New York, N.Y., 1798. Engraving; H. 13″, W. 18¾₆″. (The New York Public Library, Prints Division, I. N. Phelps Stokes Collection.)

ing to unrestrained mythologizing was complete. An iconographic study of this process, which would have to include the work of Alonzo Chappel and many others, could prove an excellent case study in the development of the mythology of nationalism. Ralph Waldo Emerson took a dim view of these attempts to rewrite history and observed the futility of arriving at the truth. In 1841 he noted in his journal:

I had occasion, in 1835, to inquire for the facts that befell on the 19th of April, 1775. Doctor [Ezra] Ripley carried me to Abel Davis and Jonas Buttrick and Master Blood [survivors of the Concord fight]. The Doctor carried in his mind what he wished them to testify, and extorted, where he could, their assent to his forewritten

history. I, who had no theory, was anxious to get at their recollections, but could learn little.[59]

The centennial celebrations of the 1870's sparked renewed interest in America's past and a concern to preserve the material culture of the early years. The Rev. Edward G. Porter of Lexington was one of the many amateur historians of the period who saw the value of working from original sources. Accordingly, in 1883, he published a portfolio of fold-out reproductions in black and white of all four of the Doolittle engravings.[60]

[59] *Journals of Ralph Waldo Emerson,* ed. Edward Waldo Emerson and Waldo Emerson Forbes (Boston and New York: Houghton Mifflin Co., 1911) , VI, 36.
[60] Edward G. Porter, *Four Drawings of the Engagement*

This was probably the first attempt to reproduce the originals rather than using a redrawn and considerably altered version. The antiquarians and collectors of the period were aware that much of the nation's material culture from the colonial and early republican periods had already disappeared and that Doolittle's engravings in particular were rare items. Porter's reproductions were not of a high quality and were not colored. The need for reproductions of good quality was met in 1902 when Charles Goodspeed employed Sidney Lawton Smith to re-engrave in color Doolittle's Lexington-Concord series in their entirety, including Doolittle's idiosyncratic drawing (Figs. 4, 6, 8, and 10).[61] Goodspeed borrowed one original from the Pequot Library of Southport, Connecticut, and the other three from the Bangor Historical Society. (The latter were subsequently lost in a fire and could possibly have been from the set owned by Reuben Brown.) A limited edition of seventy-five prints, all hand-colored, was published in 1903, and the plates were destroyed. To the unobserving these might pass for originals, but Goodspeed was careful to include in two places on each print the circumstances of publication. Lightly printed below the legend is the inscription "Published by Charles E. Goodspeed, Boston, 1903. / Re-engraved by Sidney L. Smith." In the lower left corner, where it could not be trimmed without taking off the legend too, is a wreath enclosing the set number, which, in the set

illustrated herewith, reads "No. 68 / OF AN EDITION / OF SEVENTY-FIVE / —ONLY— / AND THE PLATE / DESTROYED." Smith was a skillful engraver and, while duplicating Doolittle's awkward drawing very well, he could not help improving the image. The result is a very clean, positive print, which more than anything else makes the re-engravings easy to distinguish from Doolittle's. The four originals and the four re-engravings are brought together and illustrated for the first time in this article, thus enabling the reader to make his own comparison. Even the re-engravings have become rare and are now collectible, which suggests the rarity of the originals. To meet the continuing demand for quality reproductions of the Doolittle prints, Goodspeed's Book Shop in 1960 published another limited edition of 225 sets printed by Meriden Gravure in collotype.[62] Since they are made from color transparencies of the set of originals in the Connecticut Historical Society, the new reproductions are even closer in over-all appearance to the originals than are the re-engravings of 1903. Due to the process used, however, there is little chance of mistaking them for the originals.

The homely appeal of Amos Doolittle's crude images continues to attract Americans. For better or for worse, our visual concept of the events of the nineteenth of April, 1775, are forever shaped by the stumbling efforts of a young Connecticut silversmith-turned-engraver. That is a sufficient legacy for any man to leave to posterity.

---

at Lexington and Concord Reproduced from Doolittle's Original Copperplate Engravings with an Explanatory Text (Boston, 1883).

[61] Goodspeed, *Yankee Bookseller*, p. 111.

[62] "Doolittle's Concord & Lexington," *The Month at Goodspeed's Book Shop*, XXXII (Oct., 1960), 2–8.

Unrecorded American Views on Two Liverpool-Type Earthenware Pitchers

J. Jefferson Miller II

CREAM-COLORED earthenware pitchers, modeled in a graceful baluster shape, were manufactured in Liverpool and elsewhere in England during the late eighteenth and early nineteenth centuries. The flowing lines of these serviceable vessels were probably derived from eighteenth-century Liverpool porcelain pitchers of the same shape (Fig. 1). The distinctive form of the Liverpool prototypes differed materially from baluster-shaped pitchers produced in other eighteenth-century English porcelain centers.[1] Although few baluster-shaped, cream-colored earthenware pitchers are marked, there is sufficient evidence to assign a Liverpool provenance to the general group, always keeping in mind the caveat that at least some were made in other parts of England. For this reason, "Liverpool-type" is the preferred term. By the last decades of the eighteenth century, Liverpool-type earthenware pitchers were being manufactured in quantity. They were frequently decorated by the transfer printing process. The production of these wares continued until the 1820's when more complicated shapes were introduced and the more durable ironstone began to replace the soft, cream-colored earthenware.

Robert H. McCauley's *Liverpool Transfer Designs on Anglo-American Pottery,* published in

1942, presented students and collectors with a comprehensive list of American themes found on transfer-printed, Liverpool-type, cream-colored wares of the eighteenth and early nineteenth centuries.[2] Since the publication of this important volume, which is now out of print, relatively few examples of these wares with American views unrecorded by McCauley have come to light. This article will discuss two Liverpool-type pitchers, both in a private American collection, that are decorated with American views of more than routine interest. To the best of the author's knowledge, these decorations have not been published before.

The first of these pitchers must be classified as atypical. In a circular reserve on the obverse side is printed *A View on Hudson River* (Fig. 2). On the reverse side is printed an *American Stage Waggon* (Fig. 3). The scenes on both sides are in purple, a distinctly unusual color for transfer printing on these wares. Most Liverpool-type pitchers incorporating these decorations were printed in black or, less frequently, in red. A second unusual characteristic occurs in the green trim on the handle, spout, and upper and lower borders. Green trim is rarely found on Liverpool-type pieces; the predominant trim colors are black, brownish-red, and gold.[3] Other than the colors, the pitcher reveals no salient feature that differentiates it from its fellows of the early nineteenth century. The body, the glaze, the form, and the construction all fall well within the usual

---

[1] For other examples of Liverpool porcelain pitchers in this shape, see Knowles Boney, *Liverpool Porcelain of the Eighteenth Century and Its Makers* (London: B. T. Batsford, 1957), Plates 1 and 2. For baluster-shaped porcelain pitchers from other English factories, see F. Brayshow Gilhespy, *Derby Porcelain* (London: MacGibbon and Kee, 1961), Fig. 50; H. Rissik Marshall, *Coloured Worcester of the First Period* (Newport, Eng.: Ceramic Book Co., 1954), Plate 42, Nos. 860 and 862; George Savage, *English Pottery and Porcelain* (New York: Universe Books, 1961), Fig. 116 (Bow).

[2] Portland, Me.: Southworth-Anthoensen Press, 1942.

[3] Two pieces in the Robert H. McCauley Collection (110 items), which is now in the Smithsonian Institution, have green trim.

range to be found in pitchers of this period that we conveniently classify as "Liverpool-type."

Both of these transfer-printed decorations were copied from a travel book first published in 1799. The *American Stage Waggon* and *View on the Hudson River* were drawn by Isaac Weld for illustrations in his *Travels through the States of North America, and the Provinces of Upper and Lower Canada, during 1795, 1796 and 1797.*[4]

Isaac Weld (1774–1856) was born in Dublin. In 1795–1797 he made an extended trip through the United States and Canada, and his account of this journey seems to have made his reputation: after the publication of his book, Weld evidently was considered an authority on the two countries. He became a member of the Royal Dublin Society and continued his career as travel writer, topographical illustrator, and geographer. He wrote both statistical studies and travel accounts of his native Ireland and, in 1801 at the request of the English government, produced a paper on the problem of diverting Irish immigration from the United States to Canada. Although he evinced no later interest in the United States, there was nothing parochial about Weld, and Ireland did not hold him for long. During the first part of the nineteenth century, he worked and lived in London and traveled extensively on the Continent. A large portion of his later years was spent in Italy.

Evidently Weld's one trip to America was sufficient, for at its conclusion he is quoted as stating that he left "without entertaining the slightest wish to revisit" the new countries in North America.[5] Although, in his travel account, he discussed many incidents of his trip in specific terms, most of his illustrations are only generally related to the text. Thus, his pleasant drawing of *View on the Hudson River* is not precisely located in his description of his trip up the Hudson (Fig. 4). On July 2, 1796, Weld embarked from New York for a three-day sail upriver aboard a seventy-ton sloop. Avoiding tedious topographical data, he contented himself with stringing together some well-worn, eighteenth-century travel book clichés,

FIG. 1. Pitcher. Liverpool, *ca.* 1765. Porcelain; H. 8″. (The Hans Syz Collection, Smithsonian Institution.)

[4] London: Printed for John Stockdale, 1799. Three succeeding editions were published in 1799, 1800, and 1807. French, German, and Dutch editions were also published. Weld's account is available on microfilm (University Microfilms, American Culture Series No. 250, Roll 26).

[5] This quotation and the biographical information on Weld are from the *Dictionary of National Biography* (New York: Macmillan Co., 1899), LX, 158–60.

FIG. 2. Pitcher Liverpool type, early nineteenth century. Earthenware; H. 9¼″. Obverse: *A View on Hudson River*. (Private collection: photo, Smithsonian Institution.)

disposing of his voyage to Albany in these generalities: "To describe all the grand and beautiful prospects presented to the view on passing along this noble river, would be an endless task; all the various effects that can be supposed to arise from a happy combination of wood and water, of hill and dale, are here seen in the greatest perfection." [6]

Weld's illustration of an *American Stage Waggon* appears in connection with his trip in such a conveyance from Philadelphia to Baltimore in November, 1795 (Fig. 5). He described two of these vehicles, the coachee and the light wagon. Clearly referring to his sketch of the wagon leaving a rural tavern marked by a sign depicting an eagle, he wrote that such wagons were

peculiar, I believe, to America; the body of it is rather longer than that of a coach, but of the same shape. In the front it is left quite open down to the bottom, and the driver sits on a bench under the roof of the carriage. There are two seats in it for the passengers who sit with their faces toward the horses.[7]

After having established the source for the prints on this unusual pitcher, one must consider all other factors concerning the object in an attempt to authenticate the work. The main question about this pitcher is whether or not it is of a later vintage—perhaps a Victorian anachronism, a reproduction, or a modern version of a Liverpool-type pitcher. Later reproductions (and fakes) are frequently crazed and poorly printed and have markedly different bodies and glazes. As previously noted, the construction, body, form, color, and glaze of this pitcher are of the quality associated with early nineteenth-century pieces. The two prints were taken from a late eighteenth-century travel account. Books of this type were standard sources for English potters seeking American scenes for the decoration of their wares, and direct copying from such travel books was common in the potteries. Finally, although purple was a rare printing color for Liverpool, it was more commonly used in Staffordshire and other parts of England. We know that cream-colored earthenware pitchers in the shape we associate with Liverpool were also made elsewhere; for example, Wedgwood specimens are frequently encountered (Fig. 6). On the basis of these factors, it can be tentatively concluded that this Liverpool-type

FIG. 3. Reverse of Figure 2: *American Stage Waggon.* (Private collection: photo, Smithsonian Institution.)

[6] Weld, *Travels* (2nd ed.; New York, 1800), p. 268.
[7] *Ibid.*, p. 27.

VIEW *on the* HUDSON RIVER.

FIG. 4. *View on the Hudson River,* from Isaac Weld's *Travels through the States of North America* (4th ed.; London, 1807). (Library of Congress: photo, Smithsonian Institution.)

AMERICAN STAGE WAGGON.

Published Dec. 21 1798, by J. Stockdale, Picadilly.

FIG. 5. *American Stage Waggon,* from Isaac Weld's *Travels through the States of North America* (4th ed.; London, 1807). (Library of Congress: photo, Smithsonian Institution.)

pitcher does date from the early nineteenth century and that it was possibly made and printed in Staffordshire rather than Liverpool.

Dating and determining the source of the second pitcher present fewer difficulties (Figs. 7 and 8). Like the first it is unmarked, but it is unquestionably a Liverpool-type, cream-colored earthenware piece with a specially ordered decoration. On one side is a poem in four stanzas with the date 1797–1798 below. The date, as will be shown, is confirmed by documentary evidence. The poem, replete with hints as to its meaning, presents an exceptional opportunity for historical detective work.

> It's Franklin, Robinson and Co.
> Imported in the Ship Ontario;
> Twelve hundred Chests of Bohea Tea,
> The best that e'er was in America.
>
> The next thing if you must know,
> Who could dislike the Ship Ontario;
> For every Chest, two Cents and half,
> Makes Heyer, King and Hodge to laugh.
>
> The Ship Ontario from India came,
> Wish ev'ry day we had one of the same;
> With the Captain bold as any horned deer,
> And Hodge the B****r, in his easy Chair.
>
> Now let us drink success unto the Ontario,
> In spite of Hodge, who is our daily foe;
> Likewise unto the foreign India Trade,
> And to these wealthy Merchants it has made.
>
> 1797–8.

Reference to standard works on eighteenth-century American commercial history was not productive, suggesting that the events alluded to in the poem were not of major significance. The India and China trades were clearly involved, so the search turned to American east coast ports.

Careful examination of directories from several cities failed to yield a clue until a 1797 New York directory disclosed that the countinghouse of Franklin, Robinson and Company was located at 279 Pearl Street.[8] The same directory showed that Ralph Hodge was inspector of the customs, and John King and Walter Heyer were revenue officers working directly under Hodge.[9] To complete the cast of characters, further research revealed that

Fig. 6. Pitcher. Wedgwood, Staffordshire, *ca.* 1795. Earthenware; H. 9¹³⁄₁₆″. (The Robert H. McCauley Collection, Smithsonian Institution.)

Franklin, Robinson and Company had three partners: Abraham and Samuel Franklin and William T. Robinson. These men were important New Yorkers. Robinson served on the board of the New York Western and Northern Canal Company, while Samuel Franklin was a director of the New York Insurance Company, as well as of the Bank of New York.[10] The firm pioneered in the India and China trades. An early historian of New York commerce noted that Franklin, Robinson and Company was one of New York's great mercantile firms during the late eighteenth century and that "they did a heavy East India business."[11]

[8] *Longworth's American Almanack New-York Registrar and City Directory* (New York: T. & J. Swords, 1797), p. 182.

[9] *Ibid.*, p. 43.

[10] These references appear in *The New York Directory and Register* of 1795 (compiled by William Duncan) and 1796 (compiled by John Low).

[11] Walter Barrett [Joseph A. Scoville], *The Old Merchants of the City of New York* (New York: Worthington Co., 1889), XI, 248. This rambling history is often inaccurate. Scoville states that Franklin, Robinson and Co. sent the first ship from New York to Canton after the Revolution. At present, authorities give this honor to *The Empress of China*, sent out by Robert Morris of Philadelphia and Daniel Parker and Co. of New York. See Jean McClure Mudge, *Chinese Export Porcelain for the American Trade* (Newark, Del.: University of Delaware Press, 1962), p. 14.

But, what happened to turn the firm so strongly against the United States Customs people in New York? On Monday, May 1, 1797, the marine intelligence column of the *New York Gazette and General Advertiser* reported the arrival, after a voyage of 128 days from Canton, of the Franklin, Robinson and Company's ship *Ontario*. Captain Wheaton of the *Ontario* gave the further news that three other New York ships—the *Confederacy*, the *Nancy Lee*, and the *Hunter*—were in Canton harbor when the *Ontario* sailed. On the following day, the *Hunter*, another Franklin, Robinson ship, under Captain Whitlock, arrived in New York having made the trip from Canton in only 108 days.[12]

It took about a month to unload and assort the cargoes. On May 12, 1797, the firm was prepared to sell the goods imported in the *Ontario* and *Hunter*, and an advertisement was run in *The Daily Advertiser:*

Imported by

Franklin, Robinson and Co.

In the ships Ontario and Hunter from Canton, and for sale by the hundred chests or smaller quantity, Bohea Teas of superior quality in chests, and half and quarter chests.

Also

Hyson and Young Hyson teas of superior quality.
Nankeens, china ware, well chosen and assorted, including some handsome blue and white table sets, rhubarb in chests, quick silver,
Excellent sugar in boxes and bags, sugar candy, etc.

This advertisement continued to run until February 3, 1798. But, it seems that a dispute over duties or other entry charges on the *Ontario's* cargo of Bohea tea took place, probably in April of 1797, when the cargo was being unloaded. The reference in the poem to "two Cents and half" for each chest of tea is puzzling. The duty on Bohea tea imported in American bottoms was ten cents a pound in 1797.[13] It is doubtful that the dispute was over the tare (the amount deducted from the duty to compensate for the weight of the chest), as the tare was arbitrarily set by statute. It can be concluded that the poem on the pitcher was inspired by some bitter disagreement between the

importers and the United States Customs inspectors in New York. Furthermore, it appears that a matter of principle was involved, since two and a half cents on twelve hundred chests amounts to only thirty dollars—an insignificant sum compared with the cargo's value. Perhaps the reference is to a payment or fee (legal or otherwise) given to the inspectors for clearing the cargo. Fur-

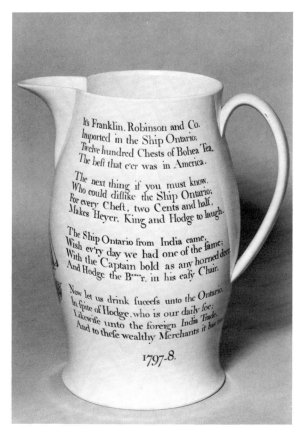

FIG. 7. Pitcher. Liverpool type, Staffordshire (?), *ca.* 1798. Earthenware; H. 11½". Obverse: A poem concerning a customs dispute. (Private collection: photo, Smithsonian Institution.)

ther research into the customs records of the period and other contemporary documents may lead to the discovery of the precise nature of this controversy.

Certainly, feelings were strong enough to encourage Franklin, Robinson and Company, some friends, or other merchants to order this transferprinted pitcher from England. More than one were probably ordered, since Liverpool-type pitchers were often purchased in small lots and presented to members of clubs or other organizations

[12] As yet the author has not ascertained whether the *Ontario* and the *Hunter* were owned or chartered by Franklin, Robinson and Co.

[13] *Longworth's Directory*, p. 25.

Fig. 8. Reverse of Figure 7, with version of the Great Seal of the United States. (Private collection: photo, Smithsonian Institution.)

such as militia companies or Masonic lodges.[14] At this time the trade between New York and Liverpool was extensive, with frequent sailings between the two great ports; therefore, the ordering and securing of specially decorated presentation pitchers would have been a simple matter.

Under the spout of the pitcher is printed a stereotyped view of a sailing vessel flying the American flag. The poem is on the obverse side, and the reverse side is decorated with a strongly conceived print of the Great Seal of the United States. This version of the Great Seal differs in detail from any in McCauley's listings. The seal itself is similar to McCauley No. 156, but a background of clouds has been added.[15] The sixteen stars over the eagle's head would seem to give some substance to the often repeated idea that pieces can be dated from the stars in the seal or flag, since there were sixteen states in the Union in 1797. But as copper printing plates were used over a considerable period of time (or recopied when worn out), such a dating theory is patently untenable. In this particular case the numbers do work out correctly.

These two Liverpool-type pitchers are of interest, of course, because they are decorated with heretofore unrecorded American views. Perhaps of more importance is the thought that research into the origins of designs found on such pieces can add to our general knowledge of the history of the early Republic. Regrettably, many of the rare presentation pieces have never been adequately investigated. Those decorated with views of the Portland Observatory, the Boston Fuseliers, and Newburyport Harbor come particularly to mind.[16] Further scholarly research in this relatively unexplored area of cultural history should provide documentation relevant to a better understanding of the material objects of the Federal Period.

[14] See McCauley, *Liverpool Transfer Designs,* frontispiece, for a pitcher made for the Boston Fuseliers. Evidently each member of this militia company received one, and about ten have survived.

[15] *Ibid.,* p. 108, No. 156 and Plate XXVIII.

[16] *Ibid.,* Nos. 251, 256, and 260.

Detail of Figure 5, page 125.

Denis A. Volozan, Philadelphia Neoclassicist

David Sellin

Unforeseen events may reduce the most affluent to poverty, and a talent for drawing may become not only an elegant accomplishment, but a means of subsistence. Many of the unfortunate victims of the French Revolution have obtained at least temporary relief from want, by the exercise of that art which formed one of the amusements of their happier days.—The Society of Artists of the United States, Constitution, 1810 [1]

IN PHILADELPHIA, on March 23, 1818, Denis A. Volozan petitioned for naturalization as an American citizen, stating that he was a native of Lyons but had been in continuous residence in the United States since arriving in Philadelphia in 1799. Two noted members of the French community, John Dubarry and Augustus Bellin, acted as character witnesses.[2] Volozan, closely involved with the Philadelphia *émigré* community, was a charter member, benefactor, and director of the Société Bien Faisance de Philadelphie, chartered in 1807 for the relief of *émigrés* in distress.[3] His marriage to Marie Victorine Rénaud de St. Félix, with the Rev. Adam Britt, S.J.,

officiating, took place in the Church of the Holy Trinity at Sixth and Spruce Streets in the presence of Jean Julien Madeleine Bacher de Boisgely, Charles Hector Brûle, François Breuil, and Pierre Nairac.[4]

By profession Volozan was an artist (apparently a versatile one) and a teacher. The city directories of 1804 and 1805 list his address as 209 South Second Street and 109 Spruce Street respectively and give his profession as "painter & architecture teacher." [5] Whether he actually practiced architecture in Philadelphia is not established, but in 1805 he seems to have been offered a commission by the French College in Baltimore. In declining he introduced, with the highest personal and professional recommendation, his good friend Maximilian Godefroy, the bearer of the letter of regret.[6] In 1807 he was listed as a "miniature painter" at the same Spruce Street address. Por-

---

[1] Anna Wells Rutledge (ed.), *Cumulative Record of Exhibition Catalogues: The Pennsylvania Academy of the Fine Arts, 1807–1870; The Society of Artists, 1800–1814; The Artists Fund Society, 1835–1845* (Philadelphia: The American Philosophical Society, 1955), p. 2.

[2] The original petition was located and transcribed by James Dallett in 1960 in the archives of the Pennsylvania Supreme Court in the City Hall of Philadelphia. Special thanks are due Mr. Dallett, who called biographical records to my attention when he was with the Philadelphia Athenaeum. Recent attempts to rediscover the original petition met with no success, and the prothonotary's office suggested, without further particulars, that the records might have been transferred to Harrisburg.

[3] The office of the society, now called The French Benevolent Society, 220 South Sixteenth Street, Philadelphia, could provide no further information.

[4] The registers of Holy Trinity Roman Catholic Church at Sixth and Spruce Streets, Philadelphia, also show that a son born to the couple on Aug. 27, 1811, was baptized on Nov. 10 in a private ceremony (Jean Baptiste Giles Reynaud de St. Félix and Marie Antoinette Charlotte Martel acting as sponsors) and was given last rites ten days later.

[5] An error in transcription in the Philadelphia directories of 1804 and 1805 presented his name "Volegau." Volozan signed his name both with and without the middle initial, *A*, but only in the church records cited is the full name given: once as Augustine, and once as Auguste. The *Aurora General Advertiser* (Philadelphia) of March 5, 1803, lists a letter in French at the post office for a "Monsieur de Vaulosan," which would be pronounced about the same as the more usual spelling, and the possibility that Volozan might have employed transliteration for American use should not be disregarded by anyone searching records in France.

[6] Letter from D. Volozan, Philadelphia, Oct. 24, 1805, to Rev. M. Dubourg, *President du colège français à Baltimore* (photostat, The Historical Society of Pennsylvania, Philadelphia).

traiture was also part of his early repertoire, for in 1806 he did a full-length portrait of the popular French general in exile, Jean Victor Moreau, "drawn from life at Morris's Hall." [7] By 1809 he had moved to 183 Walnut Street, where he was still listed in 1814, but as a "Historical Painter," a professional listing he retained when two years later he had his residence at 178 Spruce Street. Whether or not it was his original intention to earn his livelihood by his art is a matter for conjecture; but it is safe to assume that he came to America trained and educated, for a likeness done by his countryman, Charles Balthazar Julien Fevret de St.-Mémin, in the year after Volozan's arrival shows a man of amiable appearance in full maturity (Fig. 1) . [8]

Mrs. Capron, who, with Mrs. Rivardi, operated an academy in Philadelphia for the instruction of young ladies "in all the useful and ornamental branches of a polite education," advertised in 1803 the dissolution of the partnership and her subsequent removal to a "commodious situation" in Wilmington. [9] Her former associate continued the academy without her, first at 152 South Second Street, then at 204 South Front. By 1808 it had become Mrs. Rivardi's Seminary, located at 187 South Second Street, where Volozan taught the ornamental branches of painting and drawing to fashionable young ladies. "Having been very long absent this quarter it is not possible to say anything about her progress," he wrote in the appropriate spaces provided in the report card of Victorine du Pont de Nemours, dated December 31, 1807, and sent to her father in Wilmington. [10]

Perhaps in compensation for this absence, or as a friend to a patron, Volozan sent an embroidery pattern of his own design to Victorine du Pont. The design was regarded highly enough by artist and recipient that it bears the artist's signature, "invenit D. Volozan," and survives among the family papers in the Eleutherian Mills Historical Library (Fig. 2) . [11] Predating the marriage in 1813 of Victorine, it is a document from the period

FIG. 1. Charles Balthazar Julien Fevret de St.-Mémin, [Denis A.] *Volozan.* Philadelphia, 1800. Engraved medallion portrait after original drawing by the artist, from *The St.-Mémin Collection of Portraits,* ed. Elias Dexter (New York, 1862) , No. 243; Dia. 2¼". (Photo, Philadelphia Athenaeum.)

when Volozan was teaching the arts (apparently including needlework) to the young ladies at Mrs. Rivardi's Seminary.

At that time illustration was also in his stock in trade. Among the plates in *The American Artillerist's Companion,* published in 1809 in Philadelphia, are two for which Volozan supplied designs (Figs. 3 and 4) . [12] How much of the wooden articulation can be ascribed to the engraver can

---

[7] This portrait, included in the Pennsylvania Academy of the Fine Arts Annual of 1817, could have been worked up from sketches done in 1806 at Morrisville. Moreau's appearance in 1808 is recorded in Elias Dexter (ed.) , *The St.-Mémin Collection of Portraits* (New York: The editor, 1862) , No. 6.

[8] *Ibid.,* No. 243.

[9] *Aurora General Advertiser,* Jan. 20 and April 22, 1803.

[10] He signed another, dated Sept. 30, 1806. Three letters from Victorine, in Wilmington, to her sister Evelina, "at Mrs. Rivardi's Semy," offer regards to Volozan on Jan. 30, Oct. 20, and Nov. 15, 1808: Group 4, Eleuthère Irénée du Pont, Series A, Personal Correspondence, Box 5, In File, 1791–1811; Group 6, Box 2, Daughters of E. I. du Pont, Out File, 1808–1821 (Henry Francis du Pont Winterthur Manuscripts, Eleutherian Mills Historical Library, Greenville, Del.) . Milo M. Naeve, assistant director, Department of Collections, Colonial Williamsburg, provided me with this material, as well as the book illustrations from Louis de Toussard's *American Artillerist's Companion* mentioned later.

[11] Drawing from D. Volozan to Victorine du Pont, Group 6, Box 16, Daughters of E. I. du Pont, Series A (Winterthur MSS, Eleutherian Mills Historical Library) .

[12] Louis de Toussard, *American Artillerist's Companion;*

only be guessed, but the manner, scale, and detail suggest that Volozan might have had direct experience with the manoeuvres depicted, as well as with the works of Jacques Callot (1592–1635) and Frans van der Meulen (1632–1690).

Written into the constitution of the Society of Artists on its formation in 1810 was a declaration of its intention

to select, as soon as the society is organized, proper persons to teach the first elements of the arts, and particularly to establish a school for drawing in all its various branches. The connection between drawing and all the fine arts is obvious. It is the very soul of Painting and Engraving, and it is indispensable to Sculpture and Architecture. For how can an artist judge of effect unless he can produce a correct delineation of his design? [13]

One of the reasons claimed by the Society of Artists for the failure of the city's first art society, the Columbianum, was that "the principal persons engaged in the attempt were foreigners who had not resided here a sufficient length of time to form a correct opinion of the character and manners of the people of Philadelphia." [14] But that was before the arrival of Volozan in Philadelphia, and by the time the Society of Artists of the United States was formed he had apparently established himself not only as an artist but also as a Philadelphian, for his name appears on lists of members in the year of the society's foundation. [15]

The minutes of the society show that "on January 29, 1812, Messrs. Volozan and Baralett [*sic*] were appointed professors in the elementary and antique schools." [16] The following advertisement appeared in the *Aurora* on March 5, 1812:

The publick are respectfully informed, that the schools of the society for the instruction in the various branches of drawing, &c. will be opened at the Pennsylvania Academy of the Fine Arts, on Tuesday the 7th of April next, under the superintendance and direction of Denis A. Volozan, F.S.A. and John J. Barralet, F.S.A. who have been duly elected professors of the Elementary and Antique schools. Persons desirous of becoming pupils of the schools of the society, will please to apply to John Vallance at the Academy, Chestnut street, near Eleventh, where they will receive particular information respecting terms of admission, &c.
By order of the Board of Fellows

D. A. Volozan
J. J. Barralet
Professors

And on April 29, 1812, the same paper carried another announcement:

THE FINE ARTS

The publick are respectfully informed, that the schools of the Society of Artists of the United States, for instruction in the various branches of drawing, have now commenced at the Pennsylvania Academy of the Fine Arts. The Elementary schools on Monday, Wednesday

---

or, Elements of Artillery: Treating of all Kinds of Firearms in Detail, and of the Formation, Object and Service of the Flying Horse Artillery, Preceded by a Dissertation on Cannon (Philadelphia: C. & A. Conrad & Co., 1809), III, Plates XXV and XXVI. Another print is described by David McNeely Stauffer, *American Engravers on Copper and Steel* (New York: The Grolier Club, 1907), II, 156, No. 930: "Sacred Harmony / Line, vign. In center, a harp in clouds; two cupids / above bearing a ribbon inscribed 'Laus Deo'; radiating / rays. 7.10 x 6.9 / Insc. over, *Sacred Harmony*, below *Volozan, Del.–D. Edwin / Sculpt.*" Efforts to locate the print have not been successful.
[13] Rutledge, *Cumulative Record*, p. 1.
[14] *Ibid.*, p. 2. The Columbianum was established on Dec. 29, 1794, the first concerted attempt by artists in America to hold professional exhibitions and instruction. Robert E. Pine's cast of the *Medici Venus,* already infamous in Philadelphia, was the nucleus of a cast collection for instruction in the antique. Adolf Wertmuller, whose *Ariadne* scandalized proper Philadelphia, was a charter member. An attempt to introduce a life class split the group so hopelessly that it lasted less than a year.
[15] Society of Artists File, Oct. 27 and Nov. 7, 1810 (The Pennsylvania Academy of the Fine Arts, Philadelphia [hereafter PAFA]). Much of the material in the archives of PAFA was called to my attention by the late Frances

Lichten and located for me by Louise Wallman, registrar. Joseph T. Fraser, Jr., director of the academy, kindly permitted me to remove *Homer Singing His Poems* from the University of Pennsylvania, where it had been in dark corridors for twenty years, and had it restored by Theodore Siegl, the conservator of the academy.
[16] Society of Artists File, Jan. 29, 1812 (PAFA).

Fig. 2. Denis A. Volozan, Embroidery Pattern. Philadelphia, 1806–1813. Pencil on paper; H. 7⅞", W. 9¾". (Winterthur MSS, Eleutherian Mills Historical Library: photo, Winterthur.)

FIG. 3. Volozan, *A Division of Horse Artillery at Full Speed.* Philadelphia, 1809. Engraving, Plate XXV from Louis de Toussard, *American Artillerist's Companion;* H. 3¾", W. 9⅛". (Photo, Winterthur.)

FIG. 4. Volozan, *Horse Artillery Wurst Caisson.* Philadelphia, 1809. Engraving, Plate XXVI from Louis de Toussard, *American Artillerist's Companion;* H. 3¾", W. 9⅛". (Photo, Winterthur.)

and Friday—the hours of tuition from 7 o'clock to 9 o'clock P.M. under the direction of professor Volizan [*sic*]. The Antique school on Tuesday, Thursday and Saturday from 6 till 8 o'clock A.M. under the direction of professor Barralet.

By order of the Board of Fellows

Robert Mills, sec'ry

Volozan was one of the twenty original Fellows of the Society of Artists; and in March, 1812, when the Pennsylvania Academy of the Fine Arts established its rival body of distinguished artists, the Pennsylvania Academicians, Volozan was also among them,[17] enabling him to list himself with the designation "FSA and PA. Historical and Landscape painter" in the catalogue of the Second Annual Exhibition of the Society of Artists of the United States and the Pennsylvania Academy of the Fine Arts, held in 1812. The Fellows of the Society regulated its projected schools and public exhibitions, and the schools and exhibitions of the Pennsylvania Academy were to be under the regulation of the Pennsylvania Academicians. Volozan, therefore, was in a position of real influence in the eventual merger of these activities.[18] Furthermore, his appointment to teach drawing gave him an opportunity to work with a more professional group than the girls at Mrs. Rivardi's.

The First Annual Exhibition of the Society of Artists of the United States, held at the Pennsylvania Academy of the Fine Arts in 1811, also permitted him to exhibit among his peers. That year he showed paintings entitled *Homer Singing His Poems, Angelica and Medor,* and the *Death of Cleopatra,* as well as two bucolic subjects, *The Cottage* and *The Creek.* From 1812 to 1817 the list of his exhibited works include crayon portraits of Washington, a lady, a gentleman, and a Saint Joseph; a drawing entitled *Magnanimity of Henry IV under the Walls of Paris;* several landscapes in gouache; and, also in that medium, two classical

subjects, *Jupiter and Leda* and *Jupiter and Calisto.* Classical subjects include a copy of Nicolas Poussin's *Testament of Eudamidas of the City of Corinth,* a *Last Moments of Oedipus,* an *Ariadne Abandoned by Theseus,* and an *Antigone, or the Affectionate Sister.* There was also the portrait of Moreau, already mentioned, and a *Rinaldo and Armida.* After 1817 Volozan disappears from the exhibition records, being represented only once, in 1828 (perhaps *in absentia*), with a water color *Landscape with Gothic Church.*[19]

"It is particularly regrettable," wrote Virgil Barker, "that nothing is known about his history pictures except their titles, for they anticipate the academic stock in trade of the entire nineteenth century in Europe, even more than in this country." [20] A number of paintings, however, were accompanied in the catalogues of their exhibitions by extensive descriptions, probably supplied by the artist, so a great deal can be reconstructed about subject and content.[21] Selections from the entry for *Death of Cleopatra* follow:

The queen was already dead and laid upon a couch of state: one of the women (Iras) who usually attended her was likewise dead, the other (Charmion) was expiring: but while the messenger of Octavian entered the chamber, observing that the crown had fallen from her mistress's head, she made an effort with what strength she had to replace it. . . . This is the action of the piece. Behind the queen's bed is seen a marble pedestal supporting a statue in bronze of Julius Caesar. . . . In one of the corners of the piece through a door opening into another room, a part of Anthony's tomb is discovered which she had been strewing with flowers, and on a table beside Charmion are the remains of flowers, some Egyptian vases, and the basket of fruit in which the fatal asp was brought. See Plutarch's life of Anthony and Ferguson's Roman Republic.

After a long history concerning the *Affectionate Sister* the catalogue of 1817 goes on to specify that:

The action which the picture represents is when the guards sally from their ambuscade to arrest the unsuspicious Antigone. In the background are seen her companions hurried away by fear. Prince Hemon, struck with despair and astonishment, sinks into the arms of

---

[17] Resolution of the Board of Directors of the Society of Artists, March 9 to 13, 1812 (PAFA).

[18] Letter from Thomas Sully, Jan. 13, 1812, to Joseph Hopkinson, Society of Artists File (PAFA): "Dear Sir, Mr. Volozan, Mr. Miles and myself are appointed by the Society of Artists a committee, for the purpose of arranging with the Board of Directors of the Academy the extent of power which the Society may use over the books and other materials in the Academy for the use in their schools." This reference is probably to the casts, as well as the "case of books and engravings," given to the academy by Napoleon (General John Armstrong to the Board of Directors, Dec. 28, 1810 [PAFA]).

[19] Rutledge, *Cumulative Record,* pp. 239 ff.

[20] Virgil Barker, *American Painting* (New York: Macmillan Co., 1950), pp. 284 and 285.

[21] Exact references to the catalogues are to be found in Rutledge, *Cumulative Record.*

his follower. The action is under the walls of Theba, and near the tomb of Eteocles. See Sopocles Antigone and Noel's Mithological Dictionary.

Quite a lot can be determined from documents and other sources about Volozan's style. The titles of only two pictures exhibited in 1812, *Soul Fed and Made Happy by Love* and *Soul, under the Form of a Butterfly, Agitated and Tormented by Love,* fit the rococo image of the *émigré* drawing master capable of turning out a military manoeuvre or an embroidery pattern. Not old enough on his arrival in Philadelphia to have been trained in the banished rococo style but old enough to have been exposed to a decade of official French neoclassicism, Volozan copied Poussin and was proud of the fact. Of his known classical subjects, the majority have an overtone of noble tragedy requisite for the "stately mode." In addition, the artist had a predilection for archaeological detail. "He had a fine classical knowledge of art," wrote a New Orleans dealer in 1894, when he approached the academy about selling a painting signed "D. A. Volozan. 1812. Phila."

The subject is a Roman woman finding a Roman soldier asleep on the Bank of a River and she approach [*sic*] him with a poniard to kill him & a Cupid is trying to stay her hand, in distance is a city on the bank of the river. It is in a good state of preservation, and has been hung here [New Orleans] for fifty years. The other is a young Roman Warrior inscribing his love on a tree & the woman looking on, this latter is not for sale. Size of each is 44 in. by 34 inches.[22]

Apparently in New Orleans since the 1840's, these paintings were doubtless the *Rinaldo and Armida* (from Tasso, *Jerusalem Delivered*) and *Angelica and Medor* (from Ariosto, *Orlando Furioso*) exhibited in 1814 and 1811 respectively. The catalogues describe them both, adding interesting detail to the earlier: "[*Angelica and Medor*] are represented as intoxicated with their felicity, mutually engraving their names on a tree; Love crowns them, and Fidelity (under the emblem of a dog) defends them against inconsistancy, who (represented by a butterfly) endeavours to approach them. See Orlando Furioso."

In the same meeting that named Volozan a Pennsylvania Academician (along with William Rush, Thomas Sully, Charles Willson Peale,

James Peale, Rembrandt Peale, Thomas Birch, Benjamin Latrobe, John Wesley Jarvis, Maximilian Godefroy, Gilbert Stuart, Washington Allston, John Vanderlyn, Benjamin West, John Singleton Copley, John Trumbull, Robert Mills, and others), the officers of the academy "resolved that every Academician shall be expected to deposit, as the property of the Pennsylvania Academy, a specimen of his talents, whether he be a painter, sculptor, architect, or engraver."[23] Since Volozan accepted the honor, it follows that he presented a work. It is possible that he chose as the example to represent him the first of his paintings listed in the catalogue of the first annual exhibition of 1811, *Homer Singing His Poems* (then for sale), for it is in the permanent collection of the academy, where it has been exhibited repeatedly in all three of its buildings since 1834 (Fig. 5).[24] A pair of paintings in the art museum of Rosario, Argentina (Figs. 6 and 8), one of them signed and dated "D.A.V. Phila. 1814" (Fig. 7) and the other inscribed "Philadelphia. MDCCCXIV," can safely be assigned to Volozan. The signed painting corroborates the authorship of the documented but unsigned work, for they are certainly by the same hand.[25]

It must be admitted at the outset that *Homer Singing His Poems* is not a great painting. Figures gesticulate, frozen into classic postures by muscles that are all in tension, while compositional unity

---

[22] Letter from Armand Hawkins, New Orleans, March 18, 1894, to the PAFA (PAFA).

[23] Resolution of the Board of Directors, March 9 to 13, 1812 (PAFA).

[24] The catalogue entitled *First Annual Exhibition of the Society of Artists of the United States* (Philadelphia, 1811) states: "Homer, according to some historians, was so poor towards the latter end of his life, that he visited different cities of Greece, singing his poems, and begging for support. The artist having seized on this idea, represents the prince of poets, poor and blind, singing his immortal lays. He stands in the middle of a public square at Argos, surrounded by monuments erected to the memory of those heros he has celebrated."

The only serious paint loss in the painting is above the extended arm of the figure second from the right, which is surprising considering that the painting has been subjected to a major fire and a slashing at the PAFA and to a twenty-year loan to the University of Pennsylvania, where it was hung in a dark corridor of College Hall (Conservation Record of Theodore Siegl, Feb. 21, 1967 [PAFA]). As a student, I saw it between classes, and in 1961 I requested its return for examination and restoration. It reappeared on the academy walls for the first time in many years in Oct., 1967, in the exhibition "The First Forty Years."

[25] These paintings came to my attention fortuitously in 1959, when they were sent to me, as a curator in the Department of Painting of the Philadelphia Museum of Art, for identification.

FIG. 5. Volozan, *Homer Singing His Poems*. Philadelphia, *ca.* 1811. Oil on canvas; H. 32″, W. 41″. (Pennsylvania Academy of the Fine Arts.)

is dissipated by the unselective proliferation of archaeological detail and accessories, as well as by the irrelevant focus of the perspective; the poet's hands at the lyre hold none of the spell that Jacques-Louis David conjured up in his *Death of Socrates,* with which this painting invites comparison.[26] The Rosario pictures also suffer from one or more of these defects.

That being said, it must be realized that, given the time and place of execution, these paintings have an importance disproportionate to their artistic merit. They reveal the artist to have been completely familiar with the academic neoclassicism of Joseph Marie Vien and David—a familiarity he must have had on his arrival in Philadel-

phia in 1799 at a time when Vanderlyn still had several years of study in Paris before him. The portrait of Homer, details of dress such as the Belvedere sandals, and the Rosario Diana (taken from Polyclitus' Amazon) could all have been drawn from the academy cast collection; but there was nothing in America that could have prepared him to combine his motifs in this manner. Volozan was apparently the pioneer of this style of painting in America, a painter for whom line was the basis of a style rather than a method of execution and for whom classic antiquity was rivaled by only Poussin and David.[27] The Poussinesque ar-

[26] The Metropolitan Museum of Art, New York.

[27] Philadelphia, more than any other city in the United States, had been exposed to the hard-edge, linear techniques of neoclassicism through the contact of Matthew Pratt,

Fig. 6. Volozan, *Atalanta and Hippomenes*. Philadelphia, 1814. Oil on canvas; H. 35¼″, W. 26½″. (Museo Municipal de Bellas Artes, Rosario, Argentina.)

chitectural landscape of the *Homer* offers a tantalizing hint of what Volozan might have produced as a landscapist, not to mention as an architect. It is too Vitruvian, perhaps, for Achaia, but not for Philadelphia, Baltimore, or Washington in the opening year of the nineteenth century.

In the general rivalries and politics of the Philadelphia art world—the squabbles among artists, between artist and amateur, between artist and lay patron—the Society of Artists was unable to survive four years. With the failure of the society, Volozan seems to have become a competitor of the Pennsylvania Academy of the Fine Arts. The following advertisement appeared in the *Aurora*, Saturday, November 5, 1814:

D. A. Volozan has the honor to inform the public that he has removed to No. 173 Spruce st. where his DRAWING & PAINTING ACADEMY will be open as usual. For young ladies—Every Tuesday, Thursday and Saturday, from half past 2 till half past 4 P.M. For young gentlemen—Every Monday, Wednesday and Friday, from 5 to 7 P.M.

N.B.—To accommodate the professional young men who cannot pay full price, he will open a school for them the 1st. inst. for half price—to be paid in advance. Days of tuition Tuesday, Thursday and Saturday, from 7 to 9 in the evening.[28]

Volozan did not exhibit at the fifth annual of the Pennsylvania Academy in 1815, nor did Barralet or Mills. One reason can be found in another announcement in the *Aurora* of May 5, 1815, originally placed on April 10:

D. A. Volozan has the honor to inform the public that he has hired the Apolodorian Gallery, Swanwick Street, corner of Walnut above 6th for the exhibition of a valuable collection of elegantly Framed Historical Paintings, Landscapes, Drawings, &c. executed by himself, and by eminent artists, which may be seen from nine in the morning, till six in the afternoon. The exhibition is to continue for six weeks, after which time the said collection will be disposed of.—Such persons as may be inclined to favor the owner's intention will be made acquainted with the plan of sale, at the place of exhibition, where it may be seen. Admittance 25

Henry Benbridge, and Charles Willson Peale with Benjamin West in his most neoclassic period. West's *Penn's Treaty with the Indians* (PAFA), excepting narrative detail, is of the purest neoclassicism, and, while further removed in subject, so is *The American School* by Matthew Pratt (The Metropolitan Museum of Art, New York). C. W. Peale, who was the moving spirit behind the foundation of both the Columbianum and the PAFA, was most successful in his hard-edge painting modeled in opaque pigments in the neoclassic technique. "The Italians say, give me a true outline and you can fill it up with turd," he wrote to

his son Rembrandt; and to another painter he said, "I hope your likenesses please. Let that be well settled before you attempt to fill up your outline." He also thought that "a good painter of either portrait or history must be well acquainted with the Grecian and Roman statues, to be able to draw them at pleasure from memory." See Charles Coleman Sellers, *Portraits and Miniatures by Charles Willson Peale* (Philadelphia: The American Philosophical Society, 1952), pp. 13, 9, 11, respectively.

[28] D. Volozan, receipts for two quarters' tuition of Miss Josephine Soulier, May 2 and Dec. 29, 1815, to Mr. Soulier

Fig. 7. Detail of Signature on Figure 6. (Museo Municipal de Bellas Artes, Rosario, Argentina.)

FIG. 8. Volozan, Unidentified Classical Subject. Philadelphia, 1814.
Oil on canvas; H. 35¼", W. 26½". (Museo Municipal de Bellas
Artes, Rosario, Argentina.)

cents. Subscribers to the plan of sale shall be entitled to free access as often as it may please them during the time of exhibition.[29]

Thus the exhibition at the Apolodorian Gallery was being held when the academy opened its own annual without the participation of many Fellows of the defunct Society of Artists. Whatever spirit of bitterness or rivalry might have caused this confrontation, it seems to have been resolved be-

fore the next academy annual in 1817, when Volozan was represented by eight works.

The following year the artist became a citizen; the year after, he moved to 12 Prune Street. Shortly thereafter his name ceased to appear in Philadelphia records. It is possible that a search in New Orleans might reveal interesting material. There are many avenues left unexplored, so an assessment of Volozan's position in American art would be both premature and outside the scope of an article intended simply as an introduction to the man and his painting. Hopefully, someone will make a thorough study of this artist, who merits attention, now that there is a basis for stylistic analysis and a framework for historical research.

(The Historical Society of Pennsylvania, Philadelphia).
Volozan's regular fee for drawing tuition in 1815 was fifteen dollars a quarter, including materials, plus one dollar for fuel.

[29] Reference listed in H. Glenn Brown and Maud O. Brown, *A Directory of the Book-Arts and Book Trade in Philadelphia to 1820* (New York: The New York Public Library, 1950), p. 121.

Catharine Macaulay, An Eighteenth-Century Clio

Claire Gilbride Fox

IN THE vestibule of the eighteenth-century Blackwell Parlor at The Henry Francis du Pont Winterthur Museum stands a charming biscuit statuette of Catharine Macaulay Graham, England's first woman historian. Although little known today, she was a woman of such distinction that in her time she was universally referred to as "the celebrated Mrs. Macaulay." This Chelsea-Derby figure (Figs. 1 and 2), manufactured about 1775 in the pottery works of William Duesbury, is one of many forms of art that reflect the esteem accorded Mrs. Macaulay in that era. The name and face of "Kate" Macaulay were familiar to almost every well-read man and woman of the late eighteenth century. With the publication of her *History of England . . . ,* she displayed her radicalism both by her republican writings and by her entrance into the masculine world of national and international politics.[1] To the Americans whose cause she championed, and to English liberals, she was a woman of inspiration. To the conservative British thinker, however, she was a source of amusement and irritation. With the appearance of her first volume of history, Catharine Macaulay became the subject of engravings in books and periodicals, of numerous portraits, of a life-size wax model, of a marble statue of monumental proportions, and, not unexpectedly, of caricature. That she was represented in porcelain along with England's greatest heroes and men of letters was a singular honor.

Had Mrs. Macaulay's convictions been of a more conservative nature, she perhaps would never have achieved notoriety. But this woman was not only an advocate of constitutional liberty, she was a skillful writer whose views were widely circulated through strongly biased republican historiography and pamphlets. It was this rapidly growing body of literature that fortified the eighteenth-century English radicals and the American colonists in their struggle for liberty. Applying the ominous lessons learned from the decline of the Roman Republic, Catharine Macaulay sought to indicate parallels to the complex problems that so characterized eighteenth-century politics. The furor and surprise over a woman's daring to write, much less interpret history, undoubtedly enhanced the value of her works as political propaganda. Even though many Englishmen regarded both Catharine Macaulay and her writings with a smile, many of her ideas were quite alarming to defenders of the status quo, comprised of both Tories and Whigs. Her calls for reform included the eventual elimination of hereditary titles, redistribution of large landholdings, and changes in the laws of inheritance. In addition, she wrote

[1] Before the War for Independence, five volumes of Mrs. Macaulay's eight-volume history had been published. The first two volumes, entitled *The History of England from the Accession of James I to that of the Brunswick Line* appeared as follows: Vol. I (London: Printed for J. Nourse, 1763); and Vol. II (London: Printed for Mrs. Macaulay and sold by J. Nourse, 1765). The three succeeding volumes, entitled *The History of England from the Accession of James I to the Elevation of the House of Hanover* were published thus: Vol. III (London: Printed for Mrs. Macaulay and sold by W. Johnson, I. Dodsley, T. Davies, T. Cadwell, 1767); Vol. IV (London: Printed for Mrs. Macaulay and sold by W. Johnson, I. Almon, Robertson and Roberts, T. Cadwell, 1768); Vol. V (London: Printed for Edward and Charles Dilly, 1781); Vols. VII and VIII (London: Printed by A. Hamilton, Jun., and sold by C. Dilly, G. Robinson, J. Walter and R. Faulder, 1781–1783).

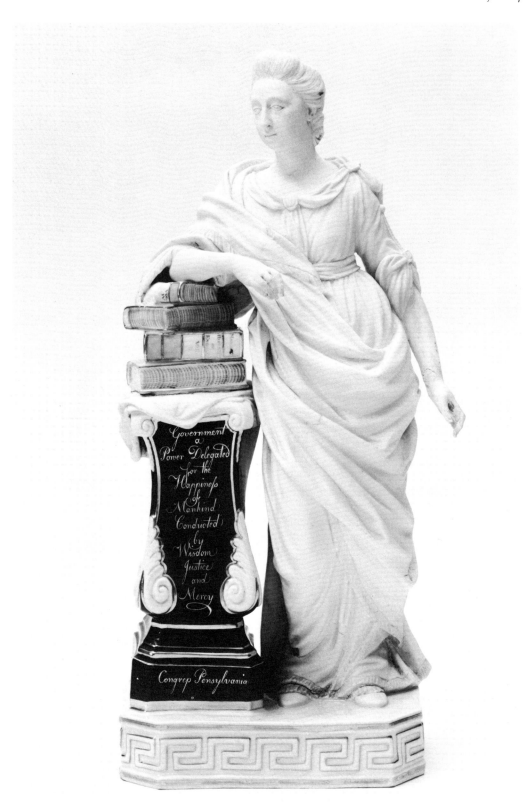

Fig. 1. William Duesbury, Figure of Catharine Macaulay. Chelsea-Derby, England, 1775–1780. Porcelain; H. 13″, W. 6¾″, D. 3¾″. (Winterthur 57.1393.)

Fig. 2. Duesbury, Detail of Figure 1.

hereditary, superiorities; that authors should be protected through the use and enforcement of copyright; and that suffrage requirements should be liberalized.[3] Underlying Mrs. Macaulay's historical and political writings was the implicit warning that the expansion of the British Empire would inevitably create an insatiable lust for luxuries that would result in the further deprivation of liberties, in moral depravity and selfishness, and in the eventual disintegration of the civilization itself.[4]

This daring woman was born Catharine Sawbridge, daughter of a wealthy country squire, on March 23, 1731, at the family seat of "Ollantigh" in Kent. In common with most daughters in privileged families, she was not given a formal education; but, from browsing through her father's library, she began early to nourish an unladylike interest in the political world. Like her brother John, who became a liberal member of Parliament, she developed an intense admiration for the Roman Republic. When twenty-nine years old, the independent and self-educated Catharine married the recently widowed Dr. George Macaulay, a Scotsman of liberal political views. Undoubtedly the busy London physician encouraged his wife to develop her literary talents, and, since he was able to appreciate such an unconventional woman, their marriage was a happy one.

The first volume of Catharine Sawbridge Macaulay's *History of England* appeared in 1763, the year that marked the beginning of seriously mounting tension between Great Britain and her American colonial empire. With the appearance of this book, which Thomas Hollis helped her prepare, it became immediately apparent that this serious, talented young matron identified herself with the cause of liberty.[5] Hollis, a close friend of Doctor and Mrs. Macaulay, arranged with the Florentine artist J. B. Cipriani to employ the decorative and iconographic device of a Roman coin in the frontispiece.[6] This adaptation of a coin struck by Brutus following the assassination of Caesar was appropriately chosen and entirely consistent with the theme of *The History of England*.

that shorter sessions of Parliament were a necessity, demanded that elections be conducted in a far more democratic and honest manner, and insisted that a member of Parliament was responsible to his constituency.[2] Also controversial, but less unsettling, were her beliefs that real distinctions of men should result from "natural," not

[2] The most complete biography of Mrs. Macaulay yet to appear is that by Mildred Chaffee Beckwith, "Catharine Macaulay: Eighteenth-Century English Rebel. A Sketch of Her Life and Some Reflections on Her Place among the Historians and Political Reformers of Her Time" (unpublished Doctoral dissertation, Ohio State University, 1958). Unfortunately, few of Mrs. Macaulay's private papers are available to scholars, and she must, therefore, be seen almost solely through the eyes of others. An exceedingly well-written and entertaining biographical account of the British historian is that by Lucy Martin Donnelly, "The Celebrated Mrs. Macaulay," *William and Mary Quarterly*, 3rd ser., VI (April, 1949), 173–207.

[3] Beckwith, "Catharine Macaulay," pp. 140–62 and 196.
[4] *Ibid.*, pp. 140–217 *passim*.
[5] Over a period of many years Thomas Hollis provided Mrs. Macaulay, as he did other writers, with considerable source material intended to advance the cause of liberty.
[6] Beckwith, "Catharine Macaulay," p. 14.

Published 12.ᵗʰ March, 1800. by LAURIE & WHITTLE *.53, Fleet Street, London.*

FIG. 3. *Catharina Macaulay.* Engraving published March 12, 1800, by Laurie & Whittle, 53 Fleet Street, London; bound into an extra-illustrated edition of Boswell's *Life of Johnson;* H. 4¼″, W. 3¾″. This engraving is the reverse of an engraving by Basire, after a design by Cipriani, that appeared as the frontispiece to Volume I of the 1766 edition of Catharine Macaulay's *History of England.* (Rare Book Division, The New York Public Library, Astor, Lenox and Tilden Foundations.)

The presentation of this object—which showed a profile of Catharine Macaulay with Roman coiffure, adorned with antique jewelry and surrounded by a wreath of laurel—set the tone for the pages that followed (Fig. 3).[7]

In 1764, the year following the publication of Volume I of *The History of England,* and presum-

---

[7] Beneath the larger emblem of Mrs. Macaulay portrayed as Libertas, Cipriani reproduced a smaller reverse of the coin that depicted a consul escorted by two lictors, in turn preceded by the *accensus.* Directly below the seal appeared the inscribed name of Brutus. The selection of this particular coin was not by chance, for thinking men were both troubled with and intrigued by the violent solution chosen by Brutus and Cassius. For the original design of the coin, see H. Noel Humphreys, *The Coin Collector's Manual* (London: H. G. Bohn, 1853), I, 297.

FIG. 4. Jonathan Spilsbury, *Catharine Macaulay.* London, 1764. Engraving after painting or pastel by Catherine Read; H. 14″, W. 10″. (Courtesy of the Trustees of the British Museum, London.)

ably in response to popular interest and demand, numerous copies of an engraving of the controversial author appeared in English bookshops (Fig. 4). For this new portrait, the doctor's wife sat for the British painter Catherine Read (d. 1778), who was well known in fashionable London circles for her paintings of women and children. Even with artistic license, it would have been indecorous for Miss Read to portray the self-assured, intellectual Catharine Macaulay as the light-hearted and dancing Clio, as represented in *George Richardson's Iconology* (Fig. 5).[8] Instead, the artist chose to portray the thirty-two-year-old English historian as a thoughtful Roman matron who had exchanged the more frivolous trumpet and laurel for a scroll of the Magna Carta, ink, and quills. This popular print, engraved by Jonathan Spilsbury, was reissued in 1767. The fame of

---

[8] See Fig. 77, Plate XXI, *George Richardson's Iconology; or, A Collection of Emblematical Figures* (London: Printed for the author, by G. Scott, 1779).

FIG. 5. Dancing Clio. London, 1776. Fig. 77, Plate XXI from *George Richardson's Iconology;* H. 5¼", W. 4¼". (Photo, Winterthur.)

FIG. 6. Williams, *Catharine Macaulay. In the Character of a Roman Matron lamenting the lost Liberties of Rome.* London, ca. 1770. Engraving, after painting by Catherine Read, that appeared in the *London Magazine,* July, 1770; H. 6½", W. 4⅝". (The New York Public Library, Astor, Lenox and Tilden Foundations.)

Catharine Macaulay continued to grow, and English readers were introduced to another portrait by Catherine Read, which appeared in the *London Magazine,* July, 1770. Mrs. Macaulay, by now a wealthy widow, is portrayed somewhat sentimentally "In the Character of a Roman Matron lamenting the lost Liberties of Rome" (Fig. 6).[9] Symbolic details include a funeral urn, and a volume of the law of the people clutched in the subject's left hand.

Whether by design or chance (or perhaps both), Mrs. Macaulay's books and pamphlets, engravings of her likeness, and her widespread reputation as an excellent hostess added immensely to her fame. Unlike other celebrated English literary women of her time, Kate Macaulay preferred to move almost totally in masculine society, a deci-

sion perhaps enforced by circumstances and interest. As an attractive widow who had been left securely endowed by her physician husband and who added substantially to that income through earnings derived from the sale of her writings, she doubtless appealed to many men. Her most ardent admirers appear to have come from the ranks of men chiefly concerned with social, economic, and political reform.

A self-educated woman, and assuredly a zealous supporter of human rights and liberty, Catharine Macaulay was not without personal charm. An intimate friend described her as a woman with elegant manners,

delicate in her person, and with features if not perfectly beautiful, so fascinating in their expression, so deservedly to rank her face among the higher order of countenances. Her height was above the middle size, inclining to tall; her shape slender and elegant; the contour of her face, neck, and shoulders, graceful. The

[9] Dr. Macaulay died Sept. 16, 1766.

form of her face was oval, her complexion delicate, and her skin fine; her hair was of a mild brown, long and profuse; her nose between the Roman and the Grecian; her mouth small, her chin round, as was the lower part of her face, which made it appear to more advantage in front than in profile. Her eyes were beautiful as imagination can conceive, full of penetration and fire, but their fire softened by the mildest beams of benevolence; their colour was a fine dark hazel, and their expression the indication of a superior soul.[10]

Isaac Smith, Jr., cousin of Abigail Adams, corroborated the observation that Mrs. Macaulay, although a handsome woman, was not beautiful, and wrote to John Adams in 1771 that the female historian "is not so much distinguished in company by the beauties of her person, as the accomplishments of her mind."[11]

Mrs. Macaulay's magnetic personality was undoubtedly more interesting than her physical appearance. Many idealistic and impressionable young American men who were studying, traveling, or visiting England on business had heard of Mrs. Macaulay's hospitality and were eager to be invited for an afternoon or evening session at her *salon*. Young Henry Marchant from Rhode Island, a protegé of Ezra Stiles, in a letter to his mentor, described the dynamic Macaulay personality after attending a session. He wrote, "Her Spirit rouses and flashes like Lightning upon the Subject of Liberty and upon the Reflexion of any Thing noble and generous—she speaks undaunted and freely lets forth her Soul—and disdains a cowardly Tongue or Pen."[12]

Mrs. Macaulay was both an enthusiastic supporter of liberty and a very knowledgeable woman with a logical mind. On another memorable occasion Marchant wrote:

Dined with the celebrated Mrs. Catharine Macaulay in company with Mr. Lee, Mr. Bond &c. The good sense and goodness of mind of this Lady are truely worthy of Admiration. I never met with a Mind so warmed and engaged in Sentiments of genuine liberty. She is no Lover of Kings—but a pure Republican. She is no Friend to Oliver Cromwell—though she ac-

knowledges his Greatness. She thinks Charles suffered justly, but pities the Man, that it should have been his Lot to fall, when others before and since his Time much more deserved it. And thought no Time ever disgraced the British Annals more than the present. Harry 8th and Elizabeth she detests and thinks Mary was a better character than that of Elizabeth. —She thinks Pitt by his Inconsistencies and Fondness of a Title &c has sullied his Glories and has barred the public from giving him those Crowns and Laurels his successful Administration would otherwise have justly claimed, and that he acts rather from sudden Motions and Impressions than from any fixt Plan or Principles.[13]

This was exactly the kind of biased interpretation of history that most American patriots appreciated. Earlier, in 1770, none other than John Adams recorded his favorable reaction to Catharine Macaulay's history when he observed in his diary:

I have read with much Admiration, Mrs. Macaulays History of England &c. It is formed upon the Plan which I have ever wished to see adopted by Historians. It is calculated to strip off the Gilding and false Lustre from worthless Princes and Nobles, and to bestow the Reward of Virtue. Praise upon the generous and worthy only.[14]

In April of that year, Richard Henry Lee wrote to his brother Arthur in London: "I have not yet got Mrs. McCauley's history. Will you be pleased to purchase it for me, and any other of her works that may be published?"[15]

For the most part, Mrs. Macaulay's books, pamphlets, and likenesses were produced in England, but presumably they were readily available, through import, in America. The popular *History of England* was published in a number of editions. Catharine Macaulay's outspoken reply to Burke, *Observations on a Pamphlet, Entitled, Thoughts on the Cause of the Present Discontents*, first published in London in 1770, went through at least

[10] Mary Hayes, *Female Biography* (London: Printed for Richard Phillips, 1803), p. 293.

[11] Letter, London, Feb. 21, 1771, quoted in *Adams Family Correspondence*, ed. L. H. Butterfield, Wendell D. Garrett, and Marjorie E. Sprague (Cambridge, Mass.: Belknap Press of Harvard University Press, 1963), I, 72.

[12] Ezra Stiles, *The Literary Diary of Ezra Stiles, D. D., LL. D., President of Yale College*, ed. Franklin Bowditch Dexter (New York: C. Scribner Sons, 1901), I, 251.

[13] *Ibid.*, p. 319.

[14] John Adams, *Diary and Autobiography of John Adams* (Cambridge, Mass.: Belknap Press of Harvard University Press, 1961), p. 360. Beckwith ("Catharine Macaulay," p. 133) has concluded that the conservatism later identified with John Adams caused him to reject Mrs. Macaulay's works during the post-Revolutionary period. In a letter written in 1789 to Dr. Richard Price, he cited various publications on history and government which were causing some confusion at the time. Among the works was Catharine Macaulay's *History of England*.

[15] *The Letters of Richard Henry Lee*, ed. James Curtis Ballagh (New York: Macmillan Co., 1911), I, 44.

five editions;[16] and her daring reprimand to the English people for their part in the suppression of liberty in America, entitled *An Address to the People of England, Scotland, and Ireland, on the Important Crisis of Affairs*, was in its fourth edition by 1776.[17]

Mrs. Macaulay's fame as a historian continued to be reflected in various art forms that indicate the peak of her career was between 1772 and 1775. In 1772 she appeared in *Ames Astronomical Diary; or Almanack for 1772* (Fig. 7). This Amer-

Mrs. CATHARINE M'CAULAY.

FIG. 7. Paul Revere (attrib.), *Mrs. Catharine M'Caulay*. Boston, 1771. Engraving from *Ames Astronomical Diary; or, Almanack for 1772*; H. 3¹³⁄₁₆″, W. 2¾″. (Courtesy of the American Antiquarian Society.)

ican engraving, presumably by Paul Revere after an unidentified likeness, depicts a handsome, elegantly coifed and gowned Catharine Macaulay in the romanticized setting of a formal English garden.[18] Her portrait was also painted by Thomas

Gainsborough, a drawing of her by Pierre Étienne Falconet was exhibited at the Society of Artists in 1772, and a full-length painting by Mason Chamberlain was shown at the Royal Academy in 1774. At least as early as 1775, her figure was modeled by Patience Lovell Wright and exhibited in the London waxworks along with representations of such celebrities as George III, Queen Charlotte, John Wilkes, and William Pitt.[19] A lifelike wax figure of Mrs. Macaulay was also shown in Philadelphia. In May, 1777, John Adams wrote to his wife that he had visited the waxworks of Mrs. Wells, the sister of Mrs. Wright, and, in one of the two chambers that constituted the exhibition, had discovered Mrs. Macaulay in the distinguished company of her contemporaries, including Chatham, Franklin, her brother John Sawbridge, and others. Interestingly, Adams acknowledged the "genius, art and taste" of the work; nevertheless, he found the scene quite disagreeable and predicted: "This Art I think will make but little Progress in the World."[20]

Catharine Macaulay had been a controversial individual since 1763, but criticism of her does not appear to have been reflected in art until 1773. At that time, a bust-length oil portrait of the historian was exhibited at the Society of Artists and was noted by Horace Walpole to be "indifferent and little like" (Fig. 8). Attributed to Richard Atkinson, it is an unflattering representation of the obviously middle-aged historian whose classically proportioned nose and heightened brow unsubtly convey the message that the sitter is, indeed, a rather unattractive intellectual of dubious charm. It cannot be said with certainty whether hours of tedious study and writing had actually altered the famous Macaulay profile, but if there was a change, it apparently made no difference to Dr. Thomas Wilson, the seventy-two-year-old prebendary of Westminster, with whom the historian made her home in Bath (soon after the portrait was exhibited) between 1774 and 1778. The generous Rev. Mr. Wilson not only adopted Mrs. Macaulay's daughter, Catharine Sophia, but put the facilities of Alfred House, including a library, at Kate Macaulay's disposal.[21]

Whatever may have been the state of her pri-

[16] London: Printed for Edward and Charles Dilly, 1770.
[17] London: Edward and Charles Dilly, 1775.
[18] Clarence S. Brigham, *Paul Revere's Engravings* (Worcester, Mass.: American Antiquarian Society, 1954), pp. 135–36.

[19] Beckwith, "Catharine Macaulay," p. 125.
[20] *Adams Family Correspondence*, II, 235.
[21] Donnelly, *William and Mary Quarterly*, 3rd ser., VI, 182–88.

FIG. 8. Portrait of Mrs. Macaulay (thought to be the portrait by Richard Atkinson exhibited at the Society of Artists Exhibition in 1773). Oil on canvas; H. 29¼″, W. 24½″. (National Portrait Gallery, London.)

vate life during her stay in Bath, Mrs. Macaulay did not neglect her American friends nor her political principles. As tension mounted between the colonies and Great Britain, this historian and pamphleteer kept up a sizable correspondence with many Americans, including her old friend Henry Marchant. In October, 1774, she wrote Marchant that she shared his alarm regarding the lack of public spirit in England, but implied that the average Englishman's apathy might force Americans to resort to drastic measures to restore lost liberties.[22] As for Mrs. Macaulay's own sympathies, she wrote that she waited "with all the anxiety which the possession of fear and hope occasion, . . . [for] the determinations of America, determination which in their opinion will either establish the power of our despot on a permanent basis, or lead to the recovery of our almost lost liberties." [23] Catharine Macaulay's openly expressed pro-American feelings were shared by her brother, and she proudly noted in her letter to Marchant that John Sawbridge "has strenuously

[22] *State of Rhode Island and Providence Plantations at the End of the Century: A History,* ed. Edward Field (Providence: Snow & Farnham, 1902), I, 224.
[23] *Ibid.*

defended the rights of America through the whole last session of Parliament, and even in some points when almost every member of the House was against him." [24]

By 1774 Mrs. Macaulay's unpopular political views understandably placed her in a precarious situation in England. The lag in the sale of her books, however, she attributed more to a pedantic literary style than to her particular kind of historical interpretation. In an attempt to remedy the situation—an attempt no doubt inspired by the generosity of Dr. Wilson—Mrs. Macaulay undertook the task of rewriting some aspects of British history in a new series. This work was entitled *The History of England from the Revolution to the Present Time, in a Series of Letters to the Reverend Doctor Wilson, Rector of St. Stephens*

[24] *Ibid.*

FIG. 9. James Caldwall, *Portrait of Mrs. Macaulay.* Bath, Eng., 1778. Engraving from the frontispiece to Volume I of *The History of England from the Revolution to the Present Time;* H. 6⅛″, W. 4¹⁄₁₆″. (The New York Public Library, Astor, Lenox and Tilden Foundations.)

of Walbrook, and Prebendary of Westminster.[25] In the frontispiece to Volume I (and only one volume appeared), an engraving by James Caldwall depicts the statuesque historian standing next to a pedestal. The engraving, exhibited at the Free Society of Artists in 1778, presents her with her right arm leaning on the first five volumes of her *History of England,* from which protrudes a paper with the inscription, "History of England." Her right hand holds a quill, and in her left hand is a letter, appropriately inscribed to "Dr. Wilson of Walbrook" (Fig. 9). A reverse of this engraving, reduced in size and supplemented by the Saw-bridge coat of arms, appeared in *The Westminster Magazine* (London), 1778. At approximately the same time that this full-length engraving of Mrs. Macaulay appeared, biscuit and glazed statuettes of the historian also became available. The blue-and-gilded biscuit figurine at Winterthur, one of the finest surviving examples, probably antedates the ceramic figures depicting Mrs. Macaulay hold-ing her letter addressed to Dr. Wilson. The Win-terthur statuette, an interesting likeness (and modeled with great skill and care), shows the historian with only her books, quill, and ink.

An example of the "Letter to Dr. Wilson" version of the statuette is the enameled and gilded figurine of Mrs. Macaulay in The Metropolitan Museum of Art (Fig. 10). In this instance, the glazed figure, dressed in white with a yellow and rose overmantle, is set upon a base with a molded fret pattern outlined in gold. Upon the delicately proportioned and ornamental pedestal are the in-scribed names, "Sydney / Hampden / Milton / Locke / Harrington / Ludlow / Marvel / Dicken-son/ Burgh / Wilson." Four volumes of history have been arranged upon drapery and are labeled "Macau / lay's / History / of England / Vol 1 / Vol 4 / Vol 6 / Vol 2." Mrs. Macaulay holds a quill in her right hand, and a letter, directed "To / Dr. Wilson / Citizen of London / & Rector of Walbrook," is held in the left. The base of the pedestal is inscribed "American Congress." An un-glazed version of this statuette is in the library of Dickinson College, Carlisle, Pennsylvania, and in this instance the books are marked "Vol. I, Vol. IV, Vol. III, and Vol. II" (Fig. 11). The numeral "88" is incised on the base. It is interesting to note that almost contemporary with the statuettes of Mrs. Macaulay as "History," the Chelsea-Derby factory was also manufacturing a far more volup-tuous Clio than Mrs. Macaulay (Fig. 12).

[25] Bath, Eng.: Printed by R. Cruttwell, 1778.

Fɪɢ. 10. Mrs. Catharine Macaulay. Chelsea-Derby, Eng., *ca.* 1770. Porcelain statuette; H. 13½". (The Metropolitan Museum of Art, Fletcher Fund, 1944.)

The inspiration commonly cited for these porcelain statuettes is the monumental sculpture of Mrs. Macaulay that Dr. Wilson commissioned for his London chapel. While there can be no doubt that there is an association of iconographic elements between the figures, engravings, and sculpture, there are also differences, particularly when the statuettes are compared with the larger work. As for the monumental figure, its presenta-tion as a gift was ill-timed and added to the scan-dal surrounding the association between the eld-erly minister and Mrs. Macaulay. Following a much-publicized birthday party, given by Dr. Wil-son in Mrs. Macaulay's honor in April, 1777, the minister prematurely erected this monument to her in St. Stephen's Church, Walbrook, on September 8, 1777 (Fig. 13). This statue of Amazonian proportions and feeling bears little relationship to the previously cited, delicately contrived engravings and ceramic figures. Albert Pierpoint, an authority on the subject, gives this rather unflattering and objective description of the monument:

The statue is not without beauty, though it is stiff and formal. The figure is draped in a loose dress or robe: the feet are in sandals; the belt plate has the caduceus of Mercury crossed with a staff on which is the Phrygian or Republican cap; on the brooch on the breast is the owl of Minerva; the hair in front and at the sides is dressed high in coronet fashion, while at the back are ringlets, some just touching the shoulders. The left elbow leans on five volumes lying on a pedestal; the right hand holds a pen, the left a scroll.[26]

The statue, formerly attributed to Bacon but now believed to have been sculptured by J. F. Moore, is housed in the Warrington Library, Warrington, England. The monument has been admired as a work of art, but it cannot be denied that its total effect is the transformation of the image of Catharine Macaulay from Clio, the young and attractive muse of history, or from a mourning Roman matron, to the formidable Minerva, goddess of war and wisdom. By the year 1777, when the statue was completed, most Englishmen would have agreed that Catharine Macaulay, the eighteenth-century Clio, had indeed accomplished many of her objectives as a propagandizing historian and pamphleteer. The controversial nature of the historian as well as the dichotomy of her personality are well revealed in the inscriptions originally chiseled on the monument but since erased. Attributed to George, Lord Lyttleton, was the following verse:

You speak of Mrs. MACAULAY;
She is a kind of Prodigy!
I revere her Abilities;
I cannot bear to hear her Name sarcastically
    mentioned:
I would have her taste the exalted Pleasure of
    universal applause.
I would have STATUES erected to her memory;
    and once in every Age I would

wish such a Woman to appear,
As proof that Genius is not confined to sex;
    but at the same time—you will pardon me—
    We want no more than
    ONE Mrs. MACAULAY.

Dr. Wilson's inscription was:

Erected by Thomas Wilson, D. D. Rector of
    this Parish, as Testimony of the high
Esteem he bears to the distinguished
    Merit of his Friend
    CATHARINE MACAULAY
    A.D. MDCCLXXVII [27]

The sensational news of the irreverent presentation was quickly circulated by *The Gazetteer and New Daily Advertiser.*[28] Details of the incident were also relayed to America, where Abigail Adams, an admirer of Mrs. Macaulay, rallied to

[27] *Ibid.,* p. 7.
[28] *The Gazetteer and New Daily Advertiser* (London), Sept. 10, 1777.

FIG. 11. Mrs. Catharine Macaulay. Chelsea-Derby (?), Eng., 1768–1770. Porcelain statuette; H. 12¼″. (Dickinson College Library, Carlisle, Pa.) The scroll is inscribed with the Magna Carta and the Bill of Rights.

[26] Reprinted from Albert Pierpoint, "Catharine Macaulay 'History' the Statue in the Warrington Town Hall," *Warrington* (Eng.) *Guardian,* March 5 and 12, 1910, p. 6.

FIG. 12. The Muse Clio. Chelsea-Derby, Eng., 1760–1765. Porcelain; L. 9″. (Courtesy of the Trustees of the British Museum, London.)

her defense. On February 15, 1778, she wrote to her cousin John Thaxter:

It gives me pleasure to see so distinguished a Genious as Mrs. Macauly Honourd with a Statue, yet she wanted it not to render her Name immortal. The Gentleman who erected it has sullied the glory of his deed by the narrow contracted Spirit which he discovers in the inscription, and if a Quotation from Lord Lyttleton (as I understand it) it is a pitty that what was meant to perpetuate the memory of that Lady should cast a shade upon the character of that Nobleman for whom heretofore I have had a great veneration. Even the most Excellent monody which he wrote upon the Death of his Lady will not atone for a mind contracted enough to wish that but one woman in an age might excell, and she only for the sake of a prodigy. What must be that Genious which cannot do justice to one lady, but at the expence of the whole Sex? [29]

In the same month, *The Morning Post* in London reported that Patience Lovell Wright was considering a return visit to America and that she would be accompanied by Dr. Thomas Wilson, Mrs. Ma-

caulay, and Dr. James Graham, her physician. The final note of political irony was summarized in the terse statement that Dr. Wilson would take along his famous monument to Catharine Macaulay and would place it "on the very spot where General Burgoyne piled his arms." [30]

The trip to America with Dr. Wilson was never realized because, in November, 1778, Catharine Macaulay married William Graham, aged twenty-one, the younger brother of her physician. Six years later, in 1784, accompanied by her second husband, the historian finally made the long-anticipated trip to the United States. During their year-long stay in America, the Macaulay Grahams, as they came to be known, were introduced to, and undoubtedly entertained by, Mr. and Mrs. Samuel Adams, Mr. and Mrs. James Warren, General and Mrs. Henry Knox, General and Mrs. Benjamin Lincoln, Mrs. James Otis, Governor and Mrs. John Langdon, Elbridge Gerry, Jabez Bowen, Richard Henry Lee, Governor George Clinton, James Monroe, Dr. Benjamin Rush, Dr. William Shippen, Jr., George Lux, Alexander McDougall,

[29] *Adams Family Correspondence*, II, 391.

[30] Beckwith, "Catharine Macaulay," p. 46.

FIG. 13. J. F. Moore, Statue of Mrs. Macaulay. Bath (?), Eng.,
1777. White marble; H. 6′. (Warrington Library, Warrington,
Eng.: photo, Guardian Photo Service, Warrington "Guardian"
series, Mackie & Co., Sankey St., Warrington, Eng.)

John Witherspoon, James Wilson, John Dickinson, William Digges, Captain John Fitzgerald, William Paca, and General and Mrs. George Washington.[31]

Of interest are the observations that Mercy Warren made about her friend when they met in 1784. Mrs. Warren wrote that she found the lady "not only a learned but a virtuous worthy character; possessed of much sensibility of heart and dignity of manners." Not only did Mrs. Macaulay Graham's "resources of knowledge seem to be almost inexhaustible," but Mrs. Warren thought her possessed of an "uncommon share of merit both as a writer and a companion." Although embarrassed by her friend's indiscreet marriage, she noted that Graham "appears to be a man of understanding and virtue."[32] A more honest appraisal, perhaps, was given in a letter from Mrs. Warren to John Adams on April 27, 1785:

I have indeed seen Mrs. Macaulay. She has been treated in Boston and its Environs with every mark of Respect. She is a Lady of most Extraordinary talent, a Commanding Genius and Brilliance of thought. This in my opinion often outruns her capacity of Expression, which is often a little too prolix both in Conversation and Composition; or rather, the Periods are a little too lengthy to please at once. I dare say this will be corrected in the future, as one of her American Friends had the Courage to tell her of it. She replied she believed the observation just, as she had always aimed more at the investigation of truth than the ornaments of style. But I think in this age of Refinement the Graces of the Letter ought to soften the harshness of the forms and prevent the mind from Fatigue while listening to the Humiliating story of Human Conduct.

We have a subscription out for an American Edition of her History down to 1744. It fills very fast and I dare say will succeed to her Wishes.

It was kind of you to wish the World would spread a Vail of Candour over a Circumstance you mentioned. Doubtless that Ladys Independency of spirit led her to suppose she might associate for the remainder of Life with an inoffensive obliging youth with the same impunity of Gentlemen of three score and ten might marry a Damsel of fifteen.[33]

There are many indications that the couple were well-received during their visit, but probably the finest and most sincere tribute of all was that paid by the *Delaware Gazette,* June 28, 1785. The reporter, an enthusiastic admirer of Mrs. Macaulay Graham, noted after her Wilmington visit, following her return from Mount Vernon, "Now satiated with the happiness she anticipated in viewing that great and good man, retires to her native country to beam afresh the splendor of heroic sentiments, in the publication of that unprecedented History on the Revolution of *America* the happy land." The writer described the respected but aging historian thus:

Her person is well proportioned, and in her countenance one may discover the traits of a bright genius.
"Slow-pacing time begins to shed
"Its silver blossoms o'er her head."
She not caring to embellish her person by any vain pomp in dress or equipage appears in quite a plain, yet elegant stile, studies the internal virtues, the elegant beauties of the mind and is an honor and an example worthy the imitation of her sex.

The Independent Journal or the General Advertiser (New York), in the edition for July 20, 1785, published the final statement about the visit to America in its report that on "Saturday last sailed his Most Christian Majesty's Packet, La Martinique for L'Orient, in which went passengers Mr. and Mrs. Macauly Graham."

The question naturally presents itself as to Mrs. Macaulay Graham's reactions to her visit in America. Undoubtedly they were mixed. She had not only met, but was entertained by, the most famous man in America, George Washington; she and her husband had been graciously received in all nine of the states they had visited. There were surely some misgivings, however, since there were not sufficient subscriptions for an American edition of her *History of England* and her projected plans for writing a history of the American Revolution were not realized. In addition, her correspondence upon her return to England reveals some disappointment with Americans because indications of the corrosive effects of love of luxury, indifference toward liberty, and the establishment of an aristocracy were already apparent.

The remaining years of Mrs. Macaulay's life

[31] Samuel Adams appears to have acted as unofficial host to the Grahams. His many letters on their behalf, as well as those provided by other acquaintances, introduced them to the most important persons on the American scene. Extant correspondence, newspaper items, and Washington's diary offer further information on the activities of the year.
[32] Letter from Mercy Warren, Dec., 1784, to Winslow Warren (Mercy Warren "Letterbook," Massachusetts Historical Society, Boston, Mass.).
[33] *Warren-Adams Letters: Being Chiefly a Correspond-* ence among *John Adams, Samuel Adams, and James Warren* (Massachusetts Historical Society Collections, Vol. LXXIII; Boston: The society, 1925), II, 254.

FIG. 14. *Mrs. Catharine Macaulay.* Engraving, published by Vernor, Hood & Sharpe, March 1, 1812; H. $4\frac{5}{16}''$, W. $2\frac{9}{16}''$. (Courtesy of the Trustees of the British Museum, London.)

were passed in relative quiet. Upon their return from America, the Grahams spent a year in southern France in the hope that her then failing health might be restored. Afterward, they settled in England where a seemingly uneventful life was, in part, devoted to Mrs. Macaulay's writing and publishing of a book on her theories on education.[34] Her sympathy for the French Revolution induced her to reply, in her last political pamphlet, to Edmund Burke's *Reflections . . . on the Revolution in France.*[35] Always interested in American affairs, she continued to correspond with her friends across the Atlantic—chief of whom were Mercy Warren and George Washington—until her death in 1791.

All in all, Mrs. Macaulay's impact on the intellectual world of the eighteenth century is difficult to assess owing to a number of factors. Certainly in England she was no heroine because of the unpopularity and final success of the cause that she espoused and because of the conduct of her private affairs. As for Mrs. Macaulay's American friends, they had grown gray just as she had since the exciting pre-Revolutionary days when a common cause inspired by the Goddess of Liberty created and cemented friendships. In post-Revolutionary America, the old patriots, such as John Adams, preferred to forget the radical days of their youth and were far more interested in solutions to political problems that would ensure stability and peace. Clio had indeed sung her song, but for many years after her death in 1791 men continued to acknowledge the fact that Catharine Macaulay's impact on eighteenth-century intellectual thought had been considerable (Fig. 14).

[34] Catharine Macaulay, *Letters on Education with Observations on Religious and Metaphysical Subjects* (London: Printed for C. Dilly, 1790).

[35] Catharine Macaulay, *Observations on the Reflections of the Right Honorable Edmund Burke, on the Revolution in France, in a Letter to the Right Hon. Earl of Stanhope* (Boston: I. Thomas and E. T. Andres, 1791).

A Checklist of the Work of Francis Shallus, Philadelphia Engraver

Mary E. Holt

FRANCIS SHALLUS was born in Philadelphia in 1773, where his grandfather Valentine had immigrated in 1747. Valentine Shallus was a successful innkeeper and left an estate of £1379.17.2 at his death. His son Jacob continued to thrive financially and socially. He served in the Continental Army as a quartermaster; and, upon leaving military service, he became assistant clerk to the Pennsylvania House of Representatives. It is believed that he was the clerk who engrossed the Constitution of the United States. These activities apparently reflect a stanch patriotism on Jacob's part that must have been shared by his wife, Elizabeth. Her obituary, which appeared in *Poulson's American Daily Advertiser*, August 4, 1818, describes her as "one of those patriotic ladies of Philadelphia, who first associated together and supplied the suffering soldiery with shirts, stockings, etc. in that eventful period of the Revolution."

Of this union, Francis was the eldest son, and apparently the only child to survive to maturity. In 1800 he married Ann Peters in Germantown.[1] There is no record of children; and, after 1824, no Shallus is listed in the Philadelphia city directory. However, a George Shallus witnessed the certificate of intestacy that Ann Peters Shallus filed in 1828, seven years after her husband's death. Whether George was a son or brother of the engraver is undetermined.

It is strange that, despite the good start he received from his father, he seems to have died impoverished, of a "painful illness," on November 12, 1821.[2] The certificate his wife filed in 1828

states that "the Whole of the Good, Chattles, Rights and Credits he died possessed of, do not in value exceed the sum of One Hundred and Fifty Dollars." There is no inventory, and the extent and expenditure of his income are subjects for speculation. One would, however, expect a larger estate in view of the successes of his grandfather and father and his many interests.

During the 1790's Shallus worked for, and may have been apprenticed to, Robert Scot, the first engraver employed by the Philadelphia Mint. Scot must have had an active shop, and probably he employed at least one or two men. As Scot's activities at the Philadelphia Mint occupied more of his time, he was forced to rely on other men to carry on the work of his shop. Scot's signed engravings are often initialed beneath the signature, and these initials indicate the workman who actually engraved the plate. Many of the plates that Scot furnished to Thomas Dobson for his *Encyclopaedia* (1798) are so identified. The majority (thirty-two) were done by Samuel Allardice, who later went into partnership with Scot. Sixteen plates, in Volumes IX through XIII, however, bear a small "FS" in script beneath the names of Scot or Scot and Allardice. A closer examination of Plates CCLXIV, CCCXVIII, and CCCLXIX reveals that "Shallus," in small letters, is cut into the plate as well as the initials "FS" (Figs. 1 and 2).[3] Shallus produced two plates for Dobson under his own name, and his association with Scot probably ended by 1797, when he was first listed in the *Philadelphia City Directory*. His position in

[1] *Poulson's American Daily Advertiser* (Philadelphia), Nov. 12, 1800.

[2] *Poulson's American Daily Advertiser*, Nov. 16, 1821.

[3] Samuel Allardice also signed his name within the plate when he worked for Scot. See *Encyclopaedia; or, A Dictionary of Arts, Sciences, and Miscellaneous Literature* (Philadelphia: Printed by Thomas Dobson, 1798).

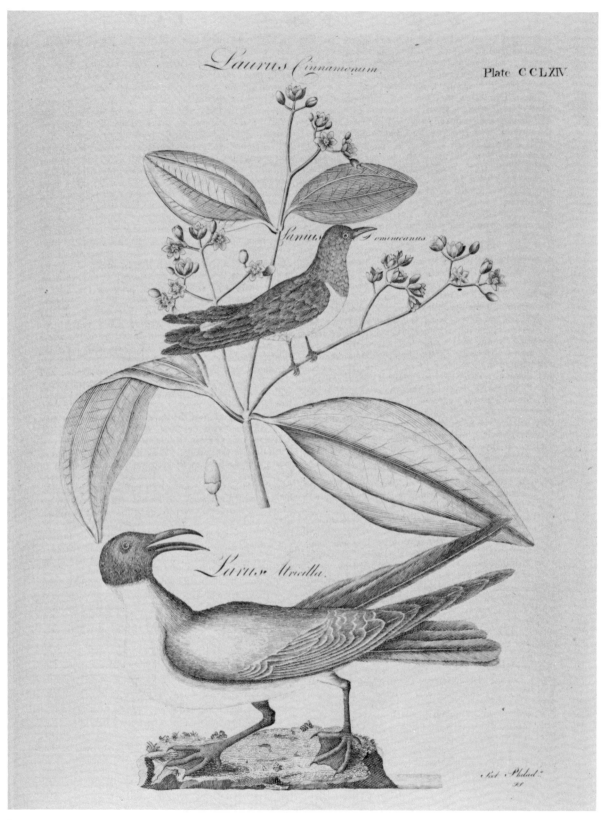

FIG. 1. Francis Shallus, Plate CCLXIV from Thomas Dobson, *Encyclopaedia,* Vol. IX. Philadelphia, 1793. Engraving; H. 9″, W. 6¹³⁄₁₆″. (Winterthur.)

Scot's shop was taken over by Benjamin Jones ("BJ" or "BI") and John Draper ("JD").

That Shallus occupied several houses during his lifetime helps to date his work, for he often included his address with his signature. In 1797 and 1798 he lived at 40 Vine Street, his family home, and from there he moved to 63 Walnut Street in 1799. There is no listing for 1800, the year in which he was married, although the *Philadelphia Trade Directory* gives the Walnut Street address. It is possible that he lived in Germantown during this time, for this small town did not become part of the city of Philadelphia until 1854. In any event, in 1801 he was listed at 104 Race Street. From 1803 through 1805 he lived at 30 Strawberry Street, and in 1806 at 12 Prune Street. He moved to 83 South Front Street in 1807, where he stayed for several years. The address for 1809 is given as 89 South Front Street; but, in that year, the Philadelphia streets were officially renumbered and this change, rather than an actual move, was probably responsible for the new number. By 1813 Shallus had again moved, this time to 49 South Third Street. In 1816 he occupied a house at 90 South Third Street, which was renumbered in 1819 to 94 South Third Street; and in 1820 "Francis Shallus, engraver" is listed at 161 Chestnut Street. The identical listing appears in 1822, the year following Shallus' death, which indicates a delay of about a year in the information supplied by the city directories.[4]

The recorded works by Shallus form only a small corpus. His earliest years were his most ac-

tive, and it seems that the circulating library he formed in 1811 engaged much of his time and interest after that date. Many of Shallus' recorded engravings are book illustrations of a scientific or technological nature. These works required plates, while the religious essays, stories, and poetry popular at that time included, at most, a frontispiece. The plates that Shallus was called upon to engrave included botanical illustrations, astronomical plates, diagrams of military tactics, and inventions (Fig. 3). City views and maps were important, especially to a new country with many unexplored regions. Atlases of every size were published, and most engravers were certain to have executed a few maps. Shallus was no exception; his illustrations are typical of his time (Fig. 4).

Shallus did little portraiture, although a portrait of George Washington is recorded, and one of Captain Cook is an illustration in a Philadelphia edition of Cook's voyages. Many of Shallus' engravings are based on English prototypes; little of his known work is fanciful. His most imaginative engraving is to be found in his trade cards (two of which were made for his wife) and in his work on metal. There are three known engravings on gold or silver: a medal presented to Victorine du Pont, a Masonic medal, and a token or medal possibly indicating membership in the Philadelphia Typographical Society.

The gold medal given to Victorine du Pont was presented to her in 1807 for excellence in her studies at Mrs. Rivardi's Seminary (Fig. 5). Whether the medal was unique or whether it was offered every year to an outstanding student is unknown. No design source for the engraving on the medal is recorded; thus, it cannot be determined whether Shallus was copying a previously established design or had created this one himself.

The Masonic medal presented to Mark Wilks Collet in 1812 is of rose gold, and the engraving is heavily laden with the secret symbols of the Masons (Fig. 6). The style of the medal is French, a rare form in America despite the close bonds be-

[4] This lag is borne out by the statement, "The Circulating Libraries of Shallus, in Third near Chestnut street, and of Phillips, in Third, opposite the mansion house hotel, contain large collections of miscellaneous books," in

FIG. 2. Detail of Figure 1 with Signature. (Winterthur.)

Thomas Wilson's *Picture of Philadelphia, for 1824, containing the "Picture of Philadelphia, for 1811, by James Mease, M.D." With All Its Improvements Since That Period* (Philadelphia: Printed by Thomas Town, 1823), p. 310. The city directory for 1811 still listed Shallus at Front Street. It would seem best when using a city directory for dating purposes to use the year preceding its issue since the information was probably collected in the year before publication.

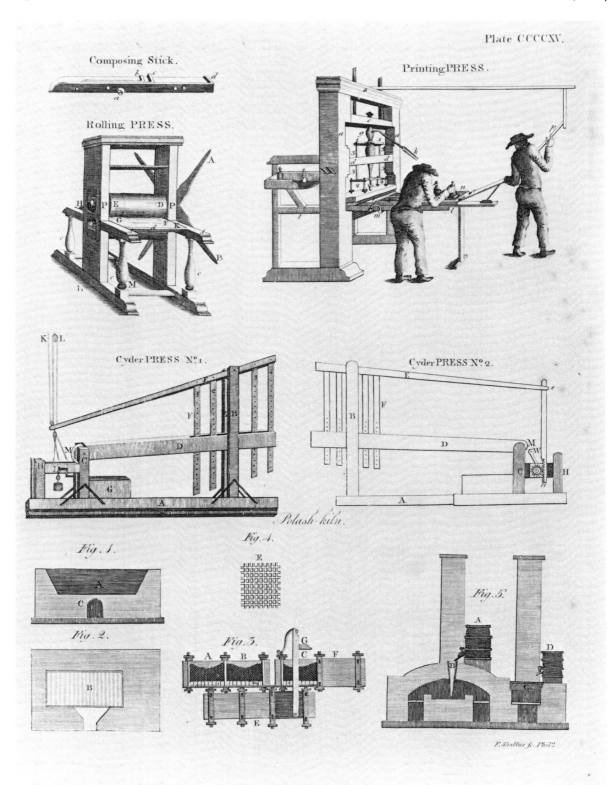

Fig. 3. Shallus, Plate CCCCXV from Thomas Dobson, *Encyclopaedia,* Vol. XV. Philadelphia, 1796. Engraving; H. 9″, W. 7⅛″. (Winterthur.)

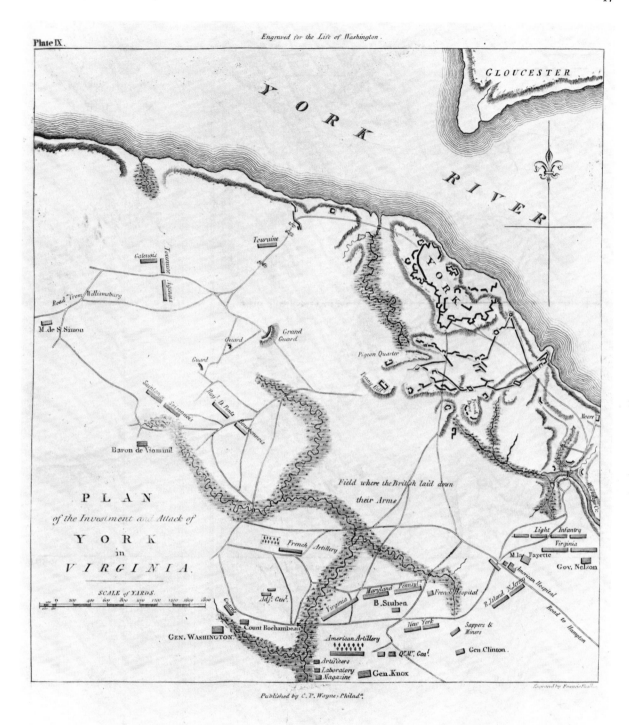

Fɪɢ. 4. Shallus, *Plan of the Investment and Attack of York in Virginia*. Philadelphia, 1807. Engraving; Plate IX from John Marshall, *Life of Washington* (Philadelphia, 1807) ; H. 10⅜″, W. 9¼″. (Winterthur.)

tween the two countries. Only one other American medal of this type is known. It is in the Masonic Library of the Grand Lodge in Philadelphia and was made for Benjamin Jones, Jr. (possibly the man who replaced Shallus as Robert Scot's assistant fifteen years earlier) , who was Third Worshipful Master of Lodge 121 in 1812. The symbols on his medal indicate this position, and these emblems could be used only by men who had presided over their lodge. This medal is similar in workmanship to the one signed by Shallus, but

cate in the 1780's. It may well have been he who introduced Shallus to the order.

The most interesting medal, and the one about which the least is known, is the medal for the Philadelphia Typographical Society (Fig. 7) . An excellent account of the society, first organized about 1789, is given in the James Mease section of *Picture of Philadelphia:*

One of the last acts of the life of the venerable Franklin, was to assist in the organization of a benefit society of Journeymen Printers, who held their meet-

Fig. 5. Shallus, Medal awarded to Victorine du Pont de Nemours. Philadelphia, 1807. Rose gold; dia. 1¾6″. (Winterthur 59.625.)

there is not enough evidence to attribute it definitely to him. Mark Wilks Collet entered Lodge 51 as an apprentice on February 13, 1812. His medal, dated July 20, 1812, may symbolize the date when he became a master in the lodge, although he apparently did not distinguish himself in the Masonic order. Shallus, on the other hand, was an active member of the Masonic order, Lodge 72, during the early 1800's, and held the positions of both secretary and president of his lodge. There is no record of his father's having been a Mason, but his teacher, Robert Scot, was active in the order and engraved a Masonic certifi-

ings during his life time at his house. This society was dissolved in the year 1795. In the year 1802, another was instituted, and incorporated in 1810, under the name of the "Philadelphia Typographical Society." It was formed not only upon the principle of mutual benefit, but also to equalise the price of labour, and thus to prevent imposition taking place upon the journeyman and employer. . . . No persons are eligible as members, who are not citizens of Pennsylvania, and who shall not have served an apprenticeship satisfactory to the board of directors, to whom he must make application in person. . . .

The members deem themselves bound to procure employment for one another in preference to those

FIG. 6. Shallus, Masonic Medal. Philalelphia, 1812. Rose gold; dia. 2⅜₆″. (Courtesy of The Henry Ford Museum, Dearborn, Michigan.)

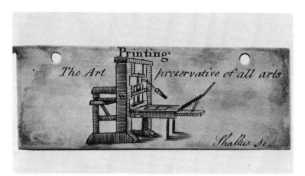

FIG. 7. Shallus, Medal for the Philadelphia Typographical Society. Philadelphia, 1789–1821. Silver; H. ⅞″, W. 2½″. (Mary E. Holt: photo, Winterthur.)

not belonging to the society; hence there is no excuse for a single member to be idle, and so much celebrity has this society obtained, that employers, not only in the city, but in all parts of the United States, when in want of good workmen, apply to the president to recommend them.[5]

Shallus engraved the medal for William Thaw, a mysterious person of whom no mention can be found in the Philadelphia directories between 1800 and 1825. He may have been one of those members who served his apprenticeship in Philadelphia and found employment elsewhere. Perhaps these medals were given to the members of the Typographical Society to commemorate incorporation; but without further evidence, no definite statement can be made. Membership was a valuable credential, and the silver medals may have been given to all members who met the stringent requirements of the society.

The Thaw medal is engraved with a press similar to that illustrated in Plate CCCCXV in Dobson's *Encyclopaedia* (Fig. 3). Possibly the legend "The Art preservative of all arts" was the motto for the Philadelphia Typographical Society,

[5] *Ibid.*, pp. 272–73.

as it was used by more than one typographer and printer, appearing as late as 1867 in an advertisement for printers' inks in *The Printers Circular,* a trade journal. The silver blank is struck with the initials "B & S" in a rectangle. This mark probably stands for the silversmiths who supplied the blank, although no such mark is recorded. During the years 1810 and 1811 a firm of jewelers, Liberty Brown and William Seale, was active. The initials of these men, and the period of their activity in Philadelphia, suggest that they may have supplied this blank to Shallus.

Three trade cards by Shallus are recorded. One was engraved for the coachmaker, Thomas Bringhurst of Germantown. The trade card for Bringhurst is one of the most skillful of the known engravings by Shallus. Unfortunately, only restrikes of the plate (Fig. 8), which is said to be preserved in the Philadelphia area, are known. No contemporary print has yet been found. This, the earliest recorded trade card by Shallus, was engraved sometime between 1809 and 1811 when he resided at 89 South Front Street. The Bringhurst family was large, and many of the members engaged in coachmaking. Although several members of the family maintained shops in the city of Philadelphia, Thomas worked only in Germantown. This fact reinforces the theory that Shallus had strong ties there, despite the lack of documentation.

The two trade cards that Shallus made for the Ann Peters Shallus Circulating Library are not so skillfully engraved. Among the last recorded works by Shallus, these cards were engraved either in 1817 or 1818 when the family was residing at 90 South Third Street. They may support the conjecture that his last illness was of fairly long duration and affected his work. It is also possible that they were hastily done while he executed the forty-one plates for *The Voyages of Captain Cook,* published in 1818 by Robert de Silver. His earlier work on the medals for Victorine du Pont and Mark Wilks Collet, as well as the Bringhurst trade card, evidence greater care and control. The cards for his wife are probably the most fanciful of his work and indicate a delight in, if not an understanding of, ornament (Figs. 9 and 10). His plump, flowing-haired women holding garlands and cornucopias are typical of the type of ornament and decoration popular during the second decade of the nineteenth century.

The circulating library was certainly a major

interest during the last ten years of Shallus' life. It must have been one of the largest in Philadelphia between 1810 and 1820. Books were popular in the city; at the time the Shallus library was active, there were at least four others in Philadelphia. Unfortunately, no catalogues survive to list the books and indicate the types of readers. One would imagine that each library contained basically the same books and did not tend to specialize, although a Mr. de la Grange ran a French circulating library during the early years of the nineteenth century.

An advertisement in *Poulson's American Daily Advertiser* on March 15, 1810, gives some idea of the size of the Shallus library. It reads in part:

Just Published, Shallus's Catalogues for the year 1810, of his new and increasing Circulating Library, Containing Upwards of 9,000 volumes of Modern Publications (With criticisms Occasionally Annexed) —No. 89,—South Front between Chestnut and Walnut Streets. . . . Philadelphia General Catalogue 218 pages price 25 cents. Select catalogue 84 pages, price 12½ cents.

The library had been operating for three years when, in 1814, it took the name "Ann Peters Shallus Circulating Library," which it continued to bear until it was closed. In 1818 the branch at 142 North Third Street was opened. This was announced in *Poulson's American Daily Advertiser* of October 12, stating:

Northern Library. Mrs. Shallus Presents her compliments to the Ladies and Gentlemen of the Northern part of the City, and begs leave to inform them that she has opened a library, for their accommodation . . .

Fig. 8. Shallus, Trade Card for Thomas Bringhurst (modern restrike). Philadelphia, 1809–1811. Engraving; H. 4¹⁵⁄₁₆", W. 3½". (Winterthur 62 × 58.)

F<small>IG</small>. 9. Shallus, Trade Card for Ann P. Shallus. Philadelphia, 1817–1818. Engraving; H. 2½″, W. 3¾″. (Courtesy of The New-York Historical Society, New York City, Bella C. Landauer Collection.)

where, she hopes, by strict attention, to merit a share of patronage, sufficient to support the undertaking. . . . The Library, No. 90 South Third Street, will also be continued as usual.

Apparently the branch did not succeed, for it is listed for only two years in the city directories. In 1821, the year of Shallus' death, the library, then located at 94 South Third Street, advertised another phase of book circulation: "Mrs. Shallus informs Gentlemen going on Voyages, that she can accomodate them with select Libraries of the most approved and interesting works, for the small sum of one or two dollars per month, or by the voyage."[6] Moreover, she had expanded the library to include hats, bonnets, caps, turbans, fans, and other fancy articles, as evidenced in the trade card.

By 1822 the library must have encountered

[6] *Poulson's American Daily Advertiser,* Aug. 11, 1821.

financial difficulties, for on February 9 she advertised in *Poulson's American Daily Advertiser:*

Mrs. S. informs her friends and the public in general, that she continues her establishment at No. 94 South Third Street, where may be had, all the latest English and American publications. . . . In consequence of the present scarcity of money, all subscriptions commenced after the first of February, 1822, will be at $5 per year, $2.75 for 6 months, and $1.50 per quarter—Payable in advance. N. B. Catalogues of the Library are just published.

Two years after this advertisement appeared, the library was closed and Ann Peters Shallus disappeared from the city directory. Probably, she returned to Germantown to live with her family, for in 1828 she filed the certificate of intestacy for her husband.

In 1816 Shallus tried his hand at publishing

when he produced, in two volumes, *Chronological Tables For Every Day in the Year*. Entries in the tables purport to give facts of historical interest for each day; one wonders, however, at some of them. One entry reads, "June 15, 1811 About 10 A.M. a fire broke out in the windsor chair makers shop, in Taylor's Alley." His father's connection with the Pennsylvania Legislature is mentioned twice. Perhaps he intended to follow this publication with others, but there is no record of later editions.

Francis Shallus' life seems typical of that led by the average educated man in the early days of the nation. A study of newspaper advertisements and city directories indicates that many craftsmen practiced more than one career. Engravers seem to have been no exception, suggesting that engraving alone was not lucrative enough to support more than a few. Shallus is especially interesting for his combination of activities. He was involved in the book trade as an illustrator, a librarian, and a publisher. That he was chosen to engrave the medal for the Philadelphia Typographical Society cannot have been accidental; he probably knew many of the members and numbered some among his friends. He was trained in a trade, but this did not lead him to specialize in his activities; he must have been a respected member of the community to have held high office in his Masonic lodge; and although he pursued a variety of interests, he achieved some measure of success and recognition in all.

FIG. 10. Shallus, Trade Card for Ann P. Shallus. Philadelphia, 1817–1818. Engraving; H. 3¾", W. 2½". (Courtesy of The New-York Historical Society, New York City, Bella C. Landauer Collection.)

Checklist

Unless otherwise noted, all sizes given are plate sizes. If the plate was not completely shown on the page, no dimension is given. Items illustrated here are marked by an asterisk.

Book Illustrations:

1793–1796

I. Thomas Dobson, *Encyclopaedia; or, A Dictionary of Arts, Sciences, and Miscellaneous Literature* (Philadelphia: Printed by Thomas Dobson, at the Stone House, No. 41, South Second Street, 1798).

A. *Volume 9* (issued in 1793).

Plate CCLII; "Scot Philad^{a} / FS"; H. $8\frac{1}{2}$″, W. $6\frac{3}{4}$″.

Plate CCLIII; "Scot. Philad^{a} / FS"; H. $8\frac{1}{2}$″, W. $5\frac{7}{8}$″.

Plate CCLVIII; "Scot Philad^{a} / FS"; H. 9″, W. $7\frac{1}{8}$″.

*Plate CCLXIV; "Scot Philad^{a} / FS / Shallus Sc."; H. 9″, W. $6\frac{13}{16}$″.

B. *Volume 10* (issued in 1793).

Plate CCLXXX; "Scot Philad^{a} / FS"; H. $9\frac{1}{4}$″, W. $7\frac{1}{4}$″.

Plate CCLXXXI; "Scot Philad^{a} / FS"; H. $9\frac{3}{8}$″, W. $6\frac{5}{8}$″.

Plate CCLXXXVII; "Scot Philad^{a} / FS"; H. $9\frac{3}{8}$″, W. $7\frac{1}{4}$″.

Plate CCLXXXVIII; "Scot Philad^{a} / FS"; H. $9\frac{5}{16}$″, W. $7\frac{1}{8}$″.

C. *Volume 11* (issued in 1794).

Plate CXCVII; "Scot Philad^{a} / FS"; H. 9″, W. $6\frac{7}{8}$″.

Plate CCC; "Scot Philad^{a} / FS"; H. $8\frac{3}{4}$″, W. $6\frac{7}{8}$″.

Plate CCCVI; "Scot Philad^{a} / FS"; H. $9\frac{1}{4}$″, W. $6\frac{7}{8}$″.

D. *Volume 12* (issued in 1794).

Plate CCCXI; "R. Scot & S Allardice / S"; H. $9\frac{3}{16}$″, W. $7\frac{3}{8}$″.

Plate CCCXIII; "R. Scot & S Allardice / S"; H. $9\frac{1}{2}$″, W. $6\frac{7}{8}$″.

Plate CCCXIV; "R. Scot & S Allardice / S"; H. $8\frac{7}{8}$″, W. $6\frac{3}{4}$″.

Plate CCCXVII; "R. Scot & S Allardice / Shallus Sc"; H. $8\frac{15}{16}$″, W. $6\frac{3}{4}$″.

Plate CCCXVIII; "R. Scot & S Allardice / Shallus sc"; H. $8\frac{1}{4}$″, W. $6\frac{3}{4}$″.

Plate CCCXIX; "R. Scot & S Allardice / S"; H. $9\frac{1}{2}$″, W. $6\frac{3}{4}$″.

E. *Volume 13* (issued in 1795).

Plate CCCLXIX; "R. Scot & S Allardice / Shallus sc."; H. $6\frac{3}{8}$″, W. $6\frac{5}{8}$″.

F. *Volume 15* (issued in 1796).

Plate CCCIV; "F. Shallus fe. Phil^{a}"; H. $8\frac{7}{8}$″, W. $6\frac{1}{2}$″.

*Plate CCCCXV; "F Shallus fe. Phil^{a}"; H. 9″, W. $7\frac{1}{8}$″.

1795

II. Oliver Goldsmith, *An History of the Earth and Animated Nature* (Philadelphia: Matthew Carey, 1795).

Volume II.

Opp. p. 36; *Buck of Juda, She Goat of Juda, Lynx.* Lower right, "Scot & Allardice"; under she goat, "Shallus"; H. $6\frac{7}{8}$″.

Opp. p. 87; *Rein Deer, Fallow Deer Female, Fallow Deer.* Lower right, "Scot & Allardice"; under reindeer, "Shallus sc"; H. 8″, W. $4\frac{1}{2}$″.

III. Smart, Goldsmith & Jackson, *The World Displayed* (Philadelphia, 1795). Page size, H. $8\frac{1}{8}$″, W. $4\frac{1}{8}$″.

A. *Volume I*—while working for Scot.

Opp. p. 79; *Columbus with 200 Foot, 20 Horse, & 20 Wolf Dogs, assisted by a body of the Islanders defeats 100,000 Indians.* Lower left, "Scot & Allardice sc."; beneath dogs, "Shallus sc"; H. $4\frac{1}{2}$″, W. $5\frac{3}{8}$″.

Opp. p. 189; *The Engagement between the Spaniards and People of Tobasco & their manner of fortifying themselves.* Lower left, "Scot & Allardice Sc"; lower left in plate, "Shallus Sc"; H. $4\frac{1}{2}$″, W. $5\frac{3}{8}$″.

B. *Volume II.*

Opp. p. 112; *Ten canoes of natives of an Island near the land of Desolation come and traffick with Captn. Davis.* Lower left, "Shallus Sc"; H. $3\frac{3}{4}$″, W. 5″.

Opp. p. 203; *Venables attacks and takes Jamaica.* Lower left, "Engraved by F. Shallus"; H. 3¾″, W. 5⅛″.

C. *Volume III.*

Opp. p. 441; *Sir Henry Middleton Escapes from the Turks.* "Engrav'd by F. Shallus"; H. 3⅞″, W. 5½″.

D. *Volume IV.*

Opp. p. 364; *A View of the City of Balbec from the South.* "F. Shallus Sculp.ͭ Phil.ᵃ"

E. *Volume V.*

Opp. p. 314; *The Tower of Horns at Ispahan.* "Engrav'd by F. Shallus"; H. 5½″, W. 3¾″.

1796

IV. The Bible (Philadelphia: Berriman, 1796).

Genesis Chap. II; [Adam and Eve]. "F. Shallus sculp.ͭ"; H. 4½″, W. 3¹⁄₁₆″·

1797

V. *Literary Museum or Monthly Magazine* (West Chester, Pa.: Derrick & Sharpless, January, 1797).

View of Herschell's Forty Foot Reflecting Telescope. "Engrav'd by F. Shallus"; H. 8¹³⁄₁₆″, W. 9⅞″.

1798

VI. *Atlas Minimus* (Philadelphia: Printed for Matthew Carey, 1798).

Page size, H. 4¾″, W. 3¾″.

Africa. "Shallus sc." (colored).

North America. "Engraved by F. Shallus."

Denmark.

1802

VII. The Bible (Philadelphia: Matthew Carey, 1802).

Plate 2A; *The Journeyings of The Children of Israel from Egypt.* . . . "F. Shallus Sculp.ͭ"; H. 19″, W. 16¾″.

Plate 3; *Canaan or the Land of Promise to Abraham and his Posterity.* "F. Shallus Sculp.ͭ"; H. 10½″, W. 8″.

Plate 10; *Map of the Assyrian, Babylonian Median and Persian Empires–D'Anville.* "Shallus sc."

VIII. S. S. Moore & T. W. Jones, *The Traveller's Directory* (Philadelphia: Matthew Carey, 1802).

Plate 1; *Philadelphia and the Commencement of the Road to New York.* "Shallus Sc."; H. 4⅝″, W. 7½″.

Plates 2 & 3; *Road from Philadel.ᵃ to New York.* "Shallus sc."; H. 7¼″.

Plates 4 & 5; *Road from Philadel.ᵃ to New York.* "Shallus sculpt"; H. 4¹⁄₁₆″, W. 7¼″.

Plates 6 & 7; *Road from Philadel.ᵃ to New York.* "Shallus sc."; H. 7½″, W. 4⅛″.

Plate 15; *Road from Philadelphia to Washington.* "Shallus sculp"; H. 7⅝″.

Plate 16; *Road from Philadelphia to Washington.* "Shallus sculp."

Plates 17 & 18; *Road from Philadelphia to Washington.* "Shallus sc."

Plates 19 & 20; *Road from Philadelphia to Washington.* "F. Shallus sc."

(These plates are also in the 1804 edition.)

1803

IX. Benjamin Smith Barton, *Elements of Botany as Outline of the Natural History of Vegetables* (Philadelphia: Printed for the Author, 1803).

Plate III; "F. Shallus Sc."; H. 7⅞″, W. 4⅝″.

Plate VIII; "F. Shallus Sc."; H. 7¹⁵⁄₁₆″.

Plate XIII; "Shallus fc'''; H. 7⅞″, W. 4⁹⁄₁₆″.

Plate XV; "Shallus sc"; H. 7⅞″, W. 4⅝″·

Plate XXII; "Shallus sc"; H. 7⅞″, W. 4⅝″.

Plate XXIII; "Shallus sc"; H. 7¹⁵⁄₁₆″.

(Plate III also in 1827 edition.)

X. A. F. M. Willich, *The Domestic Encyclo-*

paedia (Philadelphia: Abraham Small, 1803).

A. *Volume I.* Page size, H. 7⅞″, W. 4⅝″.

Opp. p. 161; *Dearborns Improved Balance.* "Shallus sc."

Opp. p. 202; *Elevation of the Longitudinal Front of the Floating Bath. Section and Elevation of the transverse side.* "Shallus sc."

Opp. p. 224; *Floating Baths at Hamburgh.* "Shallus sc."

Opp. p. 327; *Ice Boat.* "F. Shallus sculpt."

B. *Volume II.* Page size, H. 7⅞″, W. 4⅝″.

Opp. p. 273; *A Weighing Crane Invented by Mr. Ab^m Andrews.* "Shallus sc."

Opp. p. 373; *Dr. Darwins Improvements of the Drill-plough.* "Shallus sc."

Opp. p. 391; *Instruments for recovering the Drowned.* "Shallus sc."

Opp. p. 392; *Implements of Restoration from Drowning.* "Shallus sc."

C. *Volume III.* Page size, H. 7⅞″, W. 4⅝″.

Opp. p. 318; *Anatomy of the Horse.* "Shallus sc."

Opp. p. 320; *Anatomy of a Horse's Hoof.* "F.S."

D. *Volume V.* Page size, H. 7⅞″, W. 4⅝″.

Opp. p. 205; *Manning's & Knight's Turnip Drills & Transplanter.* "Shallus sc."

Opp. p. 352; *Sarjeant's Machine. Mr. Beshants' Waterwheel.* "Shallus sc."

(The 1821 edition contains the same plates.)

1805

XI. Oliver Evans, *The Abortion of the Young Steam Engineer's Guide* (Philadelphia: Fry and Kammerer, 1805).

Plate II; *Screw Mill—Invented & Patented by the Author.* "Shallus sc."; H. 4¼″, W. 3¼″.

Plate IV; *Earth Leveller.* "Shallus sc."; H. 4⅜″, W. 3¼″.

XII. *Carey's American Pocket Atlas* (Philadelphia: Matthew Carey, 1805).

Plate 20; *Louisiana.* "Shallus sc."

XIII. David Doyle, *Pinkerton's Geography* (Philadelphia, 1805).

A New Map of the World. "Shallus sc."; H. 10⅛″, W. 6⅛″.

1806

XIV. George Adams, *Lectures on Natural and Experimental Philosophy* (Philadelphia, 1806).

Volume IV.

Plate IV; *Astronomy.* "F. Shallus sc."; H. 7½″, W. 7½″.

Plate VII; *Astronomy.* "Shallus sc."; H. 7½″, W. 7¼″.

Plate IX; *Astronomy.* "F. Shallus sc."; H. 7½″, W. 8″.

Plate XII; *Astronomy.* "Shallus sc."; H. 7⅜″, W. 7½″.

(The 1807 edition also contains these plates.)

XV. James Ferguson, *Astronomy explained upon Sir Isaac Newton's Principles* (Philadelphia, 1806).

Plate XIII; "Shallus sc."; H. 8⅜″, W. 9³⁄₁₆″.

1807

XVI. John Marshall, *Life of Washington* (Philadelphia: C. P. Wayne, 1807).

Plate IV; *A Plan of the Northern Part of New Jersey.* "Drawn by S. Lewis from Surveys by Order of Gen. Washington." "Engraved by F^s Shallus / Published by C. P. Wayne Philadelphia."

Plate VI; *A Map of the Country which was the scene of operations of the Northern Army.* "Engraved by F. Shallus"; H. 11⅛″, W. 9⅜″.

Plate VIII; *A Map of those parts of Virginia, North Carolina, South Carolina & Georgia which were the scenes of the most important operations of the Southern Armies.* "Engraved by Francis Shallus. Published by C. P. Wayne, Philadelphia."

*Plate IX; *Plan of the Investment and Attack of York in Virginia.* "Engraved by Francis Shallus. Published by C. P. Wayne, Philadelphia"; H. 10⅜″, W. 9¼″.

1809

XVII. Thomas Town, *The Complete Military Tutor containing a system of Modern Tactics* (Philadelphia: The editor, 1809).
> Plate I; "F. Shallus sc."; H. 7$^{15}/_{16}$".
> Plate VIII; "Shallus sc."; H. 7$^7/_8$", W. 4$^3/_4$".
> Plate IX; "Shallus sc."; H. 7$^7/_8$", W. 4$^7/_8$".
> Plate XII; "Shallus Sc."; H. 7$^3/_4$", W. 4$^1/_2$".
> Plate XIII; "Shallus Sc."; H. 7$^7/_8$", W. 4$^{11}/_{16}$".
> Plate XIV; "Shallus Sc."; H. 7$^7/_8$", W. 4$^3/_4$".
> Plate XV; "F. Shallus sc."; H. 7$^7/_8$".
> Plate XVI; "Shallus Sc."; H. 7$^7/_8$", W. 4$^3/_4$".

1812

XVIII. The Bible (Philadelphia: Matthew Carey, 1812).
> Opp. p. 9; *Canaan or the Land of Promise to Abraham and his Posterity.* "F. Shallus sc."; H. 10$^1/_2$", W. 7$^1/_2$".
> Opp. p. 261; *The Purveyorships In the Reign of Solomon. 1. Kings. Chap. 4.* "F. Shallus sc."; H. 10$^5/_8$".
> Opp. p. 293; *Map of the Assyrian Babylonian Median and Persian Empires from D'Anville.* "Shallus sc."
> Opp. p. 340; *The Dominions of Solomon and his Allies.* Inset: *Sheba with the Voyage to Tarshish and Ophir.* "Fr. Shallus sc."

1813

XIX. *Hall's Distiller* (Philadelphia, 1813). *Improvements by Henry Witmer upon Anderson's Patent Condensing Tub.* "Engraved by F. Shallus No. 89 South Front St. Philad."
XX. The Bible (Philadelphia: M. Carey, 1814).
> Opp. p. 340; *The Dominions of Solomon and his Allies.* Inset: *Sheba with the Voyage to Tarshish and Ophir.* "F. Shallus sc."
> (Same plate as 1812.)

1818

XXI. *A Voyage to the Pacific Ocean undertaken by the Command of his Majesty, for Making discoveries in the Northern Hemisphere; performed under the direction of Captains Cook, Clerke and Gore* (Philadelphia: Published by Robert de Silver, No. 110 Walnut Street, 1818).
> A. *Volume I.*
>> Plate 1; *Capt. James Cook, FRS.* (Not signed); H. 7$^1/_8$", W. 4$^1/_2$".
>> Plate 2; *A View of Christmas Harbour, in Kerquelen's Land.* "Shallus sc."; H. 6$^7/_8$", W. 4$^1/_2$".
>> Plate 3; *A Man and Woman of Van Diemen's Land.* "F. Shallus Engraver 90 South Third S^t. Philad^a."; H. 6$^5/_8$", W. 4$^1/_8$".
>> Plate 4; *The Inside of a Hippah, in New Zealand.* (Not signed); H. 7", W. 4$^3/_8$".
>> Plate 5; *A Man of Mangea: A Woman of Eaoo.* "Shallus sc."; H. 7$^3/_8$", W. 4$^1/_2$".
>> Plate 6; *A View at Anamooka.* "F. Shallus sc."; H. 7$^7/_{16}$", W. 4$^{13}/_{16}$".
>> Plate 7; *The Reception of Captain Cook, in Hapaee.* "E. Shallus fct." [not by Shallus; possibly by one of his apprentices]; H. 7$^3/_8$", W. 4$^{11}/_{16}$".
>> Plate 8; *A Boxing-Match in Hapaee.* "Shallus Sc."; H. 7$^3/_8$", W. 4$^7/_8$".
>> Plate 9; *A Night Dance by Women in Hapaee.* "Shallus Sc."; H. 6$^3/_4$", W. 4$^1/_4$".
>> Plate 10; *Poulaho, King of the Friendly Islands. An Opposum.* See Vol. I, p. 65 "Shallus sc."; H. 6$^{15}/_{16}$", W. 4$^3/_8$".
>> Plate 11; *Poulaho, King of the Friendly Islands, Drinking Kave.* "Shallus Sc."; H. 6$^7/_8$", W. 4$^3/_8$".
>> Plate 12; *A Flatooka, or Morai in Tongataboo.* "Shallus Sc."; H. 7$^3/_8$", W. 4$^5/_8$".
>> Plate 13; *The Natche a Ceremony in Honour of the Kings Son in Tongataboo.* "Engraved by Francis Shallus No. 90 South Third St., Philada."; H. 6$^7/_8$", W. 4$^3/_8$".

Plate 14; *A Human Sacrifice in a Morai in Otaheite.* "F. Shallus Sc."; H. 6⅞", W. 4¼".

Plate 15; *A Dance in Otaheite.* "Shallus sc."; H. 7", W. 4⅜".

Plate 16; *A View of Huaheine.* "Shallus fecit."; H. 7⅜", W. 4¾".

Plate 17; *A Morai, in Atooi.* "Shallus sc."; H. 6¹⁵⁄₁₆", W. 4¼".

Plate 18; *An Inland View in Atooi.* "Shallus sc."; H. 7⅝", W. 4⅝".

Back to back, Plate 19–Plate 20; *A Man of the Sandwich Islands Dancing. A Man of the Sandwich Islands in a Mask.* "F. Shallus sc."; H. 7", W. 4⅜".

Plate 21; *An Offering before Captain Cook in Sandwich Islands.* "Shallus sc."

Plate 22; *A Sea Otter.* "Shallus sc."; H. 6⅞", W. 4¼".

Plate 23; *A Man and Woman of Nootka Sound.* [No signature; probably not Francis Shallus]; H. 7⅞", W. 4⅝".

Plate 24; *A View of the Habitations in Nootka Sound.* "F. Shallus sc."; H. 6⅞", W. 4½".

Plate 25; *The Inside of a House, in Nootka Sound.* "F. Shallus sc."; H. 6⅞".

Plate 26; *A View of Snug Corner Cove in Prince Williams Sound.* "Shallus sc."; H. 7⅜", W. 4⅜".

Plate 27; *Man and Woman of Prince Williams Sound.* "Shallus sc."; H. 7⅞".

Plate 28; *Canoes of Oonalashka.* "Shallus sc."; H. 6⅞", W. 4½".

Plate 29; *A Man and Woman of Onalashka.* "F. Shallus Sc."; H. 6½", W. 3⅞".

Plate 30; *The Tschuktsciii, and their Habitations.* "Shallus sc."; H. 6⅞", W. 4⅜".

B. *Volume II.*

Plate 31; *Inhabitants of Norton Sound and Their Habitations.* "Shallus sc."; H. 7⅞".

Plate 32; *Natives of Oonalashka, and their Habitations.* "Shallus sc."; H. 7¼", W. 4¾".

Plate 33; *The Inside of a House in Oonalashka.* "Shallus Sc."; H. 7¼", W. 4½".

Plate 34; *Terreeobog King of Owhyhee bringing presents to Captⁿ Cook.* "F. Shallus sc."; H. 6⅞", W. 4⅜".

Plate 35; *A View of the Town and Harbour of St. Peter and St. Paul in Kamtschatka.* "Shallus sc."; H. 6⅞", W. 4½".

Plate 36; *A Man of Kamtschatka, Travelling in Winter.* "Shallus Sc."; H. 7⅛", W. 4½".

No number; edge of plate clipped. *A Man and Woman of Kamtschatka.* "Shallus Sc."; H. 7¾".

Portraits:

Engraved portrait: *"Washington* / Published by F. Shallus. Engraver No 26 Walnut S: Philad." Oval; H. 1¹⁄₃₂", W. ⅝". No date.

Landscapes:

River view. "F. Shallus aquatint." No date.

Trade Cards:

1809–1811

*I. Rectangular form with example of coachmaker's craft centered above inscription: "Thomas Bringhurst / Coachmaker / Near the Old Six Mile Stone / Germantown. / Nᵒ. 1." Evenly spaced below are depictions of two coach forms and, inscribed between, "Grav'd by F. Shallus Nᵒ 89 Sᵒ Front S: Philad:" H. 4¹⁵⁄₁₆", W. 3½".

1816–1818

*II. Woman in Empire dress holding cornucopia in right hand and leaning on oval shield in which is inscribed: "Ann P. Shallus's / Circulating / Library / Nᵒ 90 / South Third Street / Philadelphia. / For Sale / Caps, Turbans / Fans / Hats, Bonnets, and a Variety of Fancy Articles." Beneath: "Francis Shallus Engraver Nᵒ 90 South Third S: Philad:"; H. 3¾", W. 2½".

*III. Ornamental borders around oval inset with woman leaning on pedestal on which is inscribed: "A. P. Shallus / Circulating / Library / Nº. 90 South / Third Street / Philadelphia." Beneath: "Francis Shallus Engraver Nº. 90 South Third Street Philadⁿ." H. 2½", W. 3¾".

Maps:

1799 & 1801

I. *Warner & Hanna's Plan of the City and Environs of Baltimore, Respectfully dedicated to the Mayor, City Council & Citizens thereof, by the Proprietors. 1801.* "Engraved by Francis Shallus, Philadⁿ."

3 States:

    1799a. [Errata given under Note] Lower right inset—*Degan's Wharf.* H. 29½", W. 20½".

    1799b. [No errata] H. 29½", W. 20½".

    1801. Lower right inset—*View of the Market Space Canal.* H. 29½", W. 20½".

II. *Map of the State of Delaware and the Eastern Shore of Maryland . . . from Actual Survey and Soundings made in 1799, 1800 and 1801.*

Bookplates:

Bookplate for William Morris. Date and measurements not known. (Source of information: Henry W. Fincham, *Artists and Engravers of British and American Book Plates* [London, 1897].)

Medals:

1807

*I. Obverse: "Mrs. Rivardi's Semʸ. Philadelphia 1807 Desert Rewarded"
Reverse: "Victorine Dupont de Nemours / F. Shallus fecit." Dia. 1³⁄₁₆".

1812

*II. Obverse: "Mark Wilks Collet Lodge 51— July 20th 1812 Shallus fecit."
Reverse: "HT ST KS WS" Masonic medal; Dia. 2³⁄₁₆".

*III. Obverse: "Printing The Art preservative of all arts Shallus Sc."
Reverse: "Philadelphia Typographical Society." In banner, "William Thaw." Stamped "B&S" in rectangle. H. ⅞", W. 2½".

William Williams: New American Discoveries

William H. Gerdts

ONE of the most fascinating of the English artists to come to America in the middle of the eighteenth century was William Williams (active *ca.* 1747–1790). The purpose of this study is to present recently discovered paintings by Williams and to offer a suggestion concerning one of his well-known works. A number of articles concerning the facts known about the career of this rather mysterious figure have been published,[1] and it is not the intent of this writer to review them. Further research has been undertaken in regard to Williams, particularly concerning his years in England.[2] How much we know about the artist's early life depends upon the extent to which we can accept his fictionalized autobiography, *The Journal of Llewellyn Penrose, a Seaman,* as factual. Furthermore, additional problems are created by the number of American artists named William Williams. Most commonly confused with the subject of this article is William Joseph Williams (1759–1823), although he was obviously a later figure.[3]

Despite the interest aroused by Williams' paintings, scarcely more than a dozen or so are known. This number is in great contrast with the hundreds of existing paintings by his contemporary John Wollaston—whose stay in America was of a far shorter duration than the almost thirty years that Williams was active here—or even the relatively large number of works by Joseph Blackburn. Both Wollaston and Blackburn came to America later than Williams and returned to England much earlier.

Williams' artistic style, although somewhat more primitive than that of his more prolific contemporaries mentioned above, was a much livelier version of the rococo and far more personal. His stylistic approach was obviously related to that of the English "little masters" and shows the particular influence of Arthur Devis (1711–1787). This group of English artists were specialists in small, full-length portraits, either single or group, which found increasing patronage in the middle of the eighteenth century from the growing English middle class. There is also a degree of variety to his art, evidenced in part by his interest in the "conversation group." This informal, outdoor portraiture was popular in England with such artists as Devis, Zoffany, and others, but was not too common among the artists active on this side of the Atlantic.[4] Whether this was due to a lack of re-

[1] William Sawitzky, "William Williams, First Instructor of Benjamin West," *Antiques,* XXXI (May, 1937), 240–42, and "Further Light on the Work of William Williams," *The New-York Historical Society Quarterly Bulletin,* XXV (July, 1941), 101–12. See also, James T. Flexner, "The Amazing William Williams: Painter, Author, Teacher, Musician, Stage Designer, Castaway," *Magazine of Art,* XXXVII (Nov., 1944), 242–46, 276–78, and "Benjamin West's American Neo-Classicism, with Documents on West and William Williams," *The New-York Historical Society Quarterly,* XXXVI (Jan., 1952), 5–41.

[2] Professor David Dickason, Indiana University, has been working on Williams as an author and has studied his artistic career in England.

[3] George C. Groce and David H. Wallace, *The New-York Historical Society's Dictionary of Artists in America, 1564–1860* (New Haven: Yale University Press, 1957), list five artists working in America with the name William

Williams. There was also an English painter of note with this name, as well as "William Williams, the Sweet Singer of Wales"!

[4] The conversation group probably reached its apex in America at the end of the eighteenth century with the works of Henry Benbridge and the really beautiful examples of James Peale, such as the painting of the Ramsey-Polk family and that of his own family.

FIG. 1. William Williams, *Woman with Book* (Old Testament sibyl). Philadelphia, 1767. Oil on panel; H. 20¼″, W. 15¼″. (Deerfield Academy: photo, Vose Gallery.)

laxed, gracious living, such as is mirrored in the English conversation groups or whether many of the artists active in the colonies simply were not capable of dealing with the more complex compositional and spatial demands of the conversation group might be debated. Even in Williams' single portraits—such as those of the Hall children, and particularly his best-known portrait, that of Deborah Hall now in the Brooklyn Museum—his concern with accessories and landscape backgrounds was far greater than that of most of his American contemporaries and predecessors.

Although Williams' *oeuvre* has been only slightly enlarged by discoveries of recent years, his repertoire seems considerably greater than almost any other colonial artist, notwithstanding the rare classical and religious works attributed to Gustavus Hesselius, as well as the latter's Indian portraits. Of course, we know from artists' inventories and other contemporaneous reports that the paintings existent in the colonies were by no means limited to one variety, the standard portrait, and we can be almost sure that a fair number of them were the works of colonial artists rather than their European counterparts. The problem, however, is that so few nonportraits by these colonials have survived. A missing still life by Matthew Pratt, a possible landscape by Robert Feke, a unique genre painting by John Greenwood, are all tantalizing suggestions of the diversity of artistic production that might have existed in Colonial America but which now seems lost.

Of the portraits by Williams that have come to light in recent years, the most significant is that of *Master Stephen Crossfield*. It is now in the collection of The Metropolitan Museum of Art,[5] and in many ways closely resembles the Hall portraits in the Brooklyn Museum and The Henry Francis du Pont Winterthur Museum. However, the main concern here is several nonportrait depictions by Williams. The first two of these in point of time are a pair of religious works, formerly owned in the Albany area and recently by the Vose Galleries of Boston. One, a *Woman with Book,* is now in the collection of Deerfield Academy (Fig. 1); the other, *Woman with Hour Glass and Skull,* is privately owned (Fig. 2).

The two works are obviously companion pictures; both depict women, one inside a cave and the other at the entrance to a cave. They were painted before Williams left Philadelphia for New York, as noted on the *Woman with Book.* The date "1767" appears in each lower corner; however, the date in the lower left corner is not legible (Figs. 3 and 4). The two pictures, although rather crudely painted, reveal a harsh but dramatic contrast of light and dark. This contrast, together with a rather tame diagonal axis of the figures and a very free, painterly approach, suggests a basis in the baroque style of the previous century; and, indeed, it is possible (or even probable) that these works were based on prints of earlier paintings. Since this was an accepted approach for American portrait painters of the eighteenth century (in their choice of pose, costumes, accessories, and the like), it is even more probable that prints were copied when nonportrait forms were painted, where the subject models were not available. Unfortunately, however, no European source, either painting or print, has yet been found for either of these pictures.

Both paintings are undoubtedly of a religious nature: the signed and dated one represents an Old Testament sibyl, and the pendant depicts the Magdalene in her cave. The two pictures thus symbolize the Old and New Testaments respectively, and this is emphasized by the large, prominent book in each picture. The symbolism is carried further by the tall, round, Romanesque tower in the background of the painting of the sibyl (a usual iconographic representation where Romanesque forms, usually rounded, stand for the synagogue as contrasted with Gothic architectural forms for the Christian church—such symbolism reaches from the Middle Ages itself to the rounded towers in the religious works of Georges Rouault) and by a cross placed before the Magdalene. The contrast between the two figures is especially noteworthy: the opposing directions in which the figures lean; the rather intense, pathetic expression on the face of the Magdalene compared with the somewhat dreamy quality of the sibyl; and, of course, the outdoor setting of the one and the cave interior of the other.

Corresponding with this contrast of setting is that of the color scheme. The painting of the sibyl is light and brilliant, with a bright blue sky and a knoll of green grass in front of the figure. The sibyl is richly and lavishly dressed in pink and

---

[5] The Metropolitan Museum is planning to publish information about this new acquisition soon; therefore, it is not illustrated or described here. In any case, this article emphasizes Williams' nonportrait achievements in the visual arts.

FIG. 2. Williams, *Woman with Hour Glass and Skull* (Mary Magdalene). Philadelphia, *ca.* 1767. Oil on panel; H. 21″, W. 16″. (Collection of the author: photo, Vose Gallery.)

gold, with a bright vermilion shoe showing. The Magdalene, on the other hand, is a somber work painted mostly in browns and blacks, with the figure on one side and the open book on the other almost white by contrast. Further color accents are

FIG. 3. Williams, Detail of Signature (lower left) of Figure 1. (Deerfield Academy: photo, Vose Gallery.)

FIG. 4. Williams, Detail of Signature (lower right) of Figure 1. (Deerfield Academy: photo, Vose Gallery.)

the vermilion glow of the flame above and the shiny vessel below at the feet of the figure. The Magdalene is a well-composed painting, not only in view of the careful balancing of color accents and highlights, but due to the repetition of globu-

lar forms: the Magdalene's breast, the skull she holds in her hand, and the pot at her feet. The partial nudity of the figure is unconventional for the period, although certainly not unique.[6] The hourglass in the painting of the Magdalene is a rather unusual feature.

The purpose of the two panels is not known. Williams might have copied them from prints either for the decoration of a private chapel or for use in speculation or advertising. In any case, their histories prior to their recent discovery are not known.

A somewhat later painting by Williams expands his repertoire in another direction—that of landscape. His *Imaginary Landscape,* dated 1772, is now in the collection of the Newark Museum (Fig. 5).[7] The subject of landscape painting in Colonial America is fascinating and intriguing, particularly because of the variety of approaches to landscape backgrounds in colonial portraits, from the specific monuments of early Boston which appear in John Smibert's *Portrait of Francis Brinley* to the more generalized, romantic backgrounds in many of Robert Feke's portraits. Pure landscapes by Smibert, Feke, and other colonial painters are, however, almost unknown; thus the Newark painting becomes a document of historic importance as well as an intriguing work of art. The picture descended in the family of the donor, Miss Clara Lee. Curiously, an inscription on the back notes that it was painted by an early member of the family, one Samuel Stibbs, in Princeton, New Jersey, in 1769. Proper authorship was established only after recent cleaning exposed a signature and date.

It is known that Williams did, indeed, paint landscapes, for in his advertisement in the *New York Gazette and Weekly Mercury* of May 8, 1769, he noted that he undertook "painting in general, viz., History, Portraiture, landskip, sign painting, lettering, guilding and stewing smalt." By this time, Williams had moved from Philadelphia to New York, but, as we shall see, landscape painting

[6] See, for instance, the classical scenes by Gustavus Hesselius or John Singleton Copley's *Galatea* and his *Mars, Venus and Vulcan.*

[7] The painting was previously discussed and illustrated by The Newark Museum, *The Museum,* X (Winter, 1958), 12–17, and figured in the Allentown Art Museum's exhibition "The World of Benjamin West," May 1–July 31, 1962. See *The World of Benjamin West* (Allentown, Pa.: The museum, 1962), Cat. No. 38, p. 68; Illus. No. 38.

FIG. 5. Williams, *Imaginary Landscape*. Philadelphia (?) , 1772. Oil on canvas; H. 16″, W. 18½″. (Newark Museum, Gift of Miss Clara Lee, 1922.)

was not a new addition to his repertoire. (Such works as his Old Testament sibyl and his Magdalene might fall into the broad category of history painting.)

Although Williams' portraits are definitely and appropriately in the rococo style of the mid-eighteenth century, this work, along with the previously described religious panels, reverts to the baroque seventeenth century. It is a work of rich chiaroscuro contrasts, with a dramatic tonality of vermilions against dark, monochromatic tones and a glistening, dark blue-green sea, not unlike the coloration of his Magdalene. Swift diagonal move-

ment back into space, following the axis of the ships and the lines of the foaming waves, creates the illusion of deep recession. Typical of Williams' art, as for instance his better-known portraits, is the attempt at enframement within the composition: the giant tree at the right not only repeats the verticality on that side but creates a canopy above, while the base of the trunk sweeps along to the rocky foreground to define the lower part of the painting.

What is surprising in the painting is that the ships at sea and the two figures on shore (one of which points toward the ships, the sea, and the distant unknown) are more typical of the six-teenth than of the mid-eighteenth century. The tower behind the figures is of no era whatsoever. Like the synagogue tower in the painting of the sibyl, it is a round, basically Romanesque struc-ture; but, strangely, it is surmounted by a half-timbered building! This, with the background, where the outline of a distant city shows Gothic spires and towers, presents an odd—indeed fantas-tic—conglomeration of architectural styles, none of which relates to New York at the time Williams produced this work. Again, as with the sibyl and the Magdalene, the purpose of this painting is not

as the man who put into his hands, when a boy, the first books he had ever read on the subject of painting, and showed him, in specimens from his own pencil, the first oil pictures he had ever seen." [8] More specifically, landscape painting figured in West's first encounter with Williams, for the "Advertisement" in the 1815 edition of Williams' *Journal of Llewellyn Penrose* records West as stating that, as a boy, on visiting Phila-delphia "I saw a person carrying a picture, a land-scape, the first I believe I had ever seen; I was very much struck with it, and desired [him] to shew it to me; he did." [9] The fact that both the

FIG. 6. Benjamin West, *Landscape with Cow*. Philadelphia, before 1760. Oil on panel; H. 30″, W. 52″. (Pennsylvania Hospital.)

known, but the likelihood of a print source, while not impossible, is more remote.

What adds interest to this work is the compari-son it affords with the well-known *Landscape with Cow* by Benjamin West (1738–1820), now in the collection of the Pennsylvania Hospital (Fig. 6). This youthful effort by West is, of course, much earlier than Williams' landscape—probably pre-dating it by twenty years or more—but the rela-tionship between the two is striking, particularly in view of Williams' position as an early instructor of the young West. Dunlap wrote of Williams that "Benjamin West remembered him with gratitude,

Imaginary Landscape and the *Landscape with Cow* are landscapes—rare survivals, indeed, from Colonial America—suggests that West may have learned more from Williams than the portrait art. Both works involve ships at sea, but of more sig-nificance are the giant trees seen in each. Most im-portant however, is the introduction by West of three separate variations of round, Romanesque architectural forms in his painting. He may have

[8] William Dunlap, *History of the Rise and Progress of the Arts of Design in the United States* (New York: Ben-jamin Bloom, 1965), I, 30.

[9] London: John Murray, 1815; I, ix–x.

learned these from Williams, or from picture- or copybooks which Williams owned and showed him, but certainly they were not based on actual forms prevalent in colonial architecture!

The final work discussed here is Williams' well-known painting entitled *Conversation Piece,* dated 1775, which is now in The Henry Francis du Pont Winterthur Museum (Fig. 7). Many aspects of Williams' style are present here: the interest in landscape and spatial recession; the enframement of the figures by natural elements; and even a round, Romanesque tower in the right background. What does this painting signify? It has always been referred to as a "conversation piece" or a portrait of a gentleman and a lady. However, despite the fact that distorted figures were part of Williams' artistic style, the trait is carried almost to the point of caricature in this painting, particularly when compared with some of his other conversation pieces—for example, *The William Denning Family* and the painting of *John Wiley, His Mother and Sisters.* It is suggested here that, rather than a conversation piece, this might be a theatrical portrait—a depiction of two actors in an eighteenth-century stage production, which (if such is the case) was almost certainly comedy. This type of painting, rare in America until such early nineteenth-century depictions as William Dunlap's illustrations of the theatricalization of James Fenimore Cooper's *The Spy,* was not uncommon in eighteenth-century England. Contemporary British representations, from either literature or the theater, include Joseph Highmore's paintings from Samuel Richardson's *Pamela,* theatrical scenes involving such actors as David Garrick, and paintings by Philip de Loutherbourg. Added weight is given to this suggestion by the obviously theatrical nature of the scenery, which has been recognized as relating to de Loutherbourg's influence on theatrical scenery after 1772.[10] Indeed, two or three successions of

wings are noticeable, and the lighting from below again suggests the stage. In any case, theatrical qualities have long been recognized as characteristic of Williams' style. In fact, while in Philadelphia he worked on the construction of the second theater built in Southwark and painted a new set of scenery for this theater.[11] Consequently, it would not be surprising to find Williams, as a scene painter, involved in theatrical representations.

If this work, dated 1775, is a theatrical representation, the question arises as to whether it was painted in America or in England. We know that Williams returned to England sometime during the Revolution, but the exact date is not known. Theatrical events virtually ceased in America during the conflict, and in some cities they were strictly banned. Thus, it may be that the work was painted by Williams shortly after he returned to England, an event that would then have had to occur by 1775. Neither the real nor theatrical identities of the two figures are known, but it has been pointed out that the woman looks very much like Kitty Clive, the popular comedienne of the English stage.[12]

Even as a conversation piece, this work is certainly atypical of colonial art in general. With this painting, and the addition of two religious pictures and a landscape to his *oeuvre,* Williams emerges as probably the most versatile artist in the annals of American colonial art—an artist both unique and personal in style and courageous, ambitious, and inventive in the variety of his artistic themes.

---

[10] Philip H. Highfill, Jr., consultant in literature at the

Folger Shakespeare Library and professor of English literature at George Washington University, has been most helpful in analysis of the possible theatrical source for this picture. He states that "there is hardly any doubt . . . that the Williams painting represents a theatrical scene."
[11] J. Thomas Scharf and Thompson Westcott, *History of Philadelphia, 1609–1884* (Philadelphia: L. H. Everts & Co., 1884), II, 1030.
[12] A suggestion made by Professor Highfill.

FIG. 7. Williams, *Conversation Piece*. Philadelphia, 1775. Oil on canvas; H. 33³/₁₆″, W. 39⅛″. (Winterthur 58.1732.)

Detail of Figure 18, page 184.

Johann Christoph Heyne
Pewterer, Minister, Teacher

Eric de Jonge

WILLIAM PENN'S invitation to participate in his "Holy Experiment" attracted
to Pennsylvania people from all walks of
life throughout Europe. Those who dreamed of a
land where oppression for religious beliefs was not
tolerated, where a man was not a pawn in the
hands of rulers of petty principalities, and where
the archaic regulations of entrenched craft guilds
did not rule the lives of artisans and craftsmen
were countless. So strong was the appeal of Penn's
message that thousands sold themselves and their
families into bondage for many years and became
indentured servants sustained by the hope that
their day of freedom would arrive. By the second
quarter of the eighteenth century, the trickle of
non-English immigrants had grown to such proportions that ship after ship literally "dumped"
human cargo upon the wharves of colonial seaports, particularly in the city of Philadelphia.

This human cargo, coming from Central Europe, was not (as is often assumed) uniform in
religious belief, nor in customs and habits, which
were as diverse as the individuals who formed that
cargo, although a common language gave the appearance of homogeneity. The dialects and idioms
of the immigrants were varied; but basically they
were German, since High German had been, for
centuries, the *lingua franca* of artisans, craftsmen,
and others whose trades took them to many parts
of Europe. While they all spoke, understood, and
generally could read and write German, they did
not think in terms of a unified people.

In the American colonies, this unifying linguis-
tic bond was so strong that, some two hundred
years later, it still affects entire counties of the
Commonwealth of Pennsylvania, where these lan-
guage-related immigrants settled together. Surrounded by a population of predominantly Eng-

lish stock not infrequently hostile to them, they
gathered in tightly knit settlements that gradually
influenced adjacent counties. While a certain acculturation took place among themselves, they
strongly resisted the adoption of the cultural traits
and customs of their English neighbors. Although
most of these immigrants were superb farmers,
their numbers included excellent artisans and
craftsmen whose products found ready acceptance
far beyond the boundaries of their settlements.
Subsequent relocations by some of these migrants
spread to other areas many of their customs and
traditions, which were reflected in the designs and
forms of even the most basic tools and utensils.

Understandably, artisans and craftsmen fashioned their products in accordance with the skills
and designs they had learned in Europe; but the
cosmopolitan atmosphere of the larger towns, such
as Philadelphia, required some modifications.
Great numbers of newcomers passed through this
port on the way to the fertile interior of the colony, where settlements and villages in need of
specialists attracted accomplished craftsmen.

The skills of metal workers were particularly
in great demand. It had been assumed that no
accomplished pewterer had established himself
outside the Philadelphia area until a magnificent
pewter communion flagon bearing the touch "I.
C. H. Lancaster" became known in 1928. An engraved inscription on the flagon describes it as a
gift of John Dirr to the Saint Peter's Church,
Mount Joy Township, Lancaster, Pennsylvania.
The inscription is dated "1771." Attempts to identify the maker of the flagon were unsuccessful at
that time,[1] but several years later his identity was

---

[1] "The Editor's Attic," *Antiques*, XIII (Feb., 1928),
112–13.

Fig. 1. Johann Christoph Heyne (left and right) and Heinrich Mueller (center), Communion Flagons. Lancaster, Pa.; (Heyne) 1750–1753, (Mueller) *ca.* 1733. Pewter; H. 12½", top Dia. 3½", bottom Dia. 6½". (Trinity Lutheran Church, Lancaster, Pa.)

established conclusively.[2] With the discovery of this flagon, Lancaster became a "pewter town" for historians and collectors and the pewterer Johann Christoph Heyne, the central figure of a fascinating research project into the background of an American craftsman.[3]

Subsequently, three pewter communion flagons in the Trinity Lutheran Church in Lancaster served as keys in unlocking the closed doors of Heyne's life before 1757 (Fig. 1). Two of the objects were marked with Heyne's large touch (Fig. 2). It was formerly assumed that the strap-handled Bavarian flagon (made by Heinrich Mueller, a German craftsman) in the Trinity Lutheran Church had served as a model for Heyne's work and that the flagons were acquired, by special order, for the dedication of a new sanctuary in 1766. It is now concluded that neither is the case. Although their resemblance to the Mueller flagon

[2] John J. Evans, Jr., "I.C.H., Lancaster Pewterer," *Antiques*, XX (Sept., 1931), 150–53.
[3] Eric de Jonge, "Swedish Influence on American Pewter," *Antiques*, LXVII (March, 1955), 230–32.

is great, those by Heyne are probably the earliest flagons made by the then independent pewterer and were probably produced as early as 1750 or 1753. Multiple sets of flagons have been documented as early as 1754 for log churches in rural Pennsylvania smaller than Trinity in Lancaster. There is no reason to believe that these for Trinity would not predate 1766 (when the new church, allegedly planned by Trinity after a local Indian treaty of 1757 promised security, was dedicated).

The simplicity of the flagon by Heinrich Mueller suggests that it was not used as a model by Heyne. The Germanic strap handle and the plain ball thumb rest (or thumbpiece) would have been both simpler and less expensive to provide than the components of the Heyne flagons. Therefore, the departure from the Mueller design can be attributed to neither the stylistic changes that had occurred during the years intervening between the two examples (since bud-end and strap handles were fashionable concurrently in some European countries, and Heyne's shop

FIG. 2. Heyne, Large Touch, magnified five times. (Winterthur 55.623.)

equipment, probably limited, would have given preference to the selection of a strap handle [Fig. 3]), nor to Heyne's Anglo-American acculturation in the stronghold of mid-European conservatism. Therefore, a more plausible reason for the differences must be found.

A knowledge of the European training and working conditions of Heyne's day made possible a search for prototypes of these features.[4] Many puzzles involving atypical features might be solved by reconstructing the background, training, and probable itineraries of American artisans. Correlation of their apprenticeships, their former masters, their experiences as journeymen, and their travels could make possible an evaluation of stylistic motifs and designs that do not fit the pattern of their normal production or that of their localities.

Johann Christoph Heyne (to give him his German name, or Hayne, as he signed his name on occasion) was born in Saxony on December 3, 1715.[5] In accordance with custom, he was apprenticed at age fourteen. He was indentured to a still-unknown master pewterer for four years, a period mandatory under the rules of the Saxon

pewterers' guild of 1708. While a number of men named Heyne are listed on the guild rolls, Johann Christoph Heyne is not among them. In general, these rolls are reliable, but occasional discrepancies have been found. According to the late Professor Erwin Hintze (the compiler of a seven-volume work on German pewterers),[6] a Tobias Heyne served his apprenticeship in Rochlitz, Saxony, from 1698 to 1702, while a Tobias Heyne from the same Saxon town is listed on the Stockholm, Sweden, guild rolls as a journeyman from 1700 to 1703.[7] Although such a coincidence is possible, it is highly improbable.

A man named Johann Christian Heyne was a master pewterer in Rochlitz, Saxony, until 1755;[8] he must not be confused with Johann Christoph Heyne, who apparently came from Rosswein, Saxony.[9] It is not known whether the latter lived there as a youth, served his apprenticeship there, or worked there as a journeyman, for Professor Hintze lists no pewterer in Rosswein from the first half of the seventeenth century until 1736.[10]

It is difficult to understand and evaluate the motivations behind a German artisan's work and habits without a brief explanation of German guild customs and regulations.[11] These, developed over the centuries, inexorably governed the lives, traditions, and working methods of the members, to the greatest imaginable extent, far into the nineteenth century. One of the inflexible rules required a young artisan to travel for several years after finishing his apprenticeship.[12] Unless a craftsman was guild-connected, beginning with apprenticeship, he could find employment only in remote areas. Without the consent of his guild, he could not set himself up in his own shop; and often he could not marry without the approval of his peers.[13] In many localities, if his religious be-

[4] R. Wissell, *Des alten Handwerks Recht und Gewohnheit* (2 vols.; Berlin, Germany: Verlag Ernst Wasmuth, 1929).

[5] "Necrologies" (Moravian Archives, Bethlehem, Pa. [hereafter MAB]).

[6] Erwin Hintze, *Deutsche Zinngiesser und Ihre Marken* (Leipzig, Germany: Karl W. Hiersemann, 1921), I, 160–61.

[7] Albert Loefgren, *Svenska Tenngjutarehantverkets Historia* (Stockholm, Sweden: Nordiska Museets Foerlag, 1933), II, 226.

[8] Hintze, *Deutsche Zinngiesser*, I, 224.

[9] Loefgren, *Svenska Historia*, III, 483.

[10] Hintze, *Deutsche Zinngiesser*, I, 225–26.

[11] For such an explanation, see Karl Hegel, *Staedte und Gilden* (2 vols.; Leipzig, Germany: Duncker & Humblot, 1891).

[12] Eric de Jonge, "Johann Christopher Heyne: Swedish Influence on American Pewter," *Pewter Collectors' Club of America*, III, Bulletin No. 34 (May, 1955), 71–76.

[13] F. Frensdorff, *Das Zunftrecht insbesondere Norddeutschlands und die Handwerkerehre* (Leipzig, Germany: Duncker & Humblot, 1907).

Fɪɢ. 3. Heyne (left) and Mueller (right), View of Handle and Hinge Arrangement of Two Flagons of Figure 1. (Trinity Lutheran Church.)

liefs differed from those prevailing, he was not employable as a journeyman and, thus, could never aspire to become a master craftsman.[14]

Such intolerance might also have been encountered by those who adhered to a sect differing even slightly with the tenets of the prevailing denomination. In general, the reason for such blackballing was the fact that both apprentices and journeymen were considered members of the master's household; and, with church attendance compulsory, a master could not afford to have a member of his household absent from the service. These were some of the inescapable customs and roadblocks Johann Christoph Heyne encountered after terminating his apprenticeship.

While a journeyman's name might be found on pewterers' guild rolls, it would be virtually impossible to trace his perambulations through Europe. Rare, indeed, are existing work certificates for individual journeymen, and these refer only to a period of employment in a particular town. The search for an individual journeyman in the records would be virtually a lifetime task. Hintze gathered, in seven volumes, the names and touches of about twelve thousand master pewterers in Germany, Austria, Switzerland, and elsewhere, each employing many journeymen. When death terminated his work, many areas of Germany remained unsearched.

Knowing something of the guild customs, one can learn much from a careful analysis of Heyne's flagons. Workmanship, stylistic features, and designs enable one to assign objects to certain periods, to countries, and even to specific localities. Significant variants from generally accepted norms require a deeper search for their *raison d'être,* since they may be indicative of the designer's past experiences. Such is the case with the Heyne flagons. For a long time it was assumed that the bud-end handles of these flagons were indicative of his Anglo-American acculturation and that the Teutonic thumb rest was set upon a little platform to overcome the pronounced upsweep of the handle. This arrangement was unknown in Heyne's native Saxony and led to the conclusion that, unless it was his own innovation, he must have encountered it in his journeys—providing, of course, that this arrangement was an

entity and not a grouping of individual features fathered by necessity.

Bud-end handles and ball thumb rests-on-platforms, however, were indigenous to Swedish hollow ware. The "English" bud-end handle was already fashionable in Sweden by the middle of the seventeenth century, probably antedating its adaptation to the English hollow ware (Fig. 4). The ball thumb rest on a platform was equally native to Sweden, in conjunction with the continental strap handle (Fig. 5), as well as with the solid or hollow-cast handle (Fig. 6). This evidence should serve to disprove the contention that Heyne copied the Mueller flagon. There are, of course, many variants in the combination of these two distinct features. Other features (the distinctive spout and erect thumb rest), equally indigenous to Sweden, are also evident in Heyne's flagons. With these as prototypes, it is not mere surmise that the path of the young journeyman led to northern Germany and Scandinavia. It has been established that, after a year's travel, Heyne arrived in Stettin, an

FIG. 4. Petter Noren, Seventeenth-Century-Type Tankard. Hedemora, Sweden, *ca.* 1765. Pewter; H. 8½". (Nordiska Museet, Stockholm, Sweden.)

[14] O. D. Potthoff, *Kulturgeschichte des deutschen Handwerks* (Hamburg, Germany: Hanseatische Verlagsanstalt, 1938).

important German port having close trade connections with Sweden. Moreover, in 1735, he was
registered as a journeyman working for Maria
Sauer, the widow of the pewterer Jakob Sauer, in
Stockholm.[15] This was not as unusual an employment as it appears. Pewterers' guilds always took
care of their own and permitted a master's widow
to continue the operation of her late husband's
shop with the help of apprentices and qualified
journeymen. In some cases, the only restriction
imposed upon her was that a *W* (for widow) be
added to the master's touch or a deep file-cut be
made across the design of the die, both alterations
leaving distinct impressions when struck upon a
pewter object.

Heyne was still on the guild rolls in 1737, but
after that year his name can no longer be traced.
For five years he does not appear in available
records; but, in 1742, he was mentioned on the
ship's list of the snow *Catherine,* which carried
the "First Sea Congregation" of the Moravians to
Philadelphia.[16] Obviously, Heyne had joined the
Moravian Church, or *Unitas Fratrum,* sometime

[15] Loefgren, *Svenska Historia,* III, 483 and 343.
[16] "Diarium Bethlehem" (1742–1871), Vol. I (MAB).

FIG. 6. Carl Saur, I, Tankard. Stockholm, Sweden, 1735–
1781. Pewter; H. 9". (Nordiska Museet, Stockholm,
Sweden.)

between 1737 and 1742. It is possible that the
meticulous records in the headquarters of the denomination, in Herrenhut, Saxony, might tell
where and when he joined that body, what moti-
vated him, and why he was selected to join the
members of the "First Sea Congregation."

One of the establishments founded by the
Moravian Brethren was a colony of adherents at
Pilgerruhe in Holstein, Denmark. When, in 1742,
the membership of the colony had to be replen-
ished, the church chartered the snow *Catherine*
for the transport of Moravians to Pilgerruhe. The
group, chiefly Germans, was called the "First Sea
Congregation" (there were two more—one in
1743 and the other in 1749).[17] Refused admission
by the Danish government, the *Catherine* quickly
changed course and sailed from London for the
American colonies on March 15, 1742. After arriving at Philadelphia on June 7, 1742, those of
non-English descent pledged allegiance to the government. Johann Christoph Heyne's name was on
both the ship's roll and the list of oath takers.

Heyne, with the other members of the congre-

FIG. 5. Heinrich Gottfried Pschorn, Wine Pitcher.
Stockholm, Sweden, datemark 1738. Pewter; H. 9".
(Nordiska Museet, Stockholm, Sweden.)

[17] "Transactions of the Moravian Historical Society,"
Vol. I, 1876 (Whitefield House, Nazareth, Pa.).

gation, left Philadelphia for Bethlehem, Pennsylvania, which had been founded in 1741 by the Moravian Brethren after they abandoned their earlier settlement in Savannah, Georgia. Called the General Economy, it was one of the early American experiments based on religious communism and was supported by various trades (numbering thirty-two in 1747 and increasing to forty in 1752).[18]

Although Bethlehem was a small and insignificant rural Pennsylvania settlement in 1742, it had a metalworkers' shop the equal of which could not be found elsewhere in Colonial America, or in guild-controlled Europe. It was an enterprise that defied every centuries-old craft rule of the Old World in that it was an establishment where different trades worked together under one roof and where artisans of one craft—all familiar with, and well-versed in, the "mysteries" of the various metal trades—supervised those of other crafts. A deliberate attempt to establish an integrated shop, it included a blacksmith; a highly competent pewterer, Heyne; and an equally competent brazier and bell founder, Samuel Powell, from Whitechurch, England, who had joined the "First Sea Congregation" in London.

Powell, supervisor of the shop, shared his responsibilities with Abraham Boemper, a German silversmith and engraver,[19] who had more than a casual acquaintance with the pewterer's trade.[20] Boemper was born in 1705, in Herborn, Nassau, Germany, the town that produced one of America's most illustrious families of pewterers—the Wills. John Will married Johanna Judith Boemper of Herborn; and Abraham Boemper, while the New York business agent for the Moravian Brethren, might very well have engraved the tankards of John Will, his relative.

These unique surroundings and unusual men were part of Heyne's world, but he, too, was an extraordinary person. His former position as an *Ortsgeselle* in the Stockholm guild points to organizational, diplomatic, and executive abilities, as well as to an above-average literacy. The Moravian Church was aware of his talents, for records

show that, three weeks after his arrival in Bethlehem, he was sent on extended trips as a missionary and itinerant minister to care for the spiritual needs of unchurched colonists in various settlements.[21] During the following year, his activities for the church sent him to Philadelphia and York, Pennsylvania, and twice to New York.[22]

Heyne married Maria Margaret Schaefer of Tulpehocken and both served three years as supervisors of various schools established by the Moravian Church. Their work and ability as instructors were reported in laudatory terms to Count Zinzendorf in Herrenhut.[23] At intervals Heyne served as assistant minister under license. The Bethlehem daybooks, in their detailed description of happenings, list him as absent from services of the church as of February, 1747. During this absence, he assisted the minister (later bishop), Peter Boehler, in bringing the message of his church to Moravian adherents in Ireland. In Dublin, they successfully opened a hall of worship with a congregation of one hundred members.[24] After two years' missionary work in Ireland, he returned to Bethlehem in 1749 to sever his connections with the Economy, but not with the Church. No vacancy in the Bethlehem pewterer's shop existed when he departed, since Abraham Hasselberg,[25] a Swedish pewterer whom Heyne could have known during his tenure as *Ortsgeselle* in Stockholm,[26] had arrived in Bethlehem.

In 1750, Heyne settled in Tulpehocken, his wife's home town. The year of his arrival in Lancaster is still a mystery, although his name first appears on the Lancaster tax rolls in 1757. The tax rolls of Berks County, where he settled with his wife, do not carry his name; therefore, one might assume that he lived with his father-in-law, who, as a property owner, was listed.[27] Since

---

[18] "Vertheilung der Brueder in Bethlehem in ihre verschiedene Handwerke und andere Arbeiten" (MAB).

[19] Ledgers and Account Books (MAB). These list Boemper as making pewter.

[20] Letters from Cammerhoff, Epistola Undecima, 7–13 Martiis 1748, to Count Zinzendorf (MAB).

[21] "Diarium Bethlehem," Vol. I (MAB). Three trips were made: July 15, July 25, and Aug. 4, 1742.

[22] Cash Books, 1743–1749 (MAB).

[23] Letter from Cammerhoff, Epistola Septima, Sept. 25–27, 1747, to Count Zinzendorf (MAB).

[24] "Transactions of the Moravian Historical Society," Vol. I, 1876 (Whitefield House, Nazareth, Pa.).

[25] I. Acrelius, *Bescrifning om de Swenska foersamlingars forna och narwarande tilstand uti det sa kallade Nya Swerige* (Stockholm, Sweden, 1759); see also, *A History of New Sweden; or, The Settlements on the River Delaware*, trans. William M. Reynolds (Philadelphia: Historical Society of Pennsylvania, 1876), p. 430.

[26] Loefgren, *Svenska Historia*, III, 323, 331.

[27] Tax Lists 1750–1757 (Pennsylvania Historical and Museum Commission, Harrisburg, Pa.).

Heyne was not given to idleness, he must have worked as an independent pewterer while in Tulpehocken. (It should be noted that the Bethlehem pewterers were not independent but worked for the community.) Unless his Lancaster shop can be shown to have existed between 1751 and 1757, he must be listed as a Berks County pewterer. The chalice dated 1753 at the Hershey Museum and the date 1754 on the chalice of Bindnagel Church in Palmyra, Pennsylvania, are sufficient evidence of his pewtering activities prior to 1757.

Heyne was naturalized in 1761. His wife Maria Margaret died in 1764; and, six months later, he married the widow Anna Regina Steinmann, who had moved from the Moravian settlement of Lititz to Lancaster after the death of her husband. Her son, Frederick Steinmann, became the owner of the pewterer's shop after Heyne's death. The shop, until it closed its doors in 1964, was the oldest American hardware store in continuous operation. No evidence has been found to suggest that Steinmann operated the pewterer's shop. A recently discovered letter states definitely that Heyne's King Street residence, with shop, was his second location in Lancaster. Heyne's letter, dated November 6, 1767, does not mention his first address but states that "Last October 27th, I began moving into my other house." [28]

Heyne died January 11, 1781, at the age of sixty-six, and was buried in the Moravian cemetery in Lancaster, a few steps away from his shop. When the cemetery was sold in 1917, as the site for a new post office, his remains, with those of about nine hundred others, were re-interred in a common grave at the Greenwood Cemetery in Lancaster.[29] Efforts to determine the disposition of the hundreds of tombstones that were in the old cemetery, which had existed for nearly two hundred years, were unsuccessful.

No will bearing Heyne's name could be found in the Lancaster courthouse, but a combination of his shop inventory and the known pewter specimens made by him give a fair summation of the range of his work. His versatility, ingenuity, and craftsmanship rank him with his fellow country-

FIG. 7. Heyne, Canteen or Flask. Lancaster, Pa., 1775. Pewter; H. 5½", Dia. 5". (William Penn Memorial Museum, Harrisburg, Pa. 31.77.3.)

[28] Letter from J. C. Heyne, Nov. 6, 1767, to I. Horsefield in Bethlehem (MAB). Horsefield was the Bethlehem metalsmith at that time; accounts indicate that he worked as a tinsmith and pewterer.

[29] Daybooks and Account Books of the Moravian Church (Lancaster, Pa.).

man William Will. Although Will produced a greater variety of forms and designs, it must be remembered that he worked in a cosmopolitan-metropolitan environment where competition was fierce and where fashionable customers demanded the latest in design. Heyne, on the other hand, was a master in a rural area where conservative tastes prevailed. It is interesting to speculate that Will and Heyne might have discussed their trade when Colonel William Will was assigned a tour of duty as storekeeper for the Continental Army at Lancaster in 1777.

Even when one considers that Lancaster was, in Heyne's time, the largest inland town in the American colonies, it is still surprising that so many varieties of pewter objects (either known or mentioned in the inventory) came out of Heyne's shop. Identified, or attributed to him, are the following forms: a 6-inch plate; a 6½-inch plate; a 7⅞-inch plate; a canteen (Fig. 7) ; two forms of flagon; a porringer; a beaker (Fig. 8) ; a covered sugar bowl, or pyx; three forms of open chalice (Figs. 9, 10, and 11) ; three forms of covered chalice (Figs. 12 and 13) ; an open salt; and church candlesticks.[30] When objects mentioned in the inventory—spoons, pint cans, quart cans, basins, and chamber pots—are added to the list, it becomes obvious that this "country" pewterer was not only the equal of his peers in versatility but outranked many of the "city" pewterers of his day. It seems quite probable that many of the unidentified pewter objects, particularly sacramental vessels, attributed to an unknown "Pennsylvania pewterer," came from the shop on King Street in Lancaster.

Considering the period of inflation before and after the Revolutionary War, Heyne's inventory listing of £38.0.0 for molds is not impressive. In view of the varied forms and designs listed above, a much larger amount for bronze molds might be expected—that is, if he used them. Apparently he did not use them to any great extent, for it is no mere assumption that he was more the master of clay, plaster, and stone molds than of brass and bronze molds. The two ball thumb rests of his Trinity church flagons cannot prove this conten-

Fig. 8. Heyne, Beaker. Lancaster, Pa., 1754–1780. Pewter; H. 4³⁄₁₆", Dia. (base) 3⁷⁄₁₆". (Winterthur 62.603.)

[30] Four pewter church candlesticks in the collection of The Henry Francis du Pont Winterthur Museum bear Heyne's small touch. Because of the location of these touches on added panels, the author attributes these candlesticks to Heyne with reservations.

FIG. 9. Heyne, Chalice. Lancaster, Pa., 1754–1780. Pewter; H. 9″. (Collection of the author.)

FIG. 10. Heyne, Chalice. Lancaster, Pa., 1754–1780. Pewter; H. 8½". (Zion Lutheran Church, Hummelstown, Pa.)

FIG. 11. Heyne, Chalice. Lancaster, Pa., 1754–1780. Pewter; H. 8¾". (Brooklyn Museum, Brooklyn, N.Y.)

Fig. 12. Heyne, Covered Chalice. Lancaster, Pa., 1754–1780. Pewter; overall H. 11⅝". (Hill Church, Cleona, Pa.: photo by Pennsylvania Historical and Museum Commission, Harrisburg, Pa.)

FIG. 13. Heyne, Covered Chalices. Lancaster, Pa., 1754–1780. Pewter; (left) H. 8¾″ without lid, (right) H. 87⁄8″ without lid. (John H. Carter, Sr., Trevorton, Pa. [left], and Charles Swain, Doylestown, Pa. [right].)

FIG. 14. Heyne, Flagons Showing Evident Variations of Spouts, Domed Lids, and Thumb Rests. Lancaster, Pa., 1754–1780. Pewter; thumb rests (left) 1″, (right) 13⁄16″. (Hill Church, Cleona, Pa. [left], and Zion Lutheran Church, Hummelstown, Pa. [right].)

tion, for their differences could mean that they originally graced the covers of earlier German tankards, acquired in trade from a neighbor's household. However, sufficient angel-head feet are available for a painstaking comparison. They leave little doubt that they were cast in a non-metal mold, with the Mueller flagon serving as a model. Invariably, there are minor discrepancies in size and design, which could not occur had a bronze mold been used. Such variations are, no doubt, the result of the limited life of a plaster or clay mold and the correction of details that become necessary after a few castings in that medium. Confirming the theory of the nonmetallic molds are the differences in height and width of the upright thumb rests, as well as their often blunt ridges—a condition not caused by wear (Fig. 14). The great variations in shape and size of the small finials of his sugar bowl and chalice covers suggest that he did not use even a quite inexpensive bronze mold, which would have cast uniform specimens of this small detail. Obvious also are the differences in the size and designs of his flagon covers. The great variety of his chalices is entirely at odds with the low valuation of his molds (Fig. 15). It is difficult to speculate what his reasons may have been for not using metal molds, since his European training required him to design, cast, and finish such molds.

John H. Carter, Sr., of Trevorton, Pennsylvania, a long-time student of Heyne's pewter, summarized his findings concisely.[31] His typology of Heyne's chalices is based on the sequence of their discovery and avoids speculation as to their chronology (Fig. 16): Type I, the Laughlin type, named after its owner, Ledlie Laughlin, of Prince-

ton, New Jersey (1931); Type II, the Poole type, named after John W. Poole, whose pewter collection is in the Brooklyn Museum, New York (1940); and Type III, the Evans type, named after John J. Evans, Jr., Wilmington, Delaware (1941). Each type is distinguished by sufficient variants to obviate any supposition that such differences are attributable to finishing methods.

By 1966, Carter had accounted for eighteen chalices of the three types, either marked or unmarked. Of them, eight are the only covered chalices of American pewter known. Since that time, the writer has located ten more Heyne chalices, all lidless, of which some are marked with Heyne's small touch (Fig. 17). There is every indication that a continuing and systematic search will bring to light more of Heyne's pewter, particularly ecclesiastical vessels by his hand.

A most unusual display of Heyne's pewter was arranged for the West Chester, Pennsylvania, meeting of the Pewter Collectors' Club of America in 1961. On exhibit was a five-piece communion service consisting of two flagons, a 6½-inch paten, a covered sugar bowl serving as a pyx, and one Evans-type covered chalice, all marked. With the exception of one flagon, all specimens were found unused when the writer removed them from their original eighteenth-century wrappings. It was the first time (and possibly the last) that anyone of our era has been privileged to behold the unsullied sheen of pewter as applied in the shop of its fashioner in the eighteenth century (Fig. 18).

Until a future day, this is the story, however incomplete, of one of the most fascinating American pewterers of the colonial period. While some day it may be possible to reconstruct the cradle-to-grave story of an American pewterer, it is unlikely that another could leave so interesting an array of his craftsmanship as did I. C. H.

[31] John H. Carter, Sr., "The Chalices of Johann Christopher Heyne," undated and unpublished manuscript, Trevorton, Pa.

FIG. 15. Heyne, Chalices. Lancaster, Pa., 1754–1780. Pewter; left to right, H. 8⅞″ without lid, H. 8¾″ without lid, H. 9″, H. 8½″. ([Left to right], Charles V. Swain, Doylestown, Pa.; John H. Carter, Sr., Trevorton, Pa.; Collection of the author; Zion Lutheran Church, Hummelstown, Pa.)

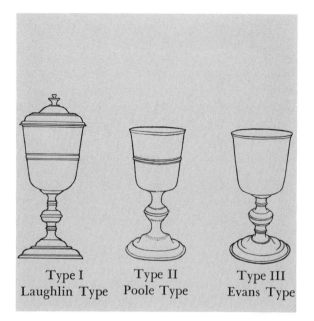

Type I
Laughlin Type

Type II
Poole Type

Type III
Evans Type

FIG. 16. John H. Carter, Sr., Drawing of Heyne Chalice Types from Unpublished Manuscript. Trevorton, Pa., n.d.

FIG. 17. Heyne, Small Touch, magnified five times. (Winterthur 62.607.)

FIG. 18. Heyne, Five-Piece Communion Service. Lancaster, Pa., 1754–1780. Pewter. (Hill Church, Cleona, Pa.)

John Hewitt, Cabinetmaker

Marilynn A. Johnson

IN 1805, on Manhattan's busy Water Street thronged with merchants and sailors, a rather slight young man named John Hewitt hung out the sign of his trade at 191 between Beekman and Burling Slips. In his life this event was not only auspicious but somewhat daring, for he was scarcely twenty-eight years old, a widower, and an expatriate without the financial backing of family or friends.

In the course of New York City history, it was an event of some interest, not so much for the aspects of his career that were unique as for those that were typical. Like countless immigrants before and after him, he had come to the new world in the hope of making a better life. Like many, he was a man whose skilled hands produced both mechanical objects, typical of those that aided America's phenomenal industrial growth during the nineteenth century, and artistic objects admired in years to come.

He had already been associated with two of the leading businessmen of the country, Nicholas Roosevelt and John Cox Stevens, and would follow a number of trades in his lifetime. He would found a flourishing cabinetmaking business with extensive export to the South; he would make a small fortune and lose it; he would patent a prize-winning and useful invention; and he would re-establish his business with one of his sons. In the mid-years of the nineteenth century, he would die in relative poverty and obscurity.

Yet, in no way can his career be considered a failure; rather, in many ways it was the fulfillment of the American dream. Not only is the record of his life an honest one, but also it reveals many of the reasons for the success of his younger son. In the latter part of the century, this son, Abram

Hewitt, as mayor of his father's adopted city, was to remember the man who had helped to inspire in him a desire for learning and a belief in a rigid code of ethics. He was to recall, not without pride, John Hewitt's simple beginnings.

Born in the village of Penkridge in Staffordshire, England, during the War of the Revolution, and raised in Cannock Chase nearby, John Hewitt was the son of a cabinetmaker who trained him and his brother Robert in the mysteries of the craft.[1] The young John must have shown talent with his hands and, perhaps, a restless desire for something more than his father's rural vocation. While still in his teens, he went to work for Matthew Boulton, a distant relative, to learn engine making at the Soho engine works of Watts and Boulton near Birmingham. At scarcely nineteen years of age, he embarked for America in 1796 with his new skill. At the Schuyler Foundry, Second River, New Jersey, he worked as a trained draftsman and pattern maker with Nicholas J. Roosevelt. This plant later became America's Soho, named in honor of the Watts and Boulton works.

With other skilled English mechanics, Hewitt worked on several significant projects during the next few years. The first of these was the construction of two engines to pump water for the new Philadelphia water system, one on the Schuylkill River and the other at Center Square. Of even more interest was the steam engine construction promoted by Colonel John Stevens. Stevens, fa-

[1] Allan Nevins, *Abram S. Hewitt, With Some Account of Peter Cooper* (New York: Harper & Brothers, 1935), pp. 3–5. Facts of John Hewitt's early life are also given in the introduction to a book by Hewitt's grandson, Edward Ringwood Hewitt, *Those Were the Days* (New York: Duell, Sloan and Pearce, 1943).

miliar with the work of John Fitch, began his own experimenting in 1796; in 1798, in partnership with Nicholas J. Roosevelt and Chancellor Robert R. Livingston, he sponsored the building of a steamboat based on plans by Livingston. Hewitt assisted in making the steam engine for the boat, which had its trial run between Belleville and New York in June, 1799, and was one of those accompanying Colonel Stevens on the wheezing, leaky craft. Despite its inadequacies, this was the second steamboat in America, and its trial run was eight years earlier than that of Fulton's *Clermont* between New York and Albany.

At some time near the end of the eighteenth century, John Hewitt left his work with Roosevelt and Stevens and returned to cabinetmaking. These first years in America were filled with uncertainty for him, and his family urged him to return to England as he had planned. In February, 1799, his brother-in-law wrote, "Since you find the trade and health of the country is so precarious, we cannot help but think you may live comfortabler among your friends, [even] if you don't get so much money." His brother's plea was even more urgent:

I respeckt you as a Brother and shoul wish to advice you as sich, and my advice to you is to come Back this Spring. For what purpas will it answer for you to stop when their is no liklewards of whe coming to you for I think you may do Better in England than where you are. As for me I have plentey of Biseness and you may have constant work whith me But I think their is a good open for you to come and Settle their.[2]

Despite his family's efforts, he did not return to England; instead, he set about making a success of his new profession by seeking in the South a new and extensive market for his products. The principal outlets of that market were to be Savannah and St. Marys, Georgia. Founded in the early eighteenth century as the capital of a debtors' colony, Savannah had become a leading mercantile center by 1800, with ships from all the major cities of the Atlantic seaboard clearing the port. As the center of a flourishing cotton trade, Savannah had particularly close ties with Liverpool,

England, and New York. St. Marys, a small town on the St. Marys River in south Georgia, was a trading center for that area and the sea islands, as well as a gateway to the territory of Florida.

Hewitt's activities during this time can be followed in both contemporary newspapers and his own accounts. By April, 1800, he was advertising in the *Columbia Museum & Savannah Advertiser:* "Mahogany Furniture for Sale by the subscriber, consisting of some elegant [pieces] of various kinds. Secretarys, oval Tables, dining do, with circular ends, night stands, portable desks warranted good   JOHN HEWITT." [3] Apparently, he was moving back and forth between Savannah and the North during this period, for the *Georgia Gazette* of October 2, 1800, listed two unclaimed letters for John Hewitt in the Savannah Post Office.

The most informative document relating to the cabinetmaking career of John Hewitt is his one surviving account book. Not only does this book tell much about Hewitt's activities during 1800–1803 and his cabinetmaking business between 1810–1813, but also it is the record of any New York craftsman-businessman of that era. From these accounts, much definite information can be acquired: the range of the furniture forms his shop was producing; the prices charged; the extent of the shop and the division of labor; the use of pattern books; the awareness of new styles, shown by sketches of forms and statements of their dimensions; Hewitt's scouting of the competition, indicated by his mention of Phyfe and Lannuier; his conscious imitation of a Phyfe style; trade to other areas, particularly Savannah and St. Marys, Georgia; and dealings in other commodities, especially lumber and veneers related to cabinetmaking.

Written in John Hewitt's hand, pages of this account book record his trading operations.[4] Many of the invoices are so obliterated that they are almost unreadable; however, those remaining show that from 1800 to 1803 he dealt in a range of

---

[2] John Hewitt Papers (Cooper Union Library, New York City [hereafter CUL]). These are a small body of papers comprising only part of the manuscript material on which Nevins based much of the first chapter of his book. The remainder of the papers have disappeared, perhaps in the fire which destroyed the Cooper-Hewitt house on Lexington Avenue.

[3] This advertisement, as well as subsequent material quoted from Georgia newspapers, is drawn from the file at the Georgia Historical Society. The author is indebted to Mrs. Lilla Hawes and Mrs. Eugene Stanley for assistance in locating this material.

[4] John Hewitt Account Book (New Jersey Historical Society, Newark, N.J.). When the author first consulted this manuscript, it was catalogued as an unidentified "Carpenter's Record Book." Hereafter it will be cited as "Account Book."

goods that he obtained in New Jersey and New York and then shipped to Savannah. Acting either as commission agent or purchaser, Hewitt traded in such articles as apples, shoes, thread, piano-fortes, clocks, screws, beer, cider, cotton bagging, stocking pantaloons, and furniture.

Although several well-known New York names occur in his accounts, one of his chief suppliers was the cabinetmaker and merchant, Matthias Bruen of Newark, New Jersey.[5] The earliest clearly decipherable accounts with Bruen, beginning in March, 1801, are two separate invoices[6] including an extensive list of wood and furniture:

To 1060 feet of Mahogany cuts 25 Cents per foot	265	
To inlaid Sideboards at 40 Dolls each	80	
To one Ditto 35 Ditto	35	
To one pair sash cornord Breakfast Tables	25	
To two pair—plain Ditto at 22 Doll per pair	44	
To two pair plain oval Breakfast Tables at 16 Dols	32	
To two pair Ditto inlaid at 22 Dols	22	
To two pair of Circular End Tables at	35	
To two Stands at 2 Doll each	4	
To one Mahogany Desk	35	
To one pair of sash cornerd Card Tables	30	
To one mahogany Bedstead Carvd post	25	
To Ditto gum sides	15	
To one feild Do witewood	10	
To one circular end without toping	17	50
To 48 feet of Vineers at 12½ Cents per foot	6	
	$680	50

Less than three weeks later, in the *Columbian Museum and Savannah Advertiser* of March 24, Hewitt offered a list of furniture for sale in Savannah, stating: "Mahogany Furniture for Sale by the Subscriber, who has just received a very handsome assortment which he will warrant in full upon reasonable terms. . . . In Bryan Street on Fells lot, above the market square, where he carries on Business, and will be able to make any piece of furniture in the above Branch." The list of items

included, in addition to many of the forms listed in the invoice from Bruen, secretaries and book-cases, dining tables, portable desks, sofas, and easy chairs.

A shipment to Savannah in December, 1801, was, perhaps, Hewitt's largest. There are a total of five invoices from four different people, all dated December 16. Again Bruen was an important furniture supplier, and the invoice, amounting to almost $1,000, is extensive and diverse.

To two inlaid sash cornerd sideboards	140	
To 1 Ditt quarter	70	
To 1 Eliptic ditto inlaid	70	
To 1 [Straight] fronted	40	
To 1 pair circular Bureaus inlaid	50	
To 1 part Ditto Ditto plain	45	
To 4 [Straight] fronted Ditto at 17 50	70	
To 1 french foot Ditto	18	75
To 1 pair of cornor basan Stands inlaid	30	
To 1 pair plain Ditto at 3.50	7	
To two Gum Candle Stands at 2.00	4	
To 1 Mahogany Ditto	3	50
To 1 Mahogany Cradle	10	
To 2 plain portable Desks	20	
To 1 Ditto inlaid	14	
To 1 pair Card Tables sash cornord	45	
To 2 pair Circular Tables Ends	35	
To 2 pair Ditto not Topd	35	
To Eight inlaid oval Tables	90	
To 1 plain Ditto	10	
To 1 pair sash cornord inlaid at 11.25	22	50
To 1 plain Table sash cornord	9	00
To 3 Squar breakfast Ditto at 7.00	21	00
To 1 pair leafes serpentine	22	
To 5 Looking Glasses at 15 Each	75	
	$962	75

This extensive transaction between Hewitt and Bruen is in contrast to the one with Adam Standley of New York for "Seventy Gross of Screws on commission at five per cent $142." From Richard Whittingham of New York, a man now chiefly remembered as either a brassfounder or a dealer in andirons, Hewitt received two invoices. The first bears the heading, "Beer Recd from Ricd Whittingham New York Dec 16th," and lists barrels of beer, while the facing page states, "Beer Sold in Savannah on Account Jno Hewitt." The second invoice seems closer to Whittingham's usual dealings, for it lists "1 Clock & Case—60, 1 Ditto Ditto—55," and states, "These are on Commissions five per cent." The final invoice of December 16 was "Recd fm Mr. James Hewitt New

[5] Margaret E. White, *Early Furniture Made in New Jersey, 1690–1870* (Catalogue of an Exhibition, Oct., 1958–Jan., 1959; Newark, N.J.: The Newark Museum, 1959), pp. 45–46. Matthias Bruen was a cabinetmaker in Newark. His shop, where he worked with his brother, Caleb, was on Broad Street south of Market.

[6] Account Book. The manuscript is not paged. The main body of it has been assigned page numbers for convenience; however, miscellaneous accounts at the back of the book run in no discernible order, and some are completely illegible or partially destroyed; therefore, no pagination has been given for entries in this section.

York." Apparently James Hewitt, like John Hewitt, Matt Bruen, and Richard Whittingham, saw the growing town of Savannah as a good potential market for his special wares, for the invoice lists:

To Music per . . .	134
To 1 Piano Forte with additional Keys	140
Case for Ditto	2.50
To a Piano Forte Common Construction	130.00
To Case for Ditto	2.50
	$409.00

The value of the last item suggests that "Case" referred to a packing case.

Although the business records are fairly extensive, the details of John Hewitt's life during this period are unclear. The concluding lines of his advertisement of January, 1801, suggest that he may have worked briefly in Savannah; however, he was not living there. He may have had a furniture shop in New Jersey, where he worked and traded; certainly he must have kept his ties there, for in 1802 he married Phoebe Tiemann, a member of a prominent New Jersey family. Later the same year, he formed a partnership with Benjamin Ansley of Savannah, who was to handle his business in the South.[7]

During that year, Hewitt received invoices from a number of cabinetmakers and merchants. In April he made note of another bill from Matt Bruen, this time for only $177 of furniture, and in May he received an invoice from Hugh McDougall for furniture, amounting to $411, to be sold on commission.[8] The forms listed include such items as, "one inlaid sideboard sash cornored" and "one Cillender Desk and bookcase doors glass." A July invoice from Bruen listed not only furniture but a "Rideing Chair," while in September Bruen billed Hewitt for "two Setts of Dining tables."

The next few years were apparently difficult for Hewitt. He and Ansley accepted too many notes for furniture sold in the South. In 1802, Savannah suffered one of its periodic yellow fever epidemics and a failure of the cotton crop. By February of 1803, Hewitt and his young bride were in actual want.[9] After 1803, Hewitt's furniture business seems to have become more stable when he sought a wider outlet for his trade and sold more furniture in New York.

During this time, Hewitt continued to trade in items other than furniture. For the most part, the account book records of the business in the South during 1802 and 1803 are too badly faded or torn to be helpful; however, two invoices from Matt Bruen in the early months of 1802 list, not furniture, but cotton bagging, bale and cord, and shoes and slippers. An invoice from Caleb Parkhurst, probably of the same period, also lists shoes and seal slippers, while a February, 1803, invoice lists, "Stocking pantaloons shipd to Mathew Shearer for the Brig Ceres bound to Savannah."

The end of this period in Hewitt's career came in late 1805 and early 1806, with a shift in the focus of his business and an end to his partnership with Ansley. In 1805, using the firm name "Hewitt and Ansley," Hewitt set up shop at 191 Water Street, New York.[10] In Savannah, the Hewitt and Ansley shop was still open in early March, 1806, when an advertisement in the *Columbian Museum and Savannah Advertiser* stated that Mathias Insley had "returned from the northward and taken his former shop in Broughton Street next door to Hewitt & Ansley," where he intended to carry on the coach, chair, and sign-painting business. On March 29, the same paper carried a notice of the "dissolution of . . . the copartnership under the firm of Hewitt & Ansley." After stating that claimants and debtors should settle their accounts, the advertisement also said that Ansley would continue his cabinet business "at his old Stand, in Broughton Street."

---

[7] Nevins, *Abram S. Hewitt,* pp. 6–7.

[8] Hugh McDougall was born in Paisley, Scotland, Dec. 22, 1770, and came to New York with his parents on the ship *Commerce* from Greenock in Feb., 1774. He was apprenticed in New York to a "Scotch" cabinetmaker, and was active in New York as a cabinetmaker from 1792 to 1798. He was first listed in New York directories in 1791 as a house and sign painter; in 1793 he was listed as a painter, gilder, and glazier. During the 1790's, he advertised as a painter and glazier at No. 92 Broadway, opposite Trinity Church. See Rita S. Gottesman, *The Arts and Crafts in New York, 1777–1799* (New York: The New-York Historical Society, 1954), II, 343. At the end of the century, he became a cabinetmaker in Newark, working there until about 1809. Apparently he retained his shop in New York, for he continued to advertise there from 1800 through 1802. See Rita S. Gottesman, *The Arts and Crafts in New York, 1800–1804* (New York: The New-York Historical Society, 1965), III, 268–69. Before 1815 he retired from cabinetmaking and moved to Hanover, N.J. The author is indebted to Carl M. Williams for all genealogical facts of McDougall's life. Mr. Williams also knows of furniture made by Hugh McDougall and still owned by McDougall's descendants.

[9] Nevins, *Abram S. Hewitt,* p. 8.

[10] *Longworth's American Almanac, New-York Register, and City Directory* (New York: David Longworth, 1805). No listing occurred for Hewitt before 1805.

Hewitt, too, continued his cabinet business at 191 Water Street. His shop seems to have been that formerly occupied by the cabinetmaker George Shipley, who died in 1803.[11] A description of the property is included in a sale notice published by Shipley's widow in New York newspapers of November and December, 1803.[12] After advertising for sale the "Stock in Trade of George Shipley, Cabinet Maker, deceased," Hannah Shipley offered:

> the lease of the premises No. 191 Water-street, between Beekman and Burling-slips, being a good established stand for the Cabinet Making Business and very convenient, running through from Water-street to Front-street, and a large gangway. The very extensive business carried on by the late Mr. Shipley renders this a very desirable object to Cabinet-Makers in general.

The location near the water and the established quality of the site were ideal for Hewitt. He also may have purchased some of Shipley's tools and supplies. The gangway to Front Street must have been particularly valuable, both for receiving shipments of mahogany and for transferring furniture from his shop to waiting ships.

Water Street was one of the most important mercantile thoroughfares of the city, with shops of many craftsmen and merchants. On the corner was E. M. Blunt's quadrant store—a landmark for seafarers—while nearby, at 192 Water Street, was the establishment of another well-known craftsman, the silversmith John Targee. Despite the prime location of the shop, Hewitt must have felt the burden of being entirely independent. Throughout 1806, he carried on the business by himself; but early in 1807 he again formed a partnership, this time with a cabinetmaker named Mandeville.[13] As before, difficulties plagued him in the first months of his partnership. In the closing days of 1807, President Jefferson, in an at-

tempt to protect American sailors who were being forcibly impressed by the British Navy and to avoid the war which public sentiment was beginning to demand, signed the Embargo Act prohibiting the sailing of ships from the United States to foreign ports. The effect of this embargo on business which, like Hewitt's, depended in large part not only on shipments to other locales but also on the well-being of the shipping industry is clear. By the end of the next year, however, Hewitt and Mandeville had recovered and opened a ware-room opposite the Exchange in Savannah, where they had on hand an assortment of furniture in addition to such items as a complete assortment of shoes for men, women, and children.

Early in 1809 Hewitt's partnership with Mandeville ended. In Savannah, Owen Strange advertised in June in the *Republic and Savannah Evening Ledger* that he had taken over the house "lately occupied by Messrs. Hewitt & Mandeville, as a ware-room, on the west side of Bull Street, near the Exchange." He stated further that he intended carrying on the cabinetmaking business, and it seems possible that either he had been associated with Hewitt and Mandeville or the location was well-known in Savannah for furniture. Hewitt alone was listed at 191 Water Street in an 1810 New York directory.

Although he had given up his wareroom in Savannah, Hewitt still maintained ties in that city. One of the more interesting examples of this is an 1810 bond of re-apprenticeship of Andrew Rodes, Jr., of Savannah.[14] Whether the young Rodes worked for Hewitt in a branch shop in Savannah or was actually working at Water Street in New York is not clear. There is, however, an "Andrew" mentioned in various places in the 1809–1812 account book, which records transactions of the Water Street shop. An analysis of this account book, the most informative document of Hewitt's career, forms the appendix to this article.

Documentation of Hewitt's personal life during these years is less clear than that of his professional life. After only a few years of marriage, Hewitt's first wife, Phoebe, died, as had their two infant sons, John and James. In 1808 Hewitt married Ann Gurnee, daughter of a farmer who lived near Haverstraw, New York. By 1812 John and

---

[11] For further information on George Shipley, see Meyric R. Rogers, "George Shipley: His Furniture and His Label," *Antiques*, LXXIX (April, 1961), 374–75.

[12] Gottesman, *Arts and Crafts, 1800–1804*, III, 152–53.

[13] The exact identity of Mandeville is not known, although it was the name of several cabinetmakers of the period. Both a Matthew and a William Mandeville are listed as cabinetmakers in early nineteenth-century New York directories. William is known to have made tables and desks for the New York Common Council, and a bill of his to William Bayard, 1811, is in The Joseph Downs Manuscript and Microfilm Collection, Division of Libraries, Winterthur Museum.

[14] Mrs. Carlton Theus, *Savannah Furniture, 1735–1825* ([n.p.]: Privately printed, 1967), pp. 58, 67.

Ann had two small children, a son Francis, lame from birth, and a daughter Sarah.[15]

During the next few years, Hewitt and his young family again entered a period of adversity. Although the account book includes entries for 1812 and 1813, there are few records to show the condition of Hewitt's business at this time. The War of 1812 must have been doubly painful to Hewitt and other English-born Americans. In addition to personal considerations, the effects on business were disastrous. Hewitt's market in Savannah virtually vanished as the South felt the effects of poor crops and a cessation of shipping. Hewitt had consistently sent furniture to St. Marys, Georgia, for the plantation market in south Georgia and Florida. From there his agent wrote of the unstable conditions in eastern Florida:

The Depredations and Murders already committed by the Indians, has not only stopped all Trade, but has occasioned a general Evacuation of all Inhabitants from St. John's River to this country, while Buildings on their plantations are Burnt, Crops destroy'd, Negroes carried off, and many have only escaped with their Lives and a small remnant of Property. Consequently my Receivals for large Demands on many of them are this season nothing, and some have commenced taking refuge under the Act of Insolvency.[16]

With the loss of his southern markets, Hewitt attempted to establish his trade with nearby points in New York State and New England. One agent took a boatload of furniture and lumber up the Hudson; another worked from Hartford, Connecticut. As in the South, customers were slow to pay, and Hewitt's situation remained precarious.

In 1815 prosperity returned after the treaty of peace. Hewitt's business picked up, only to be virtually destroyed by a disastrous fire on Water Street in 1816. After considering a move to Savannah, Hewitt rented a small place in New York and once again began cabinetmaking, supplemented with odd carpentering and dealing in cabinet brasses. He used his training as an engineer to manufacture wheels and cotton-gin parts. As in earlier years, he also acted as a jobber in lumber. He attempted to re-establish his trade in the South and collect the debts owed him.

In the autumn of 1817, Hewitt sent an agent,

William Scott, to Savannah to supervise his business there. Most of the records for this period have vanished, but Scott apparently contracted with Faries & Miller, the principal furniture dealers of Savannah, who agreed to accept the bulk of Hewitt's shop output, paying by notes due in four months. In the next six months Hewitt shipped more than $4,000 worth of furniture, but Faries & Miller proved to be poor business partners. By 1818 it was evident that they could not, or would not, pay.[17] Meanwhile, Scott continued to sell Hewitt's furniture. Two of his letters, both dated in January, 1818, comment upon the New York–Georgia furniture trade of the period.

Scott wrote his first letter after he had debarked from the ship *Prudence,* a singularly ironic name, since Hewitt's choice of her as a vessel for his precious cargo proved to be anything but prudent. Nor was his agent's business acumen any sharper at this point. Scott reported that "the Prudence got up to town yesterday having been wind bound at the mouth of the River this five days past, she will begin to unload tomorrow morning if it is fair weather. It has rained almost incessantly since I arrived here."[18] The results of this inclement weather are made clear in Scott's second letter, written four days later:

The Remainder of the furniture was landed yesterday morning. I have opened a few of the Boxes today of the most elegant piece of mark to arouse attention. I am sorry to observe that it is all injurd, more or less by the dampness of the hold and the deck's leaking. One End of the Canted Corner Sideboard is very much injurd the rosewood banding and the veneer in the End Door has all started. The Back of the Grecian Sofa has got mildewed, and I am fearfull the Rest of the articles is not in much better state. I shall try and put it in the best state I can—Oldershaws furniture is as bad as mine—Capn Tilts informs me he had an uncommon rough passage.

Scott's letters give not only a picture of the furniture which Hewitt was sending, but also an idea of the competitive situation in which Scott found himself. He was unable to find a place to reopen Hewitt's branch shop, and therefore made an arrangement with D. Williford,[19] who was will-

---

[15] Nevins, *Abram S. Hewitt,* pp. 8, 13.

[16] *Ibid.,* p. 10; quoted from the now-lost segment of the Hewitt papers.

[17] John Hewitt Papers (CUL).

[18] *Ibid.*

[19] Theus, *Savannah Furniture,* pp. 90–91, states that "the last recorded advertisement of venture furniture in Savannah ran December 18, 1819" and listed "An invoice of well made N. Y. Furniture." It was signed "D. Williford."

ing to provide storage space and sell the furniture at 4 per cent commission. Scott was optimistic and wrote Hewitt, "There is at present no great deal of furniture in Savannah [and] what their is is poor trash."

Apparently, Hewitt had expected Scott to proceed to Augusta; commenting on Hewitt's plan, Scott said:

I do not think it would answer so well at present . . . as there has been so much sent their this fall from the Northland—I forgot to mention in my former letter that their was a Mr. Warren a cabinetmaker from near Albany who came in the same vessel I did who had near four thousand Dollars worth of furniture on board of . . . he went up to Augusta with it.

Scott was confident that Hewitt would be satisfied with his decision to remain in Savannah. Transportation to Augusta, he said, was "so enormous, from 22 to 24 cent per foot," that moving the furniture to that market would not compensate for the additional expense incurred.

The closing passages of Scott's letter tell about Hewitt's associates, the furniture company of Faries & Miller, and perhaps hint at what was to come:

I have got a job at Faries & Millers. They do not yet know that you have sent out any furniture but they no doubt will in a day or two. I have never said anything to them concerning it. They get their furniture from one Clarkson in N Jersey—They talk about establishing a shop in N York next Summer and one of them to remain there, as they think they can then carry on Business to better advantage by supplying their shop here themselves—They have got but very little furniture at hand at present they are complaining of Clarkson's not attending to their orders. I understand the true reason of which is this: that Clarkson wants the money as soon as the furniture arrives here, and that, they are not willing to do. They are now indebted to him considerable and I dont expect he will send them any more untill they pay up their arrears.

Clarkson was not the only cabinetmaker to whom the firm owed money. Richard Gorham, Jacob Miller's partner during the years when the firm was called Gorham & Miller, remained in Hewitt's debt. Scott reported, "I will attend to collecting the note of 500 Dollars you sent me against Richard Gorem and remit you the money as soon as I get it."

Scott's reports are only part of the record of

John Hewitt's furniture shipments to Savannah during 1815–1817. Inward coastal cargo manifests for the Port of Savannah show that Hewitt made many shipments, most of them to the firm of Gorham & Miller.[20]

Hewitt was not the only cabinetmaker shipping furniture to Savannah for sale at this time, nor was New York the only source of furniture for Georgia merchants and planters refurbishing their homes. Cargo manifests indicate that, although the better-known New York cabinetmakers like Phyfe and Lannuier made few shipments of furniture, lesser-known craftsmen like John H. Oldershaw of New York and Abraham Cross of Newark made relatively large shipments both for

[20] Inward Coastwise Cargo Manifests for Savannah, Georgia, 1802–1805 and 1810–1820 (Collection of the Diplomatic, Legal, and Fiscal Branch, National Archives and Records Service, Washington, D.C.). Shipments made by Hewitt are as follows:
April, 1815—Hewitt to Gorham and Miller, Savannah: twelve cases furniture; three bundles bedsteads; one chair.
May, 1815—Hewitt to Gorham and Miller: three boxes of chairs.
July, 1815—Hewitt to Gorham and Miller: seven packages of furniture.
March, 1816—Hewitt to Gorham and Miller: four bedsteads; eleven boxes of furniture, aboard the *Cotton Plant*.
April, 1816—Hewitt to S. C. Dunning, Savannah: one case of furniture; one bedstead, aboard the *Adonis*.
April, 1816—Hewitt to Gorham and Miller: forty-eight mahogany boards, aboard the *Savannah Packet*.
October, 1816—Hewitt to Scott & Fahn: five cases of furniture.
   Hewitt to Gorham & Miller: nine packages of merchandise.
   Hewitt to I. W. Stark: one box of furniture.
   Hewitt to Gorham & Miller: Twenty-five boxes of furniture; one dozen chairs, aboard the *Maria*.
November, 1816—Hewitt to Jacob Miller: one case of furniture, aboard the *Mechanic*.
   Hewitt to Sampson Miles: eight bundles of chairs, aboard the *Mechanic*.
March, 1817—Hewitt to Gorham & Miller: six boxes of furniture.
April, 1817—Hewitt to Gorham & Miller: eighteen mahogany boards.
   Hewitt to H. Rogers: two cases of thirty-five mahogany boards.
The author is indebted to Mr. W. Neil Franklin of the National Archives for calling her attention to these records. The manifests, which, when examined in 1963, had not been opened since they were originally folded up, are arranged chronologically. Since then, a more thorough research of their contents has been carried out in the form of a Winterthur Program thesis. See Katharine Wood Gross, "The Sources of Furniture Sold in Savannah, 1789–1815" (unpublished Master's thesis, University of Delaware, 1967).

individual Savannah residents and for sale by agents.[21]

All this activity of trade in the South came to an end in 1818 as hard times again hit the young nation. Hewitt, in need of the $4,000 Faries & Miller had never paid, found himself in dire straits. In an attempt to better his situation, he put together a shipment of furniture to New Orleans. There, his agent said, the market was glutted. Even New York's most famous cabinetmaker, Duncan Phyfe, was reported to have lost some $2,500, having let be sold "Extensible tables for $30, Sideboardes at $40, Bureaus for almost nothing." [22]

Further tragedy was in store for Hewitt. Having known the disasters of fire and failure in business ventures, he was to learn the dishonesty of a trusted friend. Hewitt had signed notes for a fellow Englishman, one Robbins, who represented himself as a hardware merchant. He was, in fact, a kind of confidence man, engaged in a complex maneuver to avoid American tariffs on British goods. When Robbins fled to Canada, Hewitt forfeited the money on the notes he had signed, which, according to one of his letters, totaled $83,000.[23] He was never to know true prosperity again.

The 1820's were bad years for Hewitt. For

several years after the failure of his business, he and his family lived in the country near Haverstraw, New York. Periodically he appears to have tried to re-establish himself. Although there was no listing for him in the directories for 1819, he was listed as having a hardware store at 242 Water Street in 1820. In 1821 and 1822 there were again no listings, but in 1823 John Hewitt was listed at 147 Water Street. About this time Hewitt established himself as a baker. In 1824 and 1825 he must again have retired to the country, but in 1826 he was listed in city directories as proprietor of a mahogany yard on Jay Street. This listing continued until 1830.

Late in the 1820's Hewitt's fortunes began to change again when he patented a special bedstead. *Niles' Weekly Register* recorded that John Hewitt received an award for his patent bedstead at the New York Fair of 1829.[24] Apparently Hewitt's device for sleigh-type beds was a replacement for the bed screw and a "prototype for all styles of bed catches that have been developed since." [25]

By 1830 Hewitt had again become a cabinetmaker, with his shop at 20 Hudson Street and his home at 189 Duane. No doubt his patent bedstead was instrumental in his decision to return to his previous profession. Late in 1829, perhaps in hopes of having funds to set himself up again in a shop, he had employed an agent to collect the debts owed him in Savannah from a dozen years earlier. His letters to this agent, S. C. Dunning, cover the period of late 1829 through early 1830. In the first letter, Hewitt speaks of Dunning's calling on "Mesr Faries & Miller Cabinet Makers, to ascertain the best offer they will make on the debt They owe me, and also ascertain if the Presbyterian Church are paying off their debts. My demand against the church is $309 standing about 10 years."

His next letter, of March, 1830, has more than a touch of pathos:

Your favour 16th Instant has come to hand, respecting my claim on the Independent Pres Church. I think they are in a fare way of makeing themselves independent by offering to pay about one half of their just debt after having a credit of 10 years or more & shame that a poor unfortunate man with a family of a wife & seven (4 of which are now down with the scarlet

[21] Abraham Cross was a Newark, N.J., cabinetmaker. According to White, *Early Furniture,* he advertised in 1812 that he had commenced the cabinet business. In 1817 he advertised cabinet furniture, upholstering, framing; two journeymen cabinetmakers wanted. In March, 1830, Cross announced the sale of his entire stock, as "subscriber intends moving." With others, Cross was involved in shipments of furniture to the South in the second decade of the nineteenth century.

In 1816 and 1817 Cross sent four cases of furniture to William Gaston, three boxes to Hall and Hoyt, and three to D. Cooper. During the same period J. H. Oldershaw, who had once worked for Hewitt, sent thirteen boxes of furniture to C. W. Carpenter & Co., fifteen boxes of furniture to Oldershaw & Phillips, ten cases to Oldershaw & Phillips from J. H. Oldershaw and Co., and five boxes of furniture to George Jarvis.

Only two shipments of furniture by Phyfe are recorded during the years 1815–1817; the first, in October on the schooner *Ariadne,* consisted of six boxes and one bundle consigned to G. Anderson and Son of Savannah; the second, on the ship *Adonis,* left New York in late November and arrived to the attention of B. Burrows (or Burroughs) in mid-December. J. D. Bullock of Savannah is known to have purchased furniture from Lannuier in 1817. Perhaps the only Lannuier furniture sent during 1815–1817 was on the ship *Cotton Plant,* Oct. 14, 1817, when J. D. Bullock sent six packages of furniture to himself in Savannah. It is possible that his 1815 importation of two cases of furniture on the brig *Savannah Packet* also came from the Lannuier shop.

[22] Nevins, *Abram S. Hewitt,* p. 12.

[23] *Ibid.,* pp. 13–14.

[24] Oct. 24, 1829. The award was listed as a "Discretionary Premium" given at a fair under the direction of the American Institute in 1829.

[25] Thomas Hamilton Ormsbee, *The Story of American Furniture* (New York: Macmillan Co., 1934), p. 121.

fevor) should be treated thus. . . . I have every confidence in you and feel you will do all you can for me.[26]

In June, resigned to a considerable loss, Hewitt instructed his agent to compromise: "I wish you on receipt this to settle with these professing gentlemen on the best terms you can for I consider their offers do not comport with religion. My family is large and my means small, Therefore I am compelled to a settlement." Apparently, need was great for he concluded, "What settlement you make please do it as soon as possible and remit me."

Throughout the early 1830's Hewitt was not only manufacturing furniture at Hudson Street, but again shipping it to the South. His output, however, seems to have been geared as much to quantity as to quality. One of his new markets was inland Alabama, where cotton was making wealthy planters even wealthier. Letters of this period indicate that purchasers of Hewitt furniture were not always satisfied with the product. In 1834 Hewitt addressed a letter to Montgomery answering a complaint by George Wragg of Wragg & Stewart.[27] Hewitt's words show his distress at Wragg's letter, which breathed "so much disatisfaction . . . and without a just cause." Wragg was, he stated, the only person in the South for whom he would have executed such an order, and he had "even purchased a great deal of the furniture, not having time given to make it, . . . and at 10 per cent lower than the regular price." He then returned a copy of Wragg & Stewart's order and a copy of the bills for what he had purchased, as follows:

From Fredricks & Smith

Nov 22 2 Sofas	$65	$130.00
1 Secretary & Bookcase		95.00
Packing do		10.00
		$235.00

From S Carten

Nov 22 1 Sett dining		
Tables		$ 60.
1 Sideboard		50
1 Work Table		10
packing do		7
[sic]		133.00

From James Cramsey

Nov 22 2 Maho.ʸ Rocking chairs	[@]	$20	
Packing do		4	
			44.00

From Wm Cramsey

Nov 22 2 Bureaus	[@]	$30	
Packing do		6	66.00

From Bucha

Nov.ʳ 22 1 doz Chairs		$ 4	48
1 do do		2	24
Packing do			6
			78

From J. Hewitt

Nov 22 2 Maho.ʸ Bedsteads	$ 48	96	
3 Maple do	22	66	172.00
	10	10	
			728.00

Commission $556 for which
I gave my Notes for 90 days
26.00
$754

He concluded that he had

paid Five hundred & fifty six dollars . . . and charged $26 dollars for commissions. . . . As respects my bedsteads I can give you more than a dozn of names in New York that has paid me the same prices that I have charg you for the same kind of bedsteeds. You may deduct the twenty six dollars if you think I not deserving of it and if it is necessary. . . . I feel much mortified at this business and had I known nothing would have induced me to have executed the order.

A year later, in 1834, one Colonel B. B. Lamar of Montgomery complained, "The cradle you sent me is a poor concern; every time the weather is damp it will not work. . . . The tables are poor, coarse, common wood." [28]

Late in the 1830's John Hewitt's eldest son, Francis, became an independent cabinetmaker, first at 114 Bleecker Street, then at 552 Broadway, while still living with his father at 160 Duane. In 1842, for the first time, John Hewitt, Jr., listed himself in an allied trade, as an upholsterer, at 20 Hudson, the same business address as John, Sr. After 1846 John Hewitt, Sr., was no longer listed in New York, having moved to Trenton. His sons, with the exception of Abram, continued to carry on the kind of work at which he had spent almost

---

[26] John Hewitt Papers (CUL).
[27] *Ibid.*

[28] Nevins, *Abram S. Hewitt*, p. 18; quoted from the now-lost Hewitt papers.

a half century, and Francis corresponded with him in Trenton about the cabinetmaking business.

Hewitt's last years were spent in New Jersey, where he died in 1857. He was buried near a peaceful lake on the grounds of Ringwood Manor, the home of his famous son Abram and seat of the well-known Ringwood iron forges. The wheel had come full circle. More than half a century earlier, he had come to the lands of northern New Jersey as part of the influx of English engineers needed to realize the potential of America's vast natural resources. Now he lay in the same land, and his son Abram was fulfilling what John Hewitt's early life and training had promised—building railroads, managing iron works, taking his place in an industrial society. Today one can still see the grave of John Hewitt at Ringwood. The stone that bears his name gives only the simplest of inscriptions.

John Hewitt shaped objects, not events. In terms of his craft, his impress upon history is primarily that left by the records of his work. These records provide insight into the influence

of immigrant craftsmen in America, the organization of a cabinet shop, the coastal trade in furniture, the range of furniture forms of the time, the decline in popularity of various forms, and the genesis and designation of a true "Phyfe" style by the conscious imitation of this one craftsman by his contemporaries.

Yet Hewitt's story is not simply the story of a cabinetmaker. If history is the biography of great men, it is also the story of lesser men. From the lives of those who do not visibly change history one often can see more clearly the forces and events of an age. The study of John Hewitt's life shows the pattern of immigration to the new country, America's interest in engineering and mechanical progress, the South's dependence on cotton and the labor system which could produce it, the country's growing nationalism and separation from European thought, the rise of New York as a port, and the emerging of a prosperous and influential mercantile class. Therefore, the biography of John Hewitt is a chronicle of American history, a half century of growth and change.

Appendix

JOHN HEWITT unquestionably kept account books for his entire cabinetmaking career. Like most business records of his era, the majority of these have disappeared through the years. Only the title page of his 1807 accounts with Mandeville remain in the collection of Hewitt Papers at the Cooper Union Library. The greater part of a subsequent account book survives elsewhere (see Note 4). This account book, lacking its title page and any positive identification other than the character of Hewitt's handwriting and copies of his invoices at the back of the book, is a rare, and possibly a unique, document. At the present time, no other account book of a New York City cabinetmaker of the Federal Period is known.

The main body of this book gives a chronological record of furniture forms ordered from the Hewitt shop during 1809–1812. At this time, Hewitt advertised his wares: "John Hewitt / Cabinetmaker / No 191 Water Street / New York / nearly opposite E. M. Blunt's Chart and Quadrant Store / Where may be had on liberal terms, Sideboards, Secretary Bureaus, Tables, Portable Desks, and every other articles in his line, at the

shortest notice." [29] These were articles that were, perhaps, most popular with purchasers, but the range of his output was far greater. His accounts of 1809–1812 show that his principal products included bedsteads, bookcases, bureaus and secretary bureaus, chairs, cradles and cribs, desks, countinghouse desks, secretaries, sideboards, tables, and wardrobes. Within each furniture form there was a wide range in quality, price, and degree of elaboration. Page numbers assigned by the author appear in parentheses following the references.

BEDSTEADS: Listed are innumerable field bedsteads at $12.00 each, a "common bedstead" at $5.00, trundle bedsteads, "stump" bedsteads, and single and double "cotts." High post bedsteads with "carved mahogany feet posts" sold for $25.00 or $26.00. An example of the style of bedstead wealthier clients purchased was the one made "For Calvin Baker 1 high post bedstead feet post

[29] Simeon de Witt, *The Elements of Perspective* (Albany, N.Y.: Printed by H. C. Southwick, 1813), page not numbered.

mahoy & / carvd with ferrels reeded above ferrels head post mapple 7 / square room 7 ft 10 high 5 ft to 2 to top of wides with sacking bottom" (22). For the merchant Abel Buckley, Hewitt made two even more elaborate bedsteads, the first, "4 post [matched] & Carvd with head board 4 foot do 6" 6 Long by / 5 feet wide between the Joints 2 ft high to Top of the bed / on post to have ferrels & to be made in the best manner of Inch / square above the Mortes head boards to Slide"; and the second "the same as before" but "to be 2 Inches higher say 2–2 & the square . . . 18 inches instead of 16 to be releiv & in curving leafe & a square under leafes" (5). The second bedstead was one of Hewitt's better productions and ranked, perhaps, with the bed he made for the mysterious John King of Richmond, which was to have, "All the post mahoy and carv'd with drapery, & to have / between Joints. Cornice etc. 4 ft. 6 Cornice to be gilt & / light blue ground" (25). The price of $33.00 was two dollars less than the most expensive bedstead—an eight-foot-high mahogany example for B. Havens of Jenkins & Havens (28)—in Hewitt's book. After mahogany, maple seems to have been most often specified for beds. For Matt Daniels, Hewitt made a "high post Mapple bedstead 'Common Size'" (6). The bedstead he made for a Mr. Gould, in which there were "side posts to represent sattin wood" (34), may also have been made of maple.

DECEPTION BEDS: A more unusual bed form which Hewitt produced was a press, or deception, bed. For E. Quirk he made a "press bedstead . . .

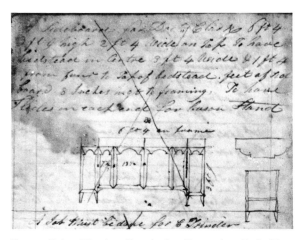

FIG. 1. John Hewitt, Sketch for Deception Bed. New York, 1810. Drawing in John Hewitt Account Book. (New Jersey Historical Society: photo, Winterthur.)

draws at bottom instead of top" (34). Another commission specified, "A press Bedstead for [Ann?] Noble to represent a secretary / carvd legs & large enough for two persons / 1 Do Single, piece to have draw in Top like the mahogany one" (3). He made his most elaborate press bedstead, for a Doctor Clarke, in the form of a sideboard (9). Not only did Hewitt give specific dimensions for it, but he also drew a clear sketch of it (Fig. 1) in his daybook. His description reads: "A Sideboard for Dr. Clarks 6 ft 4 [?] ft 9 high 2 ft 4 Wide / on Top to have bedstead in Centre 3 ft 4 Wide & 1 ft 4 from / front to top of bedstead. feet of board 8 Inches high to / framing. To have Slides in each end for basan Stand" (10).

BOOKCASES: Bookcases, although less popular than bedsteads, were also sold in the Hewitt shop. Descriptions often included dimensions and a sketch of part of the case, usually the doors. A bookcase with "sollid door" made for Thomas Freeborn cost $25.00 (21); and another, made in May, 1812, for John Harned, cost $35.00. Two sketches of the Harned case give some indication of the plan, and the phrase "glass doors No. 2" indicates that Hewitt had pattern or price books from which his customers could choose desired styles (32).

BUREAUS: Bureaus and secretary bureaus seem to have sold for $20.00 to $40.00. Hewitt produced simple bureaus priced at $20.00 for Dr. Pascalls and Dr. G. I. Miller (21, 18); Samuel Jarvis, however, paid $38.00 for his "secretary bureau fram'd and with 2 bottle draws" (33). No price is quoted for a "circular Bureau for Francis Cooper fram'd ends & reeded Legs with Balls & freze 2 ft 8 Long" (25).

CHAIRS: Chairs also are listed in a wide price range. Least expensive are the one dozen chairs at $1.00 each, which were to be sent to Timothy Hall, St. Marys, Georgia (3). A better shipment included "12 Fancey chairs" consigned to John Williamson in Savannah, at $49.00 (27). Apparently ships captains also took items on consignment, for a Captain Chase was to receive "12 chairs good [and] 2 Doz chairs cain bottoms" (31). Although these cheaper chairs probably formed the larger part of Hewitt's output, he also made fine chairs, as shown in an order for a Mr.

Maxwell of "1 Dozen Mahogany chairs with two elbows to match at $190" (7). Twelve mahogany chairs with two arms made for Francis Cooper in March, 1811, cost $191.00 (19). It is interesting to compare the price of these chairs with that of the two groups of mahogany chairs which Duncan Phyfe sold in 1807 to William Bayard and for which he charged from $12.00 to $15.00 apiece. Hewitt's chairs would seem to be of a quality comparable with that of Phyfe's. In addition to side chairs and "elbow" or armchairs, Hewitt's shop also produced easy chairs. Entries in his account book show one easy chair for Captain Newson (4), an "easey chair to be finished for Mr. Lyall" (34), and "2 easey Chairs, circular" for Mr. Harned.

CRIBS AND CRADLES: The turning skills that may have been involved in producing some of Hewitt's less expensive chairs would also have been used in the production of cribs, for which there was a large market. One child's "common crib" sold for only $7.50 (14); however, a mahogany crib with "Turned bannisters oge roof from Post to Post" sold to Mrs. Robert Whaite for $18.00 (33), and a Mr. Sadler purchased, for $19.00, a child's crib "with roof Turnd Bannister" (15). Hewitt also made a number of cradles, including one of mahogany two feet long for Thomas Gibbons (19) and a swing cradle for Mr. Harned (35).

DESKS: Desks and secretaries ranged from simple portable desks and an oval table type, of oak, at $10.00 (15), to one secretary and bookcase at $95.00 for a Mr. Cuyler (27). In between were a number of secretary bureaus and secretaries priced from $25.00 to $38.00. John King of Richmond ordered "1 Secretary 2 bookcase (like T) to have door no 12," priced at $87.50 (25). Possibly the door pattern specified is that listed as number 12 in the back of the 1811 account book.

SIDEBOARDS: One of the most popular furniture forms sold by Hewitt was the sideboard. The least expensive was a "streight" one selling for $25.00; but again they vary in price, and a number of sideboards selling for over $100.00 appear in the accounts. A sideboard "with Pedestals & cones" (20) sold for $55.00; one "streight fronted bottle draw Sideboard" for $60.00; and a "Side-board for Elias M. Stillwell for 70 Dollar" was "without bottle draws but pedestals" (1). A "French Sideboard like Phyfes" with "2 shelves in center and as many locks as possible" cost $80.00 (26). In the higher price range were Mr. Maxwell's "Mammouth Sideboard of the Best Quality" at $100.00 (7), two French sideboards at $110.00 (27) and $115.00 (18), and a sideboard at $120.00 for J[ohn] Harned (32). The majority of the sideboards ranged from $75.00 to $90.00. Hewitt made sketches of several of his sideboards, including one for John H. Shearman, another "with a shell" for Henry Newport, and two for Mr. Stannard of Heeley & Stannard.

TABLES: The furniture forms most commonly produced in the Hewitt shop were various kinds of tables. They included breakfast, card, dining, and writing tables and basin and candle stands. Hewitt was aware of the new styles in tables, and on the second page of his account book, he drew a plan for a pillar and claw breakfast table and a pillar and claw card table (Fig. 2).

Plan of a Pillar & Claw breakfast Table
Lenth 3 feet Bed 2 feet, leave 1 foot, Block
2 Inches thick & 6½ Wide, Rail 4½ Deep
Framed into blocks Drawes cock beaded & bead
over under rail with break, blocks carved
Pillar 1 ft 4 Long, & 4½ Squar for Claw
Pillar 4½ Square, to be turned all up and
to have a iron Plate—Sweep of leav 6½
from end Double eliptic, plan of Claw 11½
Sqar at Bottom, 2 in thick at Top 2¾ a
cross the Claw at Top; Claw to rise 10½ &
project 13½ the wood; plan of Pillar see under

FIG. 2. Hewitt, Sketch for Pillar of Breakfast Table. New York, 1809. Drawing in John Hewitt Account Book. (New Jersey Historical Society: photo, Winterthur.)

BREAKFAST TABLES: Several of Hewitt's customers, including John Harned, ordered the new style breakfast table. Other patrons bought pairs of breakfast tables at $30.00. These were probably like the single table "with reeded legs & castors" sold to William T. Williams for $15.00 (26). Simpler breakfast tables sold for as little as $7.50 or $9.00. A note in Hewitt's hand toward the end of the account book states, "Work to be made up 2 best piller & claw breakft Tables / 4 second dito," indicating that the shop kept on hand at least two grades of this style.

CARD TABLES: The pillar and claw card table was described: "Plan Card Table Pillar & Claw / Pillar 19½ Long & 4 in squar, Claws / the same as breakft Table, Joint Rail as / under 3 pieces 4 Inches thick & 2 skew braces / & 1 on top—Joint rail 3½ Deep / and frame as / Under" (2). Pairs of these card tables sold for $32.00 to $45.00, the most common price for them being $43.00. A pair with reeded legs was purchased by Samuel Thompson (19), while a "pair of card tables (good)" sold for $45.00 (15). Hewitt's list of work to be made up also included "2 pair best card tables" (33).

DINING TABLES: Dining tables, like card tables, were sold by the pair or, more often, by the set. It seems probable that "sett" meant three separate tables consisting of a center section and the two ends. A set of "4 ft dining Tables and leg to be reeded & to have castors" cost John King $50.00 (25), a fairly standard price. Large dining tables were made for Willaim Niblo (31, 33), who must have been furnishing a new restaurant, to judge from the various furniture pieces ordered. "Setts of Dining Tables," like breakfast tables and card tables, were also listed in Hewitt's accounts of work to be made up and kept on hand.

STANDS: Hewitt sold innumerable small tables. His designation of them varied, although the price was uniform and apparently reasonable. Candlestands sold for $5.00; however, one for George Wells was listed at $6.80 (36). Basin stands varied in price from $4.00 to the most expensive, a corner stand for John Harned, at $12.50 (32). "Wash hand stands" are also listed, and the difference between them and basin stands

is not clear. Possibly the terms were synonymous; the prices were usually similar, although one "washand stand not inclosed" for a Mr. Ogden cost $8.00 (32).

WRITING TABLES: The least common form of table recorded was the writing table. Only three are listed in the account book, and no prices are given. Dimensions, however, are explicit, as in a notation "size of a Writing Table" given on page 13 of the account book: "Lower frame 2 ft 10 Long / 2 Deep / Upper frame 1 ft 2 Deep / door —2.2 high / lower frees—.2." No catalogue description could be much clearer than Hewitt's specifications of "A Writing Table for—Gabriel Havens [30] 2 ft 1 L 1 feet 6 wide reeded legs & castors with checker board on center of top & draw" (5).

SOFAS: Among the well-known furniture forms, the rarest produced was the sofa. Only four are to be found in the accounts, and all but one were for customers outside New York. Hewitt charged $85.00 for the sofas for which prices were listed; one of them was described as a "hair cloth sofa."

WARDROBES: The shop also made at least one wardrobe; the accounts state "For Mr Castard in 2 weeks for Sep 1 Wardrobe 3 draws below 4 Trays above handsome wood for 60." Apparently the commission was completed, for a later note said, "Mr. Castards wardrobe to be sent on board the Brig Diana Capn Delamater North River below the Bath by 10 o'Clock Octo 28th" (29). Hewitt, obviously anticipating demand for the new style in this furniture form, recorded "Size of a Wardrobe French, 6 feet between Doors 4 ft Wide / outside 2 ft ends Deep, 7 hinches freeze / & pediment 7 feet Turnd part 2½ stiles" (2).

MISCELLANEOUS FORMS: In addition to the various furniture forms, the Hewitt shop also produced household accessories. One entry specified "2 cornices 3 ft 4½ between the brackets 18 hooks for curtens." Drawings of window cornices for a Mr. Greenwood are also given (4). Small house-

---

[30] In 1797 William Dunlap wrote to Joseph Byrnes of Charleston, S.C., "This packet I send by the ship Fame deliver'd to ye Captn Gabriel Havens." See *Diary of William Dunlap* (New York: The New-York Historical Society, 1929), I, 200.

hold objects were made, particularly those which had to do with food and serving—there are numbers of butler's trays, knife boxes, and tea caddies, and in one instance a bread tray. More personal articles included a "bracket for R. Charnleys Time Peice Wide 10 Inches" (9) and "A letter case for Mr. Creig with 20 holes 2 draws, to be longer than high & to have a door" (11).

Not only did Hewitt make furniture for the homes of men of the area and for consignment to the ships captains who frequented the area, but also for the proprietors of local shop rooms and counting houses. Among those listed were many well-known merchants and traders of the day. One commission led to another, as the following indicates: "For Mr. Dunlap / 1 Counting house desk same size as Baker & Schuylers except / to be 8 Inches on Top each to be made double for 58 / also top bookcases the same as J. F. DellPlaines at the same price / and two nest draws at Ditto" (27). An even more elaborate project was one "for Mr. Darling at Joshua Waddington's house corner Pearl and Pine Street: A Counting house desk 5 ft., 10 Long 4 ft broad, front rail / 6 in deep with 2 draws on each side. Top board 8 in wide a / box on Top 10 In high to 1 feet Long with 2 draws & Pidgin / holes to have railings 10 In high to have a foot rail and / to be 4 In lower than Marquands" (4).

In addition to counting house desks, Hewitt's shop made everything from "a yard stick for Oakley & Randolph" (1) to "a Packing case for Capn Chase" and "3 New Paper Sticks for Mr. Jones to be done by Monday at $1 each" (12). For an "English captain," Hewitt had an order of "A Mahogany Chest the Size of a 4 feet dining Table to be Nailed together without Lock & Hinges."

Boxes appeared to be the most popular small item sold, and the variations in them were vast. They ranged from mahogany "spitting boxes" (1, 19) to a strong box of cherry for Thomas Gibbons (19) and "a pine box 14 in 1/8 wide & 6 deep for G. Wragg to be covered in leather" (30). Hewitt also produced a box for the "New York Equtable Society 2 ft & 1 ft 2 to 1 foot Deep" (16) and for a Mr. Kerr "a Balloting Box with one hole in it and a draw" (35).

One of the more interesting of Hewitt's business commissions is contained in an entry now somewhat obscured but still partially readable: "A Sign for J. Mandeveille 12 ft . . . I Mandeville

Cabinet Maker." Possibly this refers to the same Mandeville who had been Hewitt's partner in 1807. The partnership had recently been dissolved, and apparently Mandeville was setting up his own shop, with a shop sign made by his former partner.

Among the names that recur through the account books are those of Marquand & Harriman, members of a firm of silversmiths. The company seems to have been just beginning, for over a period of almost two years Hewitt made several items of furniture for their place of business. The first, and largest, piece made for the shop was "A Countinghouse secretary Desk for Mr. Marquand . . . 6 ft Long / 4 ft 9 Wide 1 ft 10 the falls 3 ft 5 high frame, inside as / customary" (14). Hewitt included a sketch of the desk and a note of self instructions: "look at desk falls, from Mapple with Screws falls 2 ft 1/4 wide." The desk must have been successful, for, as previously noted, several other customers placed orders for desks "the same as Messrs Marquand & Harriman."

Furniture for the manufacture of silver objects was also included in the Hewitt accounts. One order "for Marquand" stipulated "4 benches 2 higher then the other" (18). Perhaps the most interesting article for the shop, however, was an object sketched and described in the closing pages of the book, "For Marquand a Wire Machine 6 feet Long 12 Inches wide [?] In thick" (35). This was a device for drawing wire to make banding for objects of silver. Since John Hewitt had considerable mechanical skill, he was a logical choice to make an item of this nature.

In addition to making furniture and mechanical devices for the business and manufacturing aspects of the Marquand company, Hewitt also made mirrored cases for the display of their wares. On page thirty-three of the account book appears the following: "For J. Marquand 2 showcases to have 2 doors to each 3 pain glass / in each door (sketch) in clear the glass front of the case to be / 6 Inches deep and to have glass in front—7 Inches Deep the back / and to be the Lock Side, and to be fixed for Looking Glass Inside."

Like Marquand & Harriman, the names "Billy Niblo" and "J. R. D. Huggins" appear frequently throughout the account book. Both men were well known at that time. Billy Niblo was already prominent in the restaurant-coffeehouse business, and John Richard Desbrosses Huggins was not only the best-known barber in New York, but also proprietor of a shop that was a favorite meeting place for other well-known men about town. One can imagine Niblo and Huggins stopping by Hewitt's shop on busy Water Street, or perhaps giving him an order when he visited them at their places of business.

Billy Niblo is not listed in the New York directories until 1814, the year in which he is thought to have opened his popular Bank Coffee House on Pine Street. Judging from the orders he placed with Hewitt, however, he was apparently setting up a restaurant or coffeehouse in 1811, or perhaps was remodeling or taking over the establishment that belonged to his father-in-law, Daniel King, "a noted publican." It is difficult to determine from William Niblo's first order whether he was furnishing a home or a public house, but the latter seems possible. He ordered the following: "1 Sett 4 ft 6 dining Tables / 4 Single field bedsteads Slatt [Bottoms] / 2 Squar breakft Tables / 3 Pine Common 3 Leged Tables / 2 Toilet Tables" (30). Shortly afterward, on August 4, 1811, he ordered a number of tables: "2 4 feet dining Tables / 1 pair circular ends / 1 pair circular card Tables [Solid] Tops / 1 pair Eliptic Do Sollid Top no castors but to be Turnd legs" (33). The number of necessary accessories continued to grow, and Niblo's next order called for: "6 Newspaper Sticks / A desk for Bar room" (33); and a subsequent order was noted requesting "A knife box Middling size mahogany." Apparently even more tables were necessary, for the next order specified: "1 Sett 4 feet dining Tables to match 5 feet Long 2 ft 4 high the / graine Leaves 22 or 24 wide to have 1 Dining Table extra."

Much of what Hewitt made for J. R. D. Huggins was obviously for his home and included "two double cotts," a swing cradle, a field bedstead (20, 21), and one sideboard.[31] In addition, however, Hewitt produced some furniture which may have been for Huggins' barber shop: "1 stool for 2 children for Huggins / 1 chair mahogany & stuffed 28 Inches Long" (24).

Although the account book record of goods produced and customers supplied by the Hewitt shop is extensive, it would be a mistake to accept this book as a complete record of the furniture made by the shop during the periods covered (1800–1803, 1809–1812). Obviously these records indicate only special orders and goods sold on credit, while the rest of the trade, furniture sold for cash from the existing stock, was not recorded in any specific way. That Hewitt kept a fair-sized inventory is clearly indicated by his reminders to himself to make up various furniture forms and by his notes in the margins next to orders that he had these forms "on hand." On one page of the account book Hewitt made a specific entry: "Workd to be made up / 2 best pillor & claw breakfe Tables / 4 Second Ditto / 2 pair best card Tables / Setts Dining Tables frame / 2 Work Stands / Secretary Bill" (33). Not only does this indicate that he kept standard furniture forms on hand but that he tried to stock at least two quality grades of each form.

Like all good tradesmen, Hewitt was aware of his competition in cabinetmaking and of the current styles that customers considered desirable. The names of the two greatest contemporary cabinetmakers, Duncan Phyfe and Charles Honoré Lannuier, occur in his accounts. One entry in the account book indicates that he had carefully considered their furniture and analyzed its proportions, for in March of 1811 he wrote: "Phyfe Collum 23 or 28 with leafe hand carv'd 2⅞ wide / Lanuas Collum 2 ft 6 to 3 ft wide" (20).

As already noted, one customer, Mr. McQueen, specified a "French Sideboard like Phyfes" (26). Other customers, like a Mr. Lawrence, asked for furniture with detailing which, until recently, has been attributed to the Phyfe shop: "1 Breakfast Table 3 ft long Castors & a leaf to be carved / on the legs and reeded" (17).

LABOR PRACTICES: Through the entries in Hewitt's account book and his notes to various employees at the back of the book, one learns something about the labor practices of his shop. Sixteen men are mentioned as being involved in the production of Hewitt furniture. A period of about two years is covered in the main portion of the entries, and an additional two years in back-of-the-book entries.[32] About two-thirds of these

---

[31] Walter Barrett [Joseph A. Scoville], *Old Merchants of New York City* (New York: Carleton, 1863), II, 63–65.

[32] The men listed, with variations in the spellings of their names, are as follows:

1) Barnes, William. Barnes is listed in New York directories from 1800 to 1804 on Reed Street and from 1804 to 1817 on Greenwich Street. A labeled breakfast table by

men were full-fledged cabinetmakers, who were apparently doing piecework in their own shops for Hewitt. Some of them, like William Barnes, had been in business several years longer than Hewitt, while others, like John Devoe (Devou, Devon), Rodney Healy, and John Donnaca (spelled Donnegha by Hewitt) were newcomers to the trade in New York and were first listed in 1811 directories.

Although the recent belief has been that by the Federal Period a division-of-labor system had begun to develop in which a man was skilled primarily in but one aspect of cabinetmaking, restricting his work to analogous forms, there is little indication of such labor practices in the Hewitt accounts.[33] On page seven of the account book, one notation seems to indicate a division of labor: "Oldershaw portable desks / Wallace tables / Andrew streight sideboards / Bill basan stands & stand tables / Tom 1 Press & sideboard

streight"; but such an implied practice is belied by later entries. Of these five men, the first was a cabinetmaker with his own shop at 30 Beekman Street, and the remainder probably worked in Hewitt's shop as journeymen. Later entries show that "Bill" was probably William Cremment, who worked on such disparate objects as a pine kitchen table and a sideboard for Henry Newport. Wallis (the "Wallace" mentioned above) made a sideboard, a kitchen table, and a harp case.

Outside the shop, a skilled cabinetmaker such as Abraham Schuyler Egerton, who was the youngest brother of the Egertons of New Brunswick, New Jersey, and probably trained at least partially in his father's shop, might have made either the elaborate French sideboard for which Hewitt paid the sum of $40.89½ or the coffin for $1.50.[34] Clearly Egerton was assisted by an apprentice, since many of the entries of "work done by Abraham Edgerton" include the appended "by boy." The boy, too, made a range of forms from "cotts" and simple bedsteads to bureaus and secretary bureaus.

Payment both to the men working within the shop and to cabinetmakers doing piecework outside was on two bases, either for individual objects made and jobs done or for working specific periods of time. The standard time wage seems to have been about one dollar a day, although the wage appears to have fluctuated somewhat according to the nature of the work. Thus Hewitt entered a credit of seventy-five cents to Abraham Egerton "by repairing a Secretary bureau 6 hours and carrying home & putting up bedstead for Mr. Havens." In May of 1813, Rodney Healy was paid the same wage, seventy-five cents, for 5½ hours of

Barn (e) s is in the collection of The Newark Museum. See The Newark Museum, *The Museum*, XIII, No. 4 (1961), 4.

2) Beers, Nathan. First listed in New York directories in 1811 on Harman Street; in 1812, as cabinetmaker, on Mulberry.

3) Bokee, Abraham. First listed as cabinetmaker in 1802 at 2 Vandewater; in 1805–1806 he was at 80 Harman Street (the 1811 location of Nathan Beers); from 1810 through 1812 he was not listed.

4) Constantine, Thomas. First listed in *Longworth's New York Directory* as a cabinetmaker at 60 Vesey Street in 1815–1816; later listed at 157 Fulton. For further information, see Lorraine Waxman (Mrs. John N. Pearce), "French Influences on American Decorative Arts of the Early Nineteenth Century" (unpublished Master's thesis, University of Delaware, 1958).

5) Cremment, William. Not listed in directories.

6) Devoe (Devon, Devou), John. Working in 1811 as a cabinetmaker at Cross, north of Mott; in 1812 as cabinetmaker at 98 Cross; in 1814 at 81 Reed.

7) Dolan, John T. First listed in *Jones Directory 1805–1806* at 65 Beekman; in 1809–1811, he was at 30 Beekman.

8) Donnaca (Donnegha), John. Listed only in 1811 as "Donnaca, John, cabinet-maker 17 Cliff."

9) Egerton, Abraham Schuyler. See Note 34.

10) Healy (Hely, Heely), Rodney. Listed in 1811 as cabinetmaker, 285 Water; no listing in 1809–1810 or 1814.

11) Nurse (first name possibly Thomas). Not listed as cabinetmaker. "Thomas Nurse, rigger" listed sporadically, and Hewitt had a "Tom" working in his shop.

12) Oldershaw, John H. Listed in New York directories, 1810–1815; in 1816 he was listed with a partner, Philips, at 30 Beekman.

13) Wallis (Wallace). Not listed in directories.

33 For a similar conclusion, see Morrison H. Heckscher, "Organization and Practice of Philadelphia Cabinetmaking Establishments, 1790–1820" (unpublished Master's thesis, University of Delaware, 1964), p. 31.

34 For initial identification of Abraham Schuyler Egerton, see W. M. Hornor, Jr., "Three Generations of Cabinetmakers," *Antiques*, XIV (Nov., 1928), 417. In this third part of his pioneer study of the Egertons, Hornor stated, "In 1802, when Matthew Egerton died, the family name was perpetuated by his three sons, Matthew, Luke, and Abraham Schuyler Egerton. Of the last, no facts remain." The inventory of Abraham Schuyler Egerton, listing tools and furniture, is in The Joseph Downs Manuscript and Microfilm Collection, Winterthur Museum. Egerton is first listed at 25 Beekman in *Longworth's New York Directory* in 1811. The firm of Loring & Egerton, cabinetmakers, is listed at the same address. In 1812 he was at 50 Beekman; in 1814 at 44 Oak; in 1816–1817 at 15 Catherine; in 1817–1818 at 12 Thomas; in 1818–1819 at 10 Beaver. The records quoted for his work for Hewitt are in Hewitt's accounts to Egerton at the back of the Account Book.

work, while he was paid for "2 days & 4 hours work at Jobing 3 37½," and, "for 4 days works, 5 87½." "Jobing" could mean almost any kind of task but seems here to refer to working with the lumber and veneers which Hewitt handled, since another entry reads, "By Jobing 125 [cuts], 37½, $1, 62½, 37½." Fairly conclusive proof that the time wage scale might change according to the task is shown by a December entry crediting Rodney Healy with $4.50 for "making a wire machin 2 days & 4 hours." The time involved was the same as that involved in the previous jobbing. The skill required was probably greater, however, and this may account for the difference of seventy-five cents or the equivalent of five to six hours of work based on the time pay scale. It seems unlikely that inflation over a period of six months would account for this great difference in the pay for the same number of man-hours.

The pay scale for objects seems to have been closely based on the New York price books of 1806 and 1811. Hewitt paid his outside suppliers approximately two-thirds of what he charged his customers for an object. Whether men like Egerton completely finished their furniture forms— varnishing or polishing—or whether Hewitt finished them is not clearly indicated in the account book.

Just as the back-of-the-book entries show Hewitt's dealings with outside cabinetmakers who did work for him, entries interspersed through the main accounts show dealings with cabinetmakers who bought or sold other related services. During 1812 Hewitt made a number of notations in his accounts, some of them among furniture orders, concerning mahogany cuts which were being sawed from logs. He indicated that he had sent logs to the mills of Silas Dean at Springfield, New Jersey, and of Jacob Barns as well as "to Joseph Meeks[35] to be saw'd at Bloomfield April 22th 1812 for William Camp,[36] and J. Hewitt [is] to

have half the profit if any from first cost." This last entry, which specified also how the logs should be cut into boards of various sizes, some for coffins and coffin tops, shows how far-flung were the connections between various cabinetmakers of the period, for William Camp lived and worked in Baltimore.

The day-by-day accounts end rather abruptly; the concluding pages of the book are used for records of individual workers. These cover a time span somewhat longer than the main body of accounts. There are also late notes made in the early 1820's when Hewitt was attempting to straighten out his precarious finances.

John Hewitt was a cabinetmaker of some prominence throughout the years covered by this account book; however, he never achieved the pre-eminence of his contemporaries, Phyfe and Lannuier. As is shown by Hewitt's words, Phyfe and Lannuier were unquestionably the arbiters of taste in that era, and their work was of a style that others tried to emulate. Unlike the large body of extant work by Phyfe and Lannuier, little Hewitt furniture survives. That which does exist can only be attributed to his shop, and these pieces are not individual enough to help in uncovering more of his work. Unless labeled pieces should be located in the future, it seems unlikely that the known body of Hewitt furniture will ever equal the body of written records of his career.

All the furniture attributed to the Hewitt shop has been inherited and passed down by Hewitt descendants. These pieces include a pair of inlaid card tables (Fig. 3) owned by the late Erskine Hewitt, grandson of John; a set of Regency-style chairs (Fig. 4) given by descendants of Hewitt to The Cooper Union Museum; and a Sheraton-style sideboard with Egyptian influence (Figs. 5 and 6) now in Ringwood Manor House, the former Abram Hewitt-Peter Cooper Mansion, in New Jersey. Also at Ringwood is a dressing table that has been so altered by the addition of a base in place of four legs, late nineteenth-century brass inlay, and incorrect brasses that little impression of its original appearance remains. An Empire breakfast table formerly at Ringwood and attributed to Hewitt in Nevin's book could not be located. In

---

[35] Joseph Meeks (1771–1868) was the founder of a famous firm of New York cabinetmakers. He was in business in New York with his brother Edward as early as 1797, having advertised in Newark, N.J., in 1793. For further information on the Meeks, see John N. Pearce, Lorraine W. Pearce, and Robert C. Smith, "The Meeks Family of Cabinetmakers," *Antiques*, LXXXV (April, 1964), 414–20.

[36] William Camp was a Baltimore cabinetmaker who was listed on Water Street in Baltimore from 1802 to 1819. His label is known; see *Baltimore Furniture, The Work of Baltimore and Annapolis Cabinetmakers from 1760 to 1810* (Baltimore: The Baltimore Museum, 1947), p. 93. For

mention of quantities of gumwood found in his inventory, see Charles F. Montgomery, *American Furniture: The Federal Period* (New York: Viking Press, 1966), p. 36.

FIG. 3. Hewitt (attrib.), Card Table (one of a pair). New York, 1800–1810. Mahogany and satinwood; H. 29½″,
W. 38″. (Present owner unknown: photo, Taylor & Dull, Inc.)

FIG. 4. Hewitt, Side Chair (one of a set of twelve). New York, *ca.* 1820. Mahogany and poplar; slip seat covered with horsehair; H. 33⅝″, W. 18¼″, D. 20⅜″. (Courtesy of The Cooper Union Museum, Gift of Mr. and Mrs. Norvin Hewitt Green.)

the possession of a descendant of Hewitt are an inlaid Pembroke table (Fig. 7) —exhibited at the Museum of the City of New York in 1956—and a set of Restauration-type chairs of the 1830's. In totality, the furniture attributed to Hewitt covers a time span of almost forty years, relatively the same period for which there are accounts and letters for his cabinetmaking activities in New York. These pieces are interesting in their own right, but doubly interesting when compared with the entries on similar pieces in the account book. It seems clear, however, that the most valuable reminders of Hewitt's work are not this small body of objects, but rather the written records of his career. Of these, the 1809–1812 account book remains the most important single document.

Fig. 5. Detail of Figure 6. (Ringwood Manor State Park: photo, Winterthur.)

Fig. 6. Hewitt, Sideboard. New York, 1810–1815. Mahogany; H. 47″, W. 80″, D. 26″. (Ringwood Manor State Park: photo, Winterthur.)

FIG. 7. Hewitt, Table. New York, *ca.* 1810. Mahogany; H. 27¾″, W. 31½″, D. 18½″ (with leaves down), D. of leaf 9½″. (Mrs. John K. Sands: photo, Community Photo Studio.)

Index

Notes on Contributors

Nancy E. Richards is an assistant curator at Winterthur Museum.

Horace L. Hotchkiss, Jr., is curator of the Corbit-Sharp House in Odessa, Delaware.

Wilford P. Cole is a doctoral candidate at the University of Delaware.

Anna Wells Rutledge is an art historian and author living in Charleston, South Carolina.

Robert G. Wheeler is director of crafts at the Henry Ford Museum and Greenfield Village.

Edgar P. Richardson, who was director of Winterthur Museum from 1962 to 1966, is a trustee of the Museum and an authority on American art, now living in Philadelphia.

Ian M. G. Quimby is registrar of Winterthur Museum.

J. Jefferson Miller, II, is associate curator of ceramics at the Smithsonian Institution.

David Sellin is gallery director, Department of Fine Arts, at Colgate University.

Claire Gilbride Fox is an assistant professor of education at Beaver College.

Mary E. Holt is librarian of The Joseph Downs Manuscript and Microfilm Collection at Winterthur Museum.

William H. Gerdts is gallery director, Department of Art, at the University of Maryland.

Eric de Jonge is chief curator of William Penn Memorial Museum in Harrisburg, Pennsylvania.

Marilynn A. Johnson is an exhibition researcher in the American Wing at The Metropolitan Museum of Art.

Portfolio 4

was composed, printed, and bound by
Kingsport Press, Inc., Kingsport, Tennessee.
The paper is Mohawk Superfine,
and the types are Baskerville and Bulmer.
Design is by Edward G. Foss.